The Cuban Americans

The Cuban Americans

Miguel Gonzalez-Pando

THE NEW AMERICANS
Ronald H. Bayor, Series Editor

GREENWOOD PRESS
Westport, Connecticut • London

Library of Congress Cataloging-in-Publication Data

González-Pando, Miguel.
     The Cuban Americans / Miguel Gonzalez-Pando.
         p.   cm.—(The new Americans, ISSN 1092–6364)
     Includes bibliographical references and index.
     ISBN 0–313–29824–6 (alk. paper)
     1. Cuban Americans.   2. Refugees, Political—United States.
     3. Cuba—Emigration and immigration.   4. United States—Emigration
     and immigration.   I. Title.   II. Series.
     E184.C97G64   1998
     975.9'3004687291—dc21   97–21448

British Library Cataloguing in Publication Data is available.

Library of Congress Catalog Card Number: 97–21448
ISBN: 0–313–29824–6
ISSN: 1092–6364

First published in 1998

Greenwood Press, 88 Post Road West, Westport, CT 06881
An imprint of Greenwood Publishing Group, Inc.

Printed in the United States of America

The paper used in this book complies with the
Permanent Paper Standard issued by the National
Information Standards Organization (Z39.48–1984).

10 9 8 7 6 5 4 3 2

Contents

Photographic Essay follows page 82

Series Foreword

Oscar Handlin, a prominent historian, once wrote, "I thought to write a history of the immigrants in America. Then I discovered that the immigrants were American history." The United States has always been a nation of nations where people from every region of the world have come to begin a new life. Other countries such as Canada, Argentina, and Australia also have had substantial immigration, but the United States is still unique in the diversity of nationalities and the great numbers of migrating people who have come to its shores.

Who are these immigrants? Why did they decide to come? How well have they adjusted to this new land? What has been the reaction to them? These are some of the questions the books in this "New Americans" series seek to answer. There have been many studies about earlier waves of immigrants—e.g., the English, Irish, Germans, Jews, Italians, and Poles—but relatively little has been written about the newer groups—those arriving in the last thirty years, since the passage of a new immigration law in 1965. This series is designed to correct that situation and to introduce these groups to the rest of America.

Each book in the series discusses one of these groups, and each is written by an expert on those immigrants. The volumes cover the new migration from primarily Asia, Latin America, and the Caribbean, including: the Koreans, Cambodians, Filipinos, Vietnamese, South Asians such as Indians and Pakistanis, Chinese from both China and Taiwan, Haitians, Jamaicans, Cubans, Dominicans, Mexicans, Puerto Ricans (even though they are already U.S. citizens), and Jews from the former Soviet Union. Although some of these people, such as Jews, have been in America since colonial times, this series concentrates on their recent migrations, and thereby offers its unique contribution.

These volumes are designed for high school and general readers who want to learn more about their new neighbors. Each author has provided information about the land of origin, its history and culture, the reasons for migrating, and the ethnic culture as it began to adjust to American life. Readers will find fascinating details on religion, politics, foods, festivals, gender roles, employment trends, and general community life. They will learn how Vietnamese immigrants differ from Cuban immigrants and, yet, how they are also alike in many ways. Each book is arranged to offer an in-depth look at the particular immigrant group but also to enable readers to compare one group with the other. The volumes also contain brief biographical profiles of notable individuals, tables noting each group's immigration, and a short bibliography of readily available books and articles for further reading. Most contain a glossary of foreign words and phrases.

Students and others who read these volumes will secure a better understanding of the age-old questions of "who is an American" and "how does the assimilation process work?" Similar to their nineteenth- and early twentieth-century forebears, many Americans today doubt the value of immigration and fear the influx of individuals who look and sound different from those who had come earlier. If comparable books had been written one hundred years ago they would have done much to help dispel readers' unwarranted fears of the newcomers. Nobody today would question, for example, the role of those of Irish or Italian ancestry as Americans; yet, this was a serious issue in our history and a source of great conflict. It is time to look at our recent arrivals, to understand their history and culture, their skills, their place in the United States, and their hopes and dreams as Americans.

The United States is a vastly different country than it was at the beginning of the twentieth century. The economy has shifted away from industrial jobs; the civil rights movement has changed minority-majority relations and, along with the women's movement, brought more people into the economic mainstream. Yet one aspect of American life remains strikingly similar—we are still the world's main immigrant receiving nation and as in every period of American history, we are still a nation of immigrants. It is essential that we attempt to learn about and understand this long-term process of migration and assimilation.

Ronald H. Bayor
Georgia Institute of Technology

Preface

The exile knows his place, and that place is the imagination.
—*Ricardo Pau-Llosa¹*

This book is about my "country." Its history began not too far back in Cuba and continues to unfold in the United States and throughout the rest of the world. This country of mine has neither a territory nor a government of its own, but its economy surpasses those of many Latin American nations, and its inhabitants enjoy the highest income per capita of that region. Perhaps mine is only an illusion of a country. I am a Cuban exile.

Together with more than a million fellow emigrés who make up the Cuban diaspora, I live outside of Cuba but still consider myself part of that nation. I yearn for its azure waters, cooling breezes, and the smell that lingered in my home's backyard after a thunderstorm. In some ways I may have become obsessed with memories of a childhood that now feels so utterly removed in time. Worse yet, I am realistic enough to know there is no going back; "imaginings"—as Gustavo Pérez Firmat cautions—"cannot sustain one indefinitely."²

Like most Cuban emigrés, I initially settled in Miami hoping this would be a short stay. As time drew longer and those expectations acquired a mythical dimension, our consuming nostalgia drove us to replicate here what we left behind when the centrifugal forces of Fidel Castro's revolution hurled us in a thousand different directions. Our enterprising spirit succeeded in recreating in Miami an approximation of what Havana was like circa 1959.

This bilingual–bicultural token capital of the Cuban Exile Country we called Little Havana. It was not like the original one; however, this was the best we could do.

I have now spent most of my life in South Florida, where I enjoy a lifestyle that reminds me of the Cuba I once left. I can walk to the corner cafeteria and savor an aromatic *café cubano*, go to the neighborhood bookstore and browse through any book, or invite friends to my home and engage in a lively political discussion. These are a few of the simple things most of my brothers and sisters on the island can no longer do; there, coffee is rationed, books are censored, and the ubiquitous secret police can burst into any gathering unannounced. Come to think of it, that is why I left. Above all, Cuban exiles in America relish freedom, even as it continues to elude us.

In this book's pages I try to capture our struggles and dreams while among good but different people whose ideals we largely share. I also try to help them understand us better, to show readers that despite our idiosyncratic differences, we all harbor the same basic aspirations: a decent life for ourselves and our children. There may not be a better place on earth for realizing that hope. Like most fellow exiles, I appreciate the opportunities this nation has offered us—more so because it has not required us to forsake the essence of who we are. If some of us no longer consider ourselves to be political exiles and have adopted a dual sense of identity as Cuban Americans, that has been our choice. I am grateful for that.

I must advise the reader at the outset that it would be utterly misleading to portray Cuban emigrés as a homogenous minority. That impression, however, has found its way into much of what has been said and written about us. Since early on, American magazines and television have contributed to glamorizing the Cuban exiles as model emigrés—white, well educated, and enterprising—and actually we were the first to encourage the so-called Cuban "success story." This emphasis on positive characteristics commonly found among the exiles has reinforced prevalent stereotypes and myths about Cuban Americans. Since the main purpose of this book is to introduce the exiles to readers unfamiliar with them, it can only glance over distinctions present within that community. For the sake of brevity, this very inquiry may at times unwittingly lead to generalizations that blur the exiles' heterogeneity and contrasting individual experiences in South Florida and elsewhere.

Truth be told, what I call the Cuban Exile Country is a much more complex phenomenon. Not all exiles, for instance, have successfully rebuilt their lives in America. Taking into account how far Cubans have come in such short time, this book often presents them as prosperous, yet Cubans, like any other group, exhibit wide socioeconomic gaps among themselves. Certainly there are significant pockets of poverty in Little Havana, Hialeah, Union City, and other areas where the exiles, particularly the elderly and newly arrived refugees, are concentrated in the United States. In addition, not all Cuban emigrés are white, at least not since the 1980 Mariel Boatlift. More significantly, nonwhite Cubans may not share the same experiences as their white counterparts, and they frequently prefer to pass for African Americans and become integrated into that community; likewise, exiles of Jewish descent have found it easier to blend in with American Jews with whom they share historical and religious backgrounds.

Beyond socioeconomic status, race, and religion, the exiles' age, gender, and contextual influences also affect, in varying degrees, relevant aspects of their acculturation in America. Young Cuban males, for example, are likely to acculturate faster than older females, as are Cubans who marry into American families. Cuban Americans who settle away from Miami's Cuban cocoon often appear to be more acculturated.

This book holds a multidisciplinary approach. Although I have conducted a survey of academic and journalistic literature, the study here is based primarily on firsthand experiences and personal insights. Because I am Cuban and have taken an active part in many crucial events that are here described, I cannot treat the emigrés as mere subjects nor tell their story in statistical terms alone—therein lies the inherent strength, as well as the weakness, of this work. As an insider, the vantage point from which I write allows me not only to complement the findings of scores of outsiders who have studied the Cuban Americans but also to delve deeply into the very soul of the community to illuminate its subjective dimensions.

I am not sure how critically objective it is possible to be when studying a group to which one belongs. I do know that I have documented my analysis of significant trends and have offered supporting testimony from representative individuals who took part in milestone events. As a safeguard of sorts against letting personal biases and opinions compromise the intellectual integrity of this work, I have asked a number of friends and colleagues to review specific chapters. I am particularly indebted to Louise Valdés-Fauli and Roberto Manzano for editorial suggestions. The photographs here have been supplied by photographer Pedro Portal. All quoted testimony comes from the archives of the Cuban Living History Project at Florida International University.

Finally, I wish to acknowledge my wife Yvette's invaluable feedback and constant encouragement; to her I dedicate this book—*con todo mi amor.*

NOTES

1. Ricardo Pau-Llosa, "Identity and Variations: Cuban Visual Thinking in Exile since 1959," in *Outside Cuba/Fuera de Cuba*, ed. Iliana Fuentes-Pérez, Graciela Cruz Taura, Ricardo Pau-Llosa (New Brunswick, N.J.: Office of Hispanic Arts, Rutgers University, 1988), 41.

2. Gustavo Pérez Firmat, *Life-on-the-Hyphen: The Cuban-American Way* (Austin: University of Texas Press, 1994), 10.

Introduction

The Cuban Exile Country—
A Drama without a Script

The experiences of the Castro-era emigrés, particularly those who consider themselves Cuban Americans and live mostly in South Florida, may resemble a drama without a script. The actors, trapped in a plot that unfolds in a surreal dimension between Cuba's past and America's future, appear to look ahead to a time that exists only in their visions of a bygone age. Driven by the constant nostalgia that consumes the cast, the never-ending performance keeps moving back and forth across the Straits of Florida. Although apparently successful in their new land, the players would rather have acted in a different setting: the island of their birth. Most may no longer feel displaced in America, but they still yearn for their homeland—even as their home is here now.

As talented performers, Cuban exiles have incorporated elements of a morality play in which they personify the spirit of enterprise with traits of the theater of the absurd, for the plot seems forever to turn as a result of events that take place in another venue. It is there, on their beloved island, where the climax must be resolved; there, the main character, played in a cameo role by Fidel Castro himself, has commanded center stage for nearly four decades. The aging protagonist, doomed by his tragic obsession with power, continues to stumble toward an uncertain conclusion. Until that final scene is played out, cast and audience alike remain transfixed by this once-heroic figure.

In their performance, the emigrés continue to change the South Florida scenery to fit their orientation. In doing so, they have turned Miami into the mythical capital of the so-called Cuban Exile Country, an illusion that extends throughout the world, its million-strong population sharing similar cultural traditions and political idiosyncrasies no matter where they have settled. Everywhere—in the United States, Europe, Asia, or Latin America—these adaptable emigrés have kept alive a collective sense of identity, insisting on remaining political exiles for as long as they could. But time is implacable: The defining bond that provided coherence to their experiences is starting to fade, even in South Florida, where most now consider themselves Cuban Americans.

The exiles and their Cuban American offspring have best displayed their enterprising talent in South Florida. It is here, on this southeastern tip of the United States, so close to the land they yearn for, where the emigré population is concentrated and draws strength from its significant numbers to cope with the formidable challenges of a destiny in exile. Here they have built their own enclave, an economically viable but politically controversial one. As a result, Greater Miami today is a unique community—part imaginary, part reality—that reflects the exiles' longings and fantasies as well as their ancestral excesses and contradictions. Therein lies the fictional quality of this dramatic performance: Despite all protestations, Cuban exiles are acting like Americans, and more so each day.

The theatrical metaphor, however, fails to do justice to the remarkable performance displayed by these determined emigrés, particularly those who came earlier and settled in Miami. What those Cubans accomplished in their first two decades of exile is as tangible as the imprint they made on every aspect of the political, cultural, economic, and social life of this century-old city. Hence, Miami has been redesigned in the exiles' image of a Havana frozen in time: a postmodern replica of the old city that may, in fact, be crumbling but never fades from their hearts. Although smaller Cuban exile colonies exist in New Jersey, New York, California, and Puerto Rico, the majority of Cuban Americans—65 percent—reside in Florida.

By most conventional measures of immigrant progress in America, the Cuban exile experience appears, on the surface, to be surprising for a largely dispossessed, politically beaten people who began their exodus less than two generations ago. How did they manage so quickly to come so far in a foreign land where language and customs were alien to many of them? What strengths have they drawn from their exile identity and from their American context? Are there meaningful differences among the four waves that make up this emigration? How have they survived, adjusted, and, ultimately, prevailed in South Florida? What, indeed, accounts for the relative prosperity of the Cuban American community?

These questions continue to challenge researchers. Some attempt to explain the success of the Cuban emigrés by emphasizing the demographic characteristics of the two earlier waves made up mostly of white entrepreneurs and professionals who belonged to the socioeconomic class best equipped to lay the foundations of the Miami enclave. Others place more weight on the initial assistance they received through the Cuban Refugee Program or the significant contributions of working women in the exile family. Although these hypotheses explain particular aspects of the dynamics of the Cuban Exile Country, there is more to the Cuban American drama.

To understand what may seem to be an improbable performance for a traveling cast forced upon America after losing their homeland, the political nature of their experience must be considered. From its initial wave, this has been a politically motivated exodus. Despite the pressure to acculturate, successive waves of emigrés have been sustained by the conviction that they were political exiles. That shared sense of identity has been the mortar that binds Cuban emigrés to each other. And from that conviction they have somehow drawn the inspiration to succeed as exiles. Even those who joined the Cuban diaspora later, although they were perhaps not really exiles in the strict sense of the word, have embraced the political identity of their predecessors.

This book begins with historical background because the exiles' experience in America is firmly grounded in the island's past—a point often neglected by researchers. Chapter 1, therefore, summarizes the Cuban republic's troubled history. Fidel Castro's revolutionary takeover, which itself triggered the onset of the Cuban diaspora, is examined in Chapter 2. A detailed chronology of the successive stages of development through which the emigrés have gone in their establishment of the Cuban Exile Country and the major influences that shaped each stage are presented in Chapter 3. Finally, the dynamics of the exiles are probed in depth from sociocultural (Chapter 4), economic (Chapter 5), and political (Chapter 6) perspectives. The epilogue at the end of the book considers the future of the Cuban emigrés. All chapters, however, are meant to complement one another, as recurrent themes are woven throughout the entire text.

After all is said and done, the Cuban Americans' drama is really a universal story of human hope in the face of adversity, not unlike that of earlier immigrants who built America. If it seems different, it is because Cuban Americans are reluctant immigrants. As such, they may have redefined in their own terms the traditional pursuit of the American Dream.

1

Historical Background

Since Europeans discovered the New World, the destinies of the United States and Cuba have been closely intertwined. Because only the Straits of Florida separates the island of Cuba from the Florida peninsula, their territories were coveted by both the Spanish and British colonial empires, which alternately governed Florida until it became a U.S. territory in 1821. Before then, the Spanish flag had waved over Florida from 1513 to 1763 and, again, from 1783 to 1821—a longer period, in fact, than has the American flag. During those two intervals of Spanish domination, fifty-two Florida governors (four of whom were born in Havana) ruled this peninsula, not to mention long stretches during which both Spanish colonies shared the same governor.

Present-day Americans, puzzled by the arrival of wave after wave of Cubans, may not remember that in 1763, when England acquired Florida from Spain, most Floridians escaped to Cuba, where each refugee family received thirty-three acres of land and a black slave to help them settle on the island. Neither do most Americans probably know that Cubans participated on their side during the American Revolution, when many Floridians again sought refuge from the war in Cuba. A century later, Cuba's own wars of independence forced tens of thousands of Cubans and Spaniards in the opposite direction. Those nineteenth-century exiles settled mostly in New York City, Philadelphia, Tampa, and Key West.

When Cuba finally won its independence in 1902, some of those Cuban exiles never returned to their homeland, opting instead to stay in Key West, Tampa, Jacksonville, and Ocala (first named "Marti City" by its Cuban founders). After that time, Cubans frequently came to Florida as students, tourists, immigrants, or political exiles; during the revolutions against Cuban dictators Gerardo Machado in the 1930s and Fulgencio Batista in the 1950s, for example, thousands of Cubans again sought haven in Florida from the island's political upheavals. Nobody, however, could have anticipated the magnitude of the Cuban exodus reaching American shores after Fidel Castro came to power in Cuba in 1959—nor would they have believed the dramatic transformation that was to take place in Miami as a result.

CUBA AND THE UNITED STATES

A History Lesson in Geopolitics

Precisely because of Cuba's location just ninety miles from the Florida Keys, its modern history has always been influenced by the United States.[1] This geopolitical reality explains the attention the United States has accorded the neighboring island since the eighteenth century. In 1868, when the spirit of independence that had already swept Latin America first drove Cubans to seek freedom from Spanish colonial rule, the United States closely followed the development of the war. From that historical juncture on, America's interest in the affairs of the island intensified.

> In Cuba the influence was Black and Spanish, but there also was a North American influence that cannot be overlooked. The first two ones cannot be disputed. The third one has been misinterpreted, because it is believed that the Cuban people have been submissive to the United States. (Translation of author's interview with Andrés Rivero Aguero, a historian who was politically active during the Cuban Republic)

Throughout the latter part of the nineteenth century, as Cubans initiated their quest for nationhood, the ultimate political fate of the island kept making headlines in the United States and occupying the attention of American politicians. In the 1890s, when José Martí sought the support of thousands of Cuban exiles in New York and Florida to organize the final campaign in Cuba's war against its Spanish colonial master, Americans kept up with such developments, even more so after insurrection again erupted on the island in February 1895. Indeed, in 1896, the U.S. Congress approved a resolution supporting the cause of the Cuban patriots, inching America closer to involving itself in the conflict.

The Spanish-American War

Shortly after the 1898 inauguration of President William McKinley, the U.S. warship *Maine* inexplicably exploded and sank during a visit to Havana's harbor. That incident triggered America's entry into the Cuban conflict. In April of that year, the U.S. Congress passed a joint resolution, which the president signed, endorsing the Cuban people's quest for freedom from the crumbling Spanish empire. A few days later, Congress declared war against Spain, and the American president ordered a naval blockade of the island.

Within two months, American military forces arrived. Fighting side by side with Cubans, they attacked Santiago de Cuba, the island's second largest city, and the U.S. Navy quickly forced the surrender of the Spanish vessels that had taken to sea. During this campaign, Colonel Theodore Roosevelt, who was leading a contingent of volunteers, the Rough Riders, distinguished himself in the assault on San Juan Hill. The actual war lasted merely a month, since the Spanish troops, already exhausted by years of combat against the Cubans, capitulated as soon as the United States flexed its military muscle. Although history has named it the Spanish-American War, this designation still infuriates Cubans, for it omits their central participation in the war effort against colonial rule.

U.S. Occupation of Cuba (1898–1902)

As a result of the military intervention of the United States in Cuba, Spain surrendered control of the island, not to the Cuban patriots, but to the United States, and the Stars and Stripes replaced the flag of Spain on the island between 1898 and 1902, much to the indignation of the Cuban people. At the conclusion of the war, the Treaty of Paris was signed by representatives of Spain and the United States, while the Cubans, who had fought long and hard to win their independence, were pointedly excluded.

Thus began the U.S. occupation of the former Spanish colony, a difficult and complex period of transition during which most Cubans feared their quest for sovereignty would be compromised by the imperialistic designs of the "Northern Colossus." It was also then that anti-American feelings first took root in the conscience of the nascent nation—a development that has cast a cloud over the relationship between the two countries ever since. The first Cuban constitution was drafted during this period of U.S. domination. But even then, the administration of President McKinley refused to grant independence to the island until the Cubans reluctantly consented to add an ominous appendix to their constitutional charter: the notorious Platt Amendment. Named after the New York senator who sponsored it, this amendment gave the United States the right to intervene in Cuba's internal affairs, thereby limiting the sovereignty of the nation from the very moment of conception.

After much political controversy around issues brought about by the imposition of the Platt Amendment, a national election was finally held, and Don Tomás Estrada Palma, the candidate supported by the United States, was elected president. On May 20, 1902, the American occupation of the island ended, and the Cuban Republic was finally born. By then, however, despite the health, educational, and infrastructure improvements carried out by the American forces on the island, the special relationship with the United States had become a permanent thorn in the nationalistic pride of the Cuban people.

THE CUBAN REPUBLIC (1902–1958)

From Independence to the Dictatorship of Gerardo Machado (1902–1933)

Born under America's shadow, the young republic was soon consumed by the need to define its political and commercial relationships with the United States. From the beginning, conflicts arising from strained relations with its powerful neighbor, internal political strife, and its rulers' obsession with remaining in power was a three-edged dagger aimed at the heart of the country's body politic. Obviously, four centuries of Spanish colonial governance had not prepared Cubans for democratic self-rule.

The first Cuban administration, to its credit, was meticulously honest, a claim that most of its successors would not be able to make; however, President Estrada Palma soon became bogged down by internal as well as external problems. After his disputed reelection in 1905, amid several opposition conspiracies, armed insurrection erupted. The overwhelmed Cuban president requested U.S. military intervention from President Theodore Roosevelt, and the United States, acting under the authority of the Platt Amendment, intervened again in Cuba. This second American occupation lasted until 1909, when a new president was inaugurated in Cuba and the U.S. armed forces left; the fledgling country was then able to resume its troubled course. Once established, however, this pattern of political instability and dependence on the United States continued to frustrate successive governments.

The period that followed the second American intervention was characterized by political excesses and recurrent revolutionary outbreaks that were to become endemic to the history of the republic. Despite its evident political malaise, however, the nation experienced considerable economic progress, particularly during World War I, when the price of sugar, Cuba's most important export product, reached unprecedented heights. The vagaries of the sugar market, from then on, determined the economic prospects of the nation; it was an industry whose fate the country could never control. In the 1920s, the postwar economic crisis added volatility to traditional party rivalries that continued to play havoc with the nation's weak political institutions. At the same time, the United States' increasing involvement in the internal affairs of the island rekindled the debate about the controversial Platt Amendment. It was during this period that the Communist party was founded, introducing a new player to the numerous forces promoting instability.

> There were times when the United States Ambassador decided fundamental issues in Cuba. For example, [Cuban] President Menocal finished his presidential period in 1917, but then decides to forcefully stay in power. . . . This gives way to a violent process, a large rebel uprising. And in that situation, the U.S. Ambassador declares that since Cuba was allied to the United States in World War I, all rebels opposing the government of President Menocal were to be considered German allies. Imagine! The opposition to Menocal died out. (Translation of author's interview with Justo Carrillo, a revolutionary leader during the republic)

Despite its recurrent troubles, the young nation was able to survive the intense factional rivalries of the time and, in 1925, a former caudillo of the war of independence, General Gerardo Machado, was elected president by a wide margin. During his otherwise productive mandate, the new president began to display an authoritarian streak and, when the end of his term of office approached, he had become not only an effective chief executive, but a ruthless ruler as well. At the conclusion of his presidential term, General Machado managed to dominate the disorganized political forces of the nation and to remain in power. He thus became the country's first full-fledged dictator.

The Revolution against Machado (1933)

The year 1933 saw the beginning of one of the most turbulent periods in the republic's brief history. The worldwide depression brought a deepening crisis to the Cuban economy, but far more unfortunate for the nation were the repressive measures carried out by the Machado regime: The university was closed, the press was censored or shut down, and political opponents were jailed, exiled, or eliminated. A wave of violence initiated by the ruling dictator was countered by the terrorist tactics of his adversaries, and political assassinations, on both sides, made their first appearance on the national scene. Violence emerged as a way of life, and from then on, it became a permanent fixture in the political affairs of Cuba.

> Towards the end of the 1920s, university students decided to get involved in politics. The students took a radical stand and as a consequence, the student body was persecuted by Machado's government. (Translation of author's interview with historian Carlos Márquez Sterling)

In September 1930, General Machado's police brutally crushed a group of protesting university students and killed one of their leaders, an incident that sparked a popular uproar against the dictatorship. That episode helped consolidate the opposition. Three years later, as the political situation worsened, the dictator, besieged by massive popular demonstrations, strikes, and mounting violence and pressured by the American ambassador and the Cuban military, finally fled the country. He left behind a tragic trail of chaos and lawlessness.

The Emergence of Batista (1933–1940)

The political vacuum created by the departure of General Machado was soon filled by an odd coalition of university professors, students, and military sergeants. During the confusing period that ensued, Fulgencio Batista, a former sergeant himself, managed to consolidate his power. With the support of the American Embassy and the Cuban military, the self-appointed Colonel Batista emerged as the real force behind a series of relatively weak civilian administrations that served largely at his will.

The revolutionary ferment lasted until the end of the decade. During those years, a radical program of social and economic reforms was initiated, and the unpopular Platt Amendment was finally revoked, while the nationalistic fervor among the revolutionaries exacerbated anti-American passions and opened the government to Communist influence. Clearly, the often-abused civil institutions were no match for the mounting chaos that spread throughout the land, as demagoguery, constant strikes, and a resurgence of political tensions brought down government after government. Such an anarchic state of affairs forced the postponement of the 1935 elections for a new constitutional convention and drove Colonel Batista to repress the unruly opposition.

When order was briefly reestablished, a fragile consensus among the political forces made possible a general election in 1936, but the new president soon ran into trouble with his army chief, the powerful Colonel Batista. The confrontation between civil authorities and the military escalated, leading to the replacement of the recently elected president. Colonel Batista had again prevailed. Despite the questionable legality of such procedures, the country managed to calm down sufficiently to hold constitutional elections in 1939.

The Constitution of 1940

With hope of putting an end to the de facto regimes that had governed the nation since General Machado interrupted the legality of the electoral process in 1928, a constitutional convention was inaugurated early in 1940. Every political tendency, from the traditional parties to the more extremist revolutionaries, including the Communist, was represented. By general agreement, the conventioneers elected university professor Ramón Grau San Martín as their president.

From its inception, the constitutional convention ran into problems because it could not overcome the traditional confrontation between moderate politicians and revolutionaries. Despite his own revolutionary credentials and his popularity, Grau lacked the procedural skills to guide the assembly. The sessions were constantly interrupted by dilatory motions and amendments that had little to do with the business at hand. Finally Grau was forced to resign, opening the way for Carlos Márquez Sterling, a longtime politician who had earlier distinguished himself as president of Cuba's Congress.

> Grau had many problems because he didn't know how to preside over an assembly. . . . Then, when Grau fell in a crisis, they nominated me—because I had been the President of Congress and had managed it well. . . . I went in during a psychological moment that was very favorable to me. . . . The assembly was then very tired . . . and wanted to finish to go into the general election. (Translation of author's interview with historian Carlos Márquez Sterling)

Under Márquez Sterling's able leadership, the constitutional convention was able to complete its task. The Constitution of 1940 represented a significant advance, particularly in the rights and protection it afforded the working class and the needy. The new charter also paved the way for a relatively calm political period, and rapid economic growth followed. This constitution, a major achievement, made the Cuban people proud that the rule of law had finally been restored in the land.

The Democratic Interlude (1940–1952)

After the approval of the new constitution, two large political coalitions, led respectively by Colonel Batista and Grau, competed for the presidency. With strong support from the workers' unions, the military, and a majority of the political parties, Batista, who had remained the country's only viable force as army chief, was elected president in 1940.

> I got in the Communist party in 1927. . . . The Communist party was part of the democratic coalition that supported Batista. . . . The development of the union struggle gave the party control of most unions in the country. (Translation of author's interview with Arnaldo Escalona, a leader in the Communist party)

Batista's presidency, however, was anything but smooth. The same problems that had plagued the nation since its independence continued to surface. Soon enough, Batista's governing social-democratic coalition was weakened by internal strife, and the nation sank into a deep economic crisis. As a result, President Batista had to contend with several conspiracies and attempts to seize power by force, and the popularity of his main political adversary, Grau, peaked again.

> One has to take into account that his was the first constitutional government that the Cuban people had since the Machado regime. . . . In that government I held the post of Minister of Education. . . . Then came the 1944 elections. Grau was again a candidate for the presidency, not against Colonel Batista, who couldn't be a candidate for reelection because of the 1940 Constitution. Dr. Grau won, won most of the provinces, and his victory was honored. The Cuban democracy was really strengthened. (Translation of author's interview with historian Andrés Rivero Aguero)

The electoral campaign of 1944 took place. Grau was elected president, and Batista, by then promoted to general, respected the popular will. Without question, the stature of Batista, the strong man who had virtually dominated the political scene since the 1933 revolution, was aggrandized when, to the surprise of many, he dutifully handed the presidency to his old foe and left the country. The general-turned-politician, however, was still young, very popular, and certainly too accustomed to the intoxicating allure of power to remain away for very long. The country was certain to hear from him again.

> The *auténticos* [Grau's ruling party] were against the Communists. They fought the Communists and we fought back. The Communist party fought mostly for control of the Workers' Union. . . . Then the *auténticos* took over the Workers' Union, tried to dissolve it, and took measures against the [Communist] party and, of course, we had to retaliate . . . by going on strike, rallying [against the government]. (Translation of author's interview with Communist party leader Arnaldo Escalona)

President Grau's administration proved to be a deep disappointment. Political corruption and violence, which once more became rampant, led to the appearance of a new evil: armed groups of gangsters who fought openly in the streets to gain political influence. The University of Havana, long a nest for revolutionaries, became the breeding ground of gangsterism.[2] The government, too weak to stop the spread of organized violence, merely presided over the rising wave of chaos while some of its ministers and leaders amassed large fortunes. The mounting public disorder continued to erode what was left of popular confidence in the besieged political institutions of the nation—no matter who was in power, the people had come to expect the same abuses.

Toward the end of Grau's presidency, his government boasted that the economy had flourished as a result of government initiatives; in fact, the bonanza was created mostly by increased world demand for sugar during the postwar years. The government's party, nevertheless, managed to prevail in the 1948 national elections, and Grau's Minister of Labor, Carlos Prío Socarrás, was elected president. With President Prío's inauguration, the so-called generation of 1930 assumed political control of the nation. The new president, young, intelligent, and very popular, was the undisputed spiritual heir to the revolutionary forces that had deposed Machado's dictatorship fifteen years earlier.

> When Prío was elected, he called me. . . . I asked him: "Carlos, what do you think about your administration? What are you going to do?" And Carlos Prío told me: "Listen Luis, I have reached the Presidency of the Republic because I made many deals. I am going to start off badly, because I have to start paying off those political debts. But I am going to finish fine." And in fact, that's what he did; during the last two years of his administration, Prío seriously attempted to end corruption and to restore public confidence in the country's

democratic institutions. (Translation of author's interview with Luis Botifoll, a newspaper publisher during the republic)

The inauguration of President Prío, like that of most of his predecessors, signaled a brief era of renewed hope for the Cuban people. He quickly instituted a much-welcomed law against gangsterism and an amnesty intended to heal the country's political malaise. As a gesture of good will, he allowed General Batista to return from his self-imposed exile in Florida. Despite his early accomplishments, however, the young president proved equally inept and just as dishonest. Old vices, particularly rampant political corruption, continued to undermine the credibility of the government. Soon, Prío's presidency would be characterized by a violent resurgence of gangsterism and the virulence of antigovernment demagogues. But even under such a cloudy political climate, the campaign for the next presidential election proceeded. After decades of political excesses and disappointments, however, the mood of the country appeared to be one of frustration; public confidence in the abused democratic institutions had sunk to an unprecedented low. The stage was set for a breakdown of the political process.

Batista's Dictatorship and Castro's Rebellion
(1952–1959)

On the morning of March 10, 1952, just a few weeks before the scheduled presidential elections were to be held, the country awoke to the news that General Batista and a group of young officers had staged a bloodless coup. Without much of a fight, President Prío sought refuge at the Mexican embassy, while the citizens, exhausted by years of recurrent political chaos, accepted this new constitutional rupture with simple resignation. The political parties, for the most part, seemed too weakened by their own internal divisions to contend with Batista's new de facto regime.

Batista's coup again sunk the nation in a constitutional limbo from which it never recovered. Under this climate of quiet discontent, the government dismantled several conspiracy threats but managed to limp forward until the morning of July 26, 1953, when a poorly armed group of about one hundred young men opposed to Batista's dictatorship staged a surprise assault against the military headquarters located in Santiago, the nation's second largest city. The intrepid action was led by Fidel Castro, an aspiring politician who had earned a reputation as somewhat of a thug during his years at the University of Havana.

Government troops crushed the improvised assault within minutes, but their ensuing hunt for the assailants still at large turned violent. There was no way to miss the atrocities of the police: Corpses were left scattered throughout Santiago as grim reminders of the mortal price of rebellion. The death toll quickly rose to about eighty, a development that so alarmed local citizens that a delegation of civic leaders convened to intercede before the Archbishop of Santiago, who appealed to the government for restraint. The city's military commander yielded to the clergy's pleas and agreed to respect the lives of the remaining assailants if the archbishop himself delivered them to the military authorities.

Within a week, most of the fugitives, including Fidel Castro himself, were delivered safely by the archbishop; the military commander kept his word and spared the lives of the surviving assailants. But the city did not return to normalcy. Indeed, the political mood of the island was never quite the same after that fateful day in 1953 that gave the opposition a brave deed to rally around and its cause a name: the 26th of July Movement. For the first time since General Batista had staged his ominous coup d'état two years earlier, a wary political feeling clouded the nation's economic contentment, while several opposition groups intensified their antigovernment activities.[3]

On November 30, 1956, all hell broke loose again in Santiago. The young opposition to the ruling dictator took over the city for several hours—an action that was staged to coincide with the arrival in the nearby Sierra Maestra mountains of an armed expedition commanded by Castro.[4] From then on, Santiago became a siege city, encircled by bearded guerillas hiding in the mountains and harassed by the urban underground from within. Political violence escalated. The citizenry largely rationalized the growing fury as fair retribution for previous acts of violence committed by either adversary, but then the savagery became more indiscriminate. By that time the population was already divided into two camps, but those who lined up with the rebel opposition were clearly emerging as the majority. The upper and middle classes, traditionally apathetic to political matters, tried to remain impartial at first, but later began to support several insurgent movements. Still, most of them distrusted Castro as much as they despised Batista.

> The different [opposition] movements that supported the revolution met in Caracas in July of 1958 and agreed to coordinate the struggle against Batista and to appoint a president. Fidel's candidate for the presidency was [Manuel] Urrutia. Someone from the *Directorio Revolucionario* vetoed Urrutia and told me: "Do you want to be our candidate?" "But, are you crazy, are you crazy? Shit! Don't you know Castro? Listen guy, you veto Urrutia and nominate me as a candidate . . . for God's sake, we'll never be able to go to Havana again."

Then, in the Caracas Pact, Urrutia was appointed; Urrutia's future presidency was legalized. (Translation of author's interview with revolutionary Justo Carrillo)

Batista's army at first refrained from pursuing the rebels into their strongholds high in the mountains, then began retreating until it found itself cornered within the military installations of Santiago. This defeatist posture allowed the rebel forces to descend from their hideaway and roam freely throughout the farmlands of the easternmost province of Oriente. The army's top brass, meanwhile, remained in Havana, far from the battlefield. The spreading crisis, indeed, had not yet reached the capital. The seat of the national government still thrived in an illusion of normalcy fostered by the economic bonanza that continued to bless the nation: Record numbers of American tourists were visiting the capital, the price of sugar was high, and the exchange rate for the Cuban peso was often greater than par with the U.S. dollar. As long as economic forecasts remained optimistic and the American ambassador stayed on the side of the ruling dictatorship, nothing seemed to worry the government partisans.

The still-optimistic mood in the capital was misleading. It ignored the misery corroding the nation's social fabric, the political hopelessness of large segments of the population, and the advancing guerillas. As the crisis escalated, Batista hurriedly scheduled a national election for November 1958. Popular sentiments, however, had already turned irrevocably in favor of the heroics of Fidel Castro, whose legend spread over the land even faster than his conquering rebel forces. The few dissenting voices that warned about this sword hanging over the island's fortunes, however, went largely unheeded, and their appeal, "ballots not bullets," sounded timid compared to the fury of the regime's repression and the revolutionary delirium. The choice between those two political evils, dictatorship and revolution, did not account for other available options: Several nonviolent alternatives were also being advanced in hopes of restoring democracy through a national election. This peaceful formula was proposed by the Partido del Pueblo Libre, a small party coalescing around the figure of Márquez Sterling, who had distinguished himself as president of the 1940 constitutional convention. His was, perhaps, the only stand remaining against the mounting tide of violence.

I was convinced that if the elections went well and I was elected, the militarism would end. But they didn't support me as they should have; I played a difficult hand. . . . Rivero Aguero [Batista's candidate] won because . . . only the government people voted. (Translation of author's interview with Carlos Márquez Sterling)

Carlos Márquez Sterling went for a solution that he thought could be institutional, thinking that in fact if the elections were to take place and a president was elected, we would put an end to Batista's dictatorship . . . and once again restore the institutional regime. And I believe that Márquez Sterling was completely right. Unfortunately, it was too late and the Cuban people did not share that hope anymore; the people thought that it was already too late to solve the problem with elections. (Translation of author's interview with newspaper publisher Luis Botifoll)

The November elections were finally held, but nothing was settled. The power of the ballot was lost in the roar of bayonets, bullets, bombs, arrests, and political assassinations. General Batista's hand-picked presidential candidate was elected, but everyone assumed the election was a fraud staged so that Batista could continue to wield the real power behind his annointed successor. After the elections, the fighting escalated and spread. The government's precarious hold was reduced to just Havana and the provincial capitals, but even in those urban pockets remaining under the army's control, the insurgents became more aggressive. In fact, the rebels were not really defeating the army in combat; the army's will to fight had collapsed.

The consensus was that the agonizing dictatorship had reached an end. That conclusion was shared by the American administration of Dwight Eisenhower. After propping up the de facto Cuban regime for years, President Eisenhower delivered a decisive one-two punch combination to General Batista. The first blow was the imposition of a demoralizing arms embargo; the second was a private letter sent to Batista in which Eisenhower withdrew his support from the discredited dictatorship. This was tantamount to signing the regime's death sentence. By then, the disintegration of the government had become so evident that all segments of society, as well as the pivotal American ambassador, had reached the point of chancing the nation's future with the charismatic Castro.

That was a difficult time for the Republic and, particularly, for us, too. I had been elected president in November, but Washington didn't want me to take over. What's more, in December 1958, President Eisenhower sent Batista a letter telling him he had to leave the presidency and adding: "We will not recognize the government of Rivero Aguero." In that letter, President Eisenhower presumed that I was going to be Batista's puppet. . . . Interestingly, President Eisenhower had recognized Batista's government, one that had risen to power through a coup d'état, but didn't want to acknowledge my government, which was the product of an election—a very controversial election, but an election nonetheless! (Translation of author's interview with Andrés Rivero Aguero)

In the wake of Washington's ultimatum, General Batista gathered a group of his closest partisans at Havana's impregnable military command on December 31, 1958. It would not be a celebration of the New Year, but the conclusion of a melodrama of excesses. That night the dictator announced to his partisans that circumstances forced him to flee the country.

> Batista started to dine. But his emotional state was such, that he couldn't swallow the first bite. He threw it back on the plate and threw the plate on the table and left. Afterward he sent for us . . . Then Batista approached me and said: "Riverito, I want you to accompany me." And that's how it was. . . . That's the end of Batista's story and, of course, ours, too. I have never seen my country since. (Translation of author's interview with Andrés Rivero Aguero)

A military guard then came in and escorted the chosen few who would accompany the First Family into exile. This caravan of the disgraced sped to three planes that awaited them on a nearby landing strip, and they took off under cover of darkness.

CASTRO'S TAKEOVER (1959)

The departure of General Batista took the country by surprise. Despite the rapidly deteriorating political conditions, few expected such a sudden collapse of his dictatorial regime. The opposition forces not aligned with Castro's movement quickly tried to seize control of the nation's capital while the guerilla leader remained in the province of Oriente, a thousand kilometers away. The citizenry, however, clamored for the bearded messiah.

The news of General Batista's departure did not reach Castro until later that morning, while he was preparing his troops for an all-out assault on Santiago. Immediately, he entered the city, where he received a reception worthy of a conquering savior. In order to prevent the consolidation of a transitional government in Havana, Castro knew he had to act quickly. Wasting no time, he announced his first "provisional" revolutionary cabinet, composed mostly of moderate politicians, declared a general strike, and proclaimed Santiago the temporary capital of the nation. With these bold measures, he succeeded in wresting the initiative from the opposition not aligned with his 26th of July Movement. Only then did Castro begin his victory march toward Havana.

The enthusiastic outpouring of support the guerilla leader received along his way was unprecedented in Cuban history. By the time he reached the capital a week later, Fidel Castro was not only in control of the seat of government, he had emerged as the unchallenged leader of the nation. He then instituted the practice of governing by speeches that lasted for hours, inciting his television audiences toward delirium. His welcomed revolutionary message was simple: He vowed to restore the Constitution of 1940 and fulfill the social justice aspirations that for too long had been denied by corrupt politicians and American imperialists—but first, he had to make sure that the culprits of the Cuban tragedy paid for their crimes. Thus, to the approving chorus of his ardent supporters, the firing squads began to dispense their peculiar brand of revolutionary justice.

To the delight of most of the nation, Castro proceeded to take on his potential adversaries one by one: first, Batista's partisans and the army, then the large American corporations and land owners, and finally, the wealthy, the entrepreneurial class, the Catholic Church, and the free press. In rapid succession, Castro implemented the initial stage of an agrarian reform, began to nationalize large land holdings and businesses, replaced his hand-picked president with a Communist puppet, and purged his own cabinet of its more moderate ministers. There was no stopping him. Those who dared even question his growing authoritarian rule and the increasing Communist influence in the government were labeled "counterrevolutionaries." Once so branded, dissenters were likely to face firing squads, long jail sentences, or a life in exile.

By the end of his initial two years of revolutionary rule, Castro had, in effect, dismantled the discredited national institutions and crushed the civil society. As a result, his rebel army and his people's militia, the judicial system, the government's bureaucracy, and the press were clearly under his absolute control. The revolution had consolidated all power, and Castro became the *Máximo Líder.*

NOTES

1. For a comprehensive historical analysis of Cuba's international relations, see Herminio Portell Vilá, *Historia de Cuba en sus relaciones con Estados Unidos y España* (Havana, 1938).

2. At that time, a young university student who belonged to one of the violent revolutionary groups, which degenerated into political gangs, gained notoriety. His name was Fidel Castro.

3. Besides Castro's own 26th of July Movement, many other groups were active against Batista. Examples are a failed 1956 conspiracy of young military officers, led by Colonel Ramón Barquín, and the 1957 attack on the Presidential Palace, staged by the students' Directorio Revolucionario.

4. After the July 26th attack in Santiago, Fidel Castro was tried and sent to prison; however, he was granted amnesty by Batista's government. Castro went into exile and, with support from former President Prío, he organized his armed expedition in Mexico.

2

Genesis of the Cuban Exile

Once upon a time there was a Republic. It had its Constitution, its laws, its freedoms. . . . Everyone could gather, talk, and write with complete freedom. . . . The people had suffered much and, if they were not happy, they longed for [freedom] and had a right to it. . . . [The people] were proud of their love for liberty and were convinced that it would be respected as something sacred.

—*Fidel Castro*[1]

THE REVOLUTION'S EARLY IMPACT ON CUBAN SOCIETY

Castro's Initial Revolutionary Measures

Almost from the start, the revolution initiated an effective, if misleading, practice: Castro would persuasively pledge that his regime was essentially humanistic, rather than Marxist, but the Communist-infiltrated government proceeded in ways that contradicted his pronouncements. The regime's actions spoke louder than the charismatic leader's public rhetoric. Clearly, there was a hidden agenda within Castro's divided inner circle.

> What Fidel was, we all knew: The undisputed caudillo of the revolution. What Fidel thought, no one knew. . . . Fidel identified with all of us. Beyond the different factions, the strongest and most powerful of which was the pro-Soviet and pro-communist commanders: Raúl [Castro], Che [Guevara]. . . . The most popular one was the CTC [Workers' Union], *Revolución* [the regime's newspaper headed by Franqui] and the 26 [the rebels' 26 of July Movement].

... What divides the two groups was ... communism. The third important group was the democratic one: Almeida, Huber Matos and Manuel Ray. . . . The conservative group was formed by leaders of civic institutions, professional associations and representatives of the upper middle class linked to the *Resistencia Cívica* (former underground opposition to Batista). . . . On guard against all of us, an enormous network of newspapers, radio stations and television and the sugar producers, landowners linked to the U.S.[2]

The *Máximo Líder*'s agenda was not revealed all at once. Instead, in long-winded, eloquent speeches, Castro promised to restore democratic freedom, eliminate social injustice, and defend the nation's sovereignty, without ever fully defining the specific measures his regime would implement. He did not have to outline his program. His captivated television audiences applauded this new style of governing by speeches and urged the popular leader to embark upon a vague revolutionary program the scope of which was not spelled out in detail. Less vague, however, was Castro's identification of the "sinister forces" opposing the revolution; he did take his time to associate each of those forces with a distinct segment of society. In retrospect, Castro was meticulously laying the foundations for handling his potential opponents as "enemies of the nation." The ploy would work to perfection.

Occasionally, after years of struggle and disappointment . . . , people decide to place their collective will-power in the hands of a single man. Ever since the death of [José] Martí, the Cubans had been searching for such an individual. Now they believed they had found one.[3]

Despite the overwhelming popular support he enjoyed, Castro was careful to avoid taking on more than one enemy at a time. Following a brilliant divide-and-conquer script, he managed to discredit and isolate his potential adversaries one by one, a strategy that prevented the early opposition from coalescing into a united front. First, he disbanded the army and jailed, executed, or forced into hiding any supporters of Fulgencio Batista who did not follow the deposed dictator into exile. Only after he had disposed of the last vestiges of the ancien régime, did he take clear aim at his next enemy: American businesses on the island. After he had nationalized U.S. investments, he felt secure enough to begin dismantling the civil society. To accomplish that crucial task, Castro needed to count on the support of the masses, so he enacted a series of populist measures, like agrarian reform, that effectively took away the property rights of landowners and the upper classes.

The infighting for political influence between moderate and pro-Communist revolutionaries meanwhile sharpened, and the debate about Castro's own convictions intensified. What seemed to be at stake was the ideological soul of the revolution. Whether by intention or not, the *Máximo Líder* appeared to remain undecided about what course the revolution would actually follow—but not for long. In a dramatic television speech aired on July 17, Castro forced the resignation of his hand-picked president Manuel Urrutia, a moderate—an action that confirmed his totalitarian nature and may well have been the turning point in the radicalization of the revolution. Soon after, other respected non-Communist leaders of the revolution followed Urrutia's unfortunate fate: *Comandante* Huber Matos resigned in October and was later tried and sentenced to twenty years; National Bank director Felipe Pazos and cabinet ministers Manuel Ray and Faustino Pérez were purged; and several independent labor leaders were replaced by Communist sympathizers. It was evident that the revolution, "like Saturn, was beginning to devour its children."[4]

After the conclusion of a high-profile visit by Soviet leader Anastas Mikoyan, ideological divisions on the island definitely solidified. By then, the independent press was coming under attack; several so-called counterrevolutionary newspapers and radio and television stations were taken over by the regime; and it became evident that the days of the rest of the "free" press were numbered.

> The combat with the press was furious. *La Marina* [a conservative newspaper] was enraged. Other newspapers were in the opposition [because of] a combination of vested interests they defended and concerns about the radicalization that were confused with correct criticism. The civil rights were violated. . . . The Revolution was turning communist.[5]

In the following months, the media, one by one, came under the regime's complete control, as did other independent institutions and the unions. Castro's next target was the Catholic Church. This step-by-step strategy, called *la revolución del callo* (the toe revolution), paid off grandly because it assured Castro the enthusiastic support of the rest of the nation against each succeeding political target. The strategy succeeded because all social classes and interest groups continued to back Castro's increasingly totalitarian measures until their own turn came about—when Castro stepped on *their* toes. Then they had no recourse but to leave the country or face the full force of revolutionary justice.

> The "counter-revolutionary" bourgeoisie and the old Batista partisans emigrated to the United States; and it's known that to the fleeing enemy, *puente*

de plata [extend a silver bridge]. Despite the depths of the Revolution and its radicalization, there was no strong opposition.[6]

Not all anti-Castro opponents, however, had left the island. Several groups of disaffected supporters of the revolution, now tied to the United States, continued to operate inside the cities and in the mountains. Perhaps the most prominent among these, the Movimiento de Rescate Revolucionario (MRR), was led by Manuel Artime and Nino Díaz. Others, like the Catholic students' Directorio Revolucionario, led by Alberto Muller, and Manuel Ray's Movimiento Revolucionario del Pueblo (MRP) made a point of proceeding with their clandestine activities without any support from the United States.

Beginning of the Diaspora (1959–1961)

Castro's effective manipulation of public opinion soon succeeded in portraying would-be adversaries of the revolutionary excesses as enemies. There was no political space for dissenters, even among his own comrades in arms —no room for compromise. His guiding dictum, "within the revolution everything, outside the revolution nothing," required supporting him unconditionally or risk being labeled a counterrevolutionary.

The *Máximo Líder*'s immense popularity allowed him to carry repression to extremes never before witnessed in Cuba, even under Batista's dictatorship. Because of the ongoing revolutionary terror, those adversely affected by each new measure could never mount an effective opposition to the popular regime. Instead, as Cubans had often done during periods of political trouble, they sought temporary exile in the United States, a decision that further weakened any internal opposition. But those leaving this time were not only from the nation's more politicized elements, but also from its economic elite—and they now had the overt encouragement of the American government, the giant Goliath whose might had been challenged by this tropical David. When their time to flee arrived, they left convinced that the American government would never allow a Communist dictatorship to exist within its sphere of influence. This geopolitical assumption, known as the "myth of the ninety miles," was soon proven to be a fallacy.

Among the first to follow Batista's partisans into exile were members of the highly educated and mostly white elite: wealthy landowners, sugar barons, industrialists, entrepreneurs, professionals, and former employees of U.S.-owned companies. But since the bulk of them belonged to the more enterprising layers of the island's socioeconomic pyramid, which was being dismantled, their leaving created an irreplaceable gap in economic productivity. Some left as soon as Castro had stepped on their proverbial toes; others felt compelled to leave by the menacing revolutionary climate. In order to come to the United States, Cubans used whatever means were available. The lucky ones obtained immigrant, student, or tourist visas; the rest left through third countries from which they applied for U.S. visas. About 14,000 unaccompanied minors arrived in the United States in 1960 and 1961 by means of the clandestine Operacion Pedro Pan.

The process of leaving was an ordeal in itself because the emigrés were often subjected to embarrassing searches. After 1961, all they were allowed to take was five dollars; they had to surrender all property to the regime. Feeling victims of the political changes taking place on the island, the emigrés in the initial exodus gave the exile community in the United States its lasting political character. The timing of the initial exodus also coincided with mounting tensions between the United States and the Soviet Union. Naturally, Cubans arriving from the Communist-leaning regime saw themselves caught in that international conflict, and both the Eisenhower and Kennedy administrations enthusiastically embraced them as freedom fighters. The exiles, in turn, effectively became willing pawns of the Cold War. They had no other choice.

CAUGHT IN THE COLD WAR

The U.S.–Cuba Conflict

After his takeover in 1959, Castro wasted no time in unleashing a war of words against the United States, placing his regime on a collision course with Washington. He had always personally abhorred Americans, and the feeling was reciprocated by the Republican administration. When Castro briefly visited the United States on April 15, President Eisenhower, who was playing golf in Carolina, declined to meet with him. The Cuban leader, however, was not one to be slighted so pointedly.

A few months after his return to Havana, Castro's tirades against American imperialism gradually intensified. Reciprocal recrimination followed. In the wake of the May agrarian reform, when Washington insisted on "prompt" compensation to the U.S. companies whose land had been confiscated, Castro turned more radical. American officials, however, were still of two minds: While the U.S. State Department largely doubted the Cuban leader was a Communist, the American intelligence community and the military thought otherwise. What perhaps they did not know was that, since the summer of 1959, the *Máximo Líder* had been contemplating the acquisition of arms from the Soviet Union. In fact, it was not until November that the U.S. ambassador to Havana, Philip Bonsal, finally concluded that an understanding with Castro could no longer be expected. By then, a new wave of the nationalization of foreign companies was gathering momentum.

Toward the conclusion of the revolution's first year in power, the Cuban regime was busy making plans for a realignment of its national and international stance: Its ambassador to Washington had been "indefinitely" withdrawn, and a visit to Cuba by Soviet Vice President Mikoyan had been scheduled for February 1960. Nevertheless, the fact that the American administration still had not made up its mind about Castro was evident in the conciliatory tone of President Eisenhower's January 26 speech on Cuba. Whatever goodwill Eisenhower's softer pronunciations generated, however, was undermined by increasing paramilitary raids against the revolutionary regime staged by Cuban exiles in the United States. At such a confusing and volatile moment, Mikoyan's visit to Havana took place.

The Cuban regime spared no effort to ingratiate itself with the high-ranking Soviet visitor: Castro and a Communist party delegation welcomed Mikoyan at the airport, a Soviet scientific exhibition was staged, and a concert was organized in his honor. Although a modest trade agreement with the Soviet Union was signed, Mikoyan's visit was marred when some Catholic university students forcibly replaced with their own a wreath the Russian had placed on Martí's statue on Havana's Central Park.

> When he [Mikoyan] comes to Cuba, we go with a group of Catholic students to Central Park to place a wreath resembling the Cuban flag in order to counter Mikoyan's "sickle and hammer" wreath. Our banners read: "Hail to the revolution; down with communism." We still differentiated between the revolution and communism at that time. But when we get there we are physically attacked and apprehended. Right then we realized that there was no difference; what was being implanted in Cuba was really a Communist regime. (Translation of author's interview with Manuel Salvat)

By the end of Mikoyan's visit, Washington's interest in pursuing a rapprochement with the Cuban regime had begun to wane. Indeed, at least as early as March 17, 1960, as the hostile posturing between the two governments intensified, President Eisenhower officially authorized the Central Intelligence Agency (CIA) to begin arming and training Cuban exiles. The CIA's secret mission was to help militant Cuban freedom fighters in Miami carry out operations against the Cuban regime. Initially, the scope of such actions was relatively limited, consisting mainly of the clandestine infiltration of exiles onto the island to aid internal opposition and several guerilla groups that were sprouting up in the mountains. Despite this obvious escalation in the conflict, the advantageous U.S. quota for Cuban sugar imports ironically still remained intact. Soon enough, the quota would become a bone of contention between the two governments.

For several months, concerns over the U.S. quota for Cuban sugar had kept both sides posturing obsessively. Finally, in the summer of 1960, Cuba's "intervention" of U.S. oil refineries persuaded Eisenhower to reduce the U.S. quota for Cuban sugar, a decision that, in effect, amounted to an economic sanction against Castro. By then, the Soviets had established formal diplomatic relations with Cuba, and Prime Minister Nikita Khrushchev warned that, if it became necessary, the Soviets would use rockets to defend the revolutionary government. As a reaction to Washington's "economic aggression," the Cuban regime became even more radical and expropriated the remaining U.S. companies on the island as well as most of Cuba's private business sector.

In September 1960, Castro made a second trip to the United States. He did not, unlike during his previous visit, get a warm reception from the American people. Neither did his four-hour speech at the United Nations serve to ingratiate him this time. By attracting so much attention to himself, however, all Castro may have accomplished was to make Cuba a central issue during the U.S. presidential campaign. To be sure, Senator John F. Kennedy seized the opportunity to identify the Republican administration with the failed policies that had turned Cuba against the United States; a Democratic administration, he vowed, would aggressively enforce the Monroe Doctrine[7] and restore democracy to Cuba. That was precisely the course of action secretly embarked upon by President Eisenhower six months earlier, but because of its covert nature, Republican candidate Richard M. Nixon could not publicly divulge the administration's plans.

It was under the political shadow cast by the ongoing presidential campaign that the Eisenhower administration imposed the first commercial embargo on Cuban goods.[8] Castro reacted quickly. In rapid succession, his regime speeded up the nationalization of the remaining U.S. companies on the island, ordered a general mobilization to counter an alleged American invasion, and demanded that the United States drastically reduce its personnel at the American embassy in Havana. At the time, Castro's charges about an invasion were still technically unfounded; so far, President Eisenhower had only authorized exile covert actions against Cuba's revolutionary government. A more ominous type of escalation, nevertheless, was already brewing within the U.S. intelligence community. Indeed, by November 1960, as mutual accusations steered both nations on an increasingly belligerent path, plans for a larger-scale operation against Cuba were being hatched in Washington.[9]

The Bay of Pigs Invasion (1961)

By the time John F. Kennedy became president in January 1961, plans for an invasion were rapidly escalating, and a proposal to use Cuban exiles for a more weighty attack—actually, a conventional military landing—was finally approved. The training of exiles in the remote mountains of Guatemala under the supervision of the CIA took a new course: The would-be guerilla force created under the Eisenhower administration was reorganized into Brigade 2506, a military assault unit that included paratroopers, heavy weapons, tanks, and even some vintage B-26 airplanes.

> I arrived in exile on the 29th of June of 1960—I won't forget that date. This was after a short participation in the anti-Castro struggle inside Cuba. And I came with the definite idea to join those that I knew were already involved in the training in Guatemala to form a force to go to Cuba. So, in December of 1960, I joined those camps and began training as a paratrooper for what was eventually the Bay of Pigs' Invasion. We all went with the expectation that this was something serious, that definitely we would have control of the air as was promised by our instructors, who were Americans; we didn't know who they were exactly, but we know what happened. (Author's interview with sociologist Juan Clark)

In the month of March 1961, the number of exile recruits in Guatemala swelled to about 1,500 men, and the Bay of Pigs, an inhospitable swampy area in the southern underbelly of the island, was selected as the landing site for the invasion. Under President Kennedy, the CIA also revamped the umbrella coalition of anti-Castro organizations it had inherited from the previous administration. Early in 1961, the old Frente Revolucionario Democrático became reconstituted with disaffected members of Castro's own 26th of July Movement whose revolutionary credentials would appeal to Cubans on the island. Among its new members was Manuel Ray, who reluctantly came into the CIA's fold. The new Consejo Revolutionario Cubano, created as a sort of provisional government in exile, triggered much controversy within the politically fractured exile leadership. The *batistianos* considered it too leftist; the former *fidelistas* objected to its dependence on the CIA. Given the impending invasion, however, the Consejo's directorate ultimately closed ranks behind José Miró Cardona, the former prime minister in Castro's first revolutionary cabinet; Manuel Artime was appointed its military liaison to the CIA.

> After a brief period in Miami, I was infiltrated into Cuba on December of 1960. My mission was to help coordinate underground activities for the planned invasion. A so-called Clandestine Army was then being formed by all underground organizations for the purpose of producing an uprising upon the landing of the invasion. (Translation of author's interview with Manuel Salvat)

From its inception, the success of the invasion was heavily predicated upon two untested strategic premises: It would enjoy control of the airspace over Cuba, and it would have the backing of the Cuban people. Specifically, the plans for the invasion assumed that U.S. fighter planes piloted by Cuban exiles would provide air cover to Brigade 2506 before and during its landing; and that Cubans on the island, led by a massive underground movement, would rise against the government the moment they learned the invasion was under way. Neither of these strategic assumptions materialized; Castro effectively preempted both developments.

As planned, exiled pilots flying U.S. planes disguised to look like Cuba's own air force began to attack the island's military airfields two days before the invasion took place. This gimmick, conceived by the CIA, was to create the impression that the Cuban air force had turned against Castro. But instead of achieving the intended effect, the air raids tipped off Castro to the impending invasion. Thus forewarned, Castro's repressive apparatus rounded up more than 100,000 citizens it suspected of supporting an invasion. The massive detention, coupled with the fact that the island's underground was never notified, crippled the internal opposition to Castro and prevented its effective involvement in support of the operation.

> April 17th, for us, was a great frustration. We woke up to the news that the invasion had arrived and we, simply, were not ready. The regime was apprehending anyone who looked a bit suspicious; on that very morning, many of our own people had already been detained. On the following day, April 18th, I get caught during a routine search—I carried false identification—and I am taken to the G-2 [military intelligence unit] where I remained in limbo for 18 days, much like the rest. (Translation of author's interview with Manuel Salvat)

Once alerted, the Cuban revolutionary regime also moved on the diplomatic front, prompting the Soviet Union to denounce the American ploy before the United Nations. Unaware himself that the CIA had actually or-

chestrated those air raids, Adlai Stevenson, the American representative to
the United Nations, adamantly refuted the Soviet charges. But much to the
embarrassment of Ambassador Stevenson, the Soviets were ready to show the
damning evidence to the world. It was at that late time that President Kennedy actually learned the compromising details of the American involvement
in the invasion. The young president nevertheless allowed the landing to go
ahead, but he ordered the critical U.S. role trimmed down and cancelled the
remaining air strikes in support of the operation. The curtailment of such
critical components effectively doomed the fate of Brigade 2506. The revolutionary government quickly dispatched about 20,000 Cuban troops to re-
spond to the landing of the exile force. Without American military support,
Brigade 2506 was defeated in three days.[10] Castro decisively won the day.

> The defeat of the invasion was due to a lack of U.S. support, when it failed
> to honor the promises to provide air support and to aid the underground. Our
> fundamental error was placing Cuba's destiny on the hands of the United
> States. (Translation of author's interview with José Basulto)

To the Cuban exiles who had anxiously awaited the invasion, the U.S.
failure to live up to its commitment at the Bay of Pigs represented a harsh
blow that shook their confidence in their only ally. They felt betrayed by
President Kennedy, and to their mortification, Fidel Castro's image was aggrandized throughout the world. Now their Communist nemesis could boast
of having defeated the powerful United States and its Cuban "mercenaries"
at the Bay of Pigs. The invasion fiasco certainly gave a tremendous boost to
the revolution. It cast the bearded Cuban leader in the role of a victorious
David over the American imperialist Goliath, and it justified Castro's seeking
a formal military alliance with the Soviet Union, a move that would shortly
bring the world to the brink of nuclear holocaust.

The Cuban Missile Crisis (1962)

On October 22, 1962, after a frantic week of secret discussions at the
highest levels of government, President Kennedy appeared on national television to announce that the Soviet Union was on the verge of installing
offensive missiles in Cuba. In his dramatic broadcast to the American people,
the president denounced this action as an unprecedented Soviet provocation
and ordered an immediate naval blockade of the nearby island.

Everyone cringed in horror. This ominous development placed the American president clearly on the political defensive, for the Soviet military

buildup in Cuba had occurred during his watch. But that was the least of Kennedy's concerns; he knew the stakes were much higher. While fear gripped the rest of the world, however, most Cuban exiles welcomed the news of a potential confrontation over Cuba as an opportunity to somehow get rid of Castro once and for all. From their narrow perspective, the reaction was understandable, for it confirmed their prediction that the Cuban Communist regime would eventually open its doors to Soviet military penetration of the American continent. They felt that their suspicions had finally been validated.

The presence in Cuba of nuclear missiles capable of striking American targets from just ninety miles away was certainly a reckless Soviet move that threatened the precarious military balance between the world's two superpowers. President Kennedy, not sure what type of response would persuade the Kremlin that the United States would not tolerate missiles in Cuba, had initially opted to blockade the island, his most moderate option. Should this action fail to dissuade the Kremlin, however, it would have been necessary to consider an air strike against the missile installations or even an all-out military invasion of Cuba. And time was short, since about twenty-five Russian ships, presumably loaded with their deadly nuclear cargo, were quickly approaching the island.

The stage was set for what could develop into the first U.S.-Soviet military confrontation of the nuclear age. That unthinkable conflict, however, was temporarily avoided when the Soviet vessels stopped dead on the high seas just as they were to reach the quarantined waters around the island. Premier Khrushchev apparently "blinked," and the American president won some precious time to pursue a settlement. The confrontation, of course, had only been momentarily delayed. The more difficult issue—the actual disposal of the rocket sites nearing completion on the island—still needed to be resolved. The quid pro quo for removing those rockets, Premier Khrushchev stated in his private correspondence to President Kennedy, was the removal of the United States' own nuclear bases from Turkey and an American pledge not to invade Cuba in the future.

Castro, however, was not as inclined to compromise. Although left out of the negotiations loop between Kennedy and Khrushchev, he kept urging the Soviet premier to seize the initiative and unleash an all-out nuclear attack against the United States. When his intemperate advice was rejected, Castro personally ordered the Cuban military to use Soviet ground-to-air missiles to shoot down an American U-2 spy plane during an intelligence-gathering flight over the island. That action could have ended the short-lived respite. President Kennedy, however, decided not to retaliate in kind to the trigger-happy Cuban leader; instead, he ignored this provocation and continued to pursue a last-minute peaceful settlement of the crisis, even as he ordered the U.S. military to continue preparing for an air attack on Cuba within a few days.

On the eve of an American attack against Cuba, the White House received another message from the Kremlin: Premier Khrushchev had decided to remove all offensive missiles from the Caribbean island—much to Castro's annoyance. Thus, an imminent nuclear confrontation was averted, and the balance between the two superpowers was restored. The world had come to the brink of a nuclear war and, almost miraculously, the two world leaders had managed to avoid that horrible outcome; reason had prevailed over the whims of the Cubans on both sides of the Straits of Florida.

> After the failure of the Bay of Pigs' invasion and the Missile Crisis . . . our struggle for the liberation of Cuba was considerably weakened; only a few organizations like Alpha 66 maintained a militant attitude. Some of them helped the rebels who were in the Escambray mountains [inside Cuba] fighting against the regime and . . . carried out paramilitary operations, but all of this in a minor tone. (Author's interview with economist Antonio Jorge, a leader of the exile community)

The Cuban exiles could not find any solace in the peaceful resolution of the October missile crisis. Once more, Castro had succeeded in defying the United States' might and still remained in power. In the eyes of the Cuban exiles, the Kremlin had proven to be a more decisive ally to its friends than Washington. Indeed, the exiles' suspicion that a deal had been struck with the Soviets whereby Castro's survival would be guaranteed by the United States was eventually confirmed by the future course of events.

DAWNING OF A NEW ERA

To the Cuban exiles who already felt betrayed by President Kennedy's indecisiveness during the Bay of Pigs Invasion, the diplomatic resolution of the October missile crisis represented another wasted opportunity to free their country from communism. They felt that the American president had abandoned their cause on both occasions—and now perhaps irrevocably, for the Cuban exiles feared that the resulting internationalization of the Cuban issue made it even more difficult to get rid of the regime that enslaved their nation.

Those fears proved correct. Soon after the missile crisis, the United States virtually discontinued the military and financial assistance it had provided to the Cuban freedom fighters since the summer of 1960. Although the United States officially withdrew its support from the exiles' paramilitary operations, the CIA encouraged freedom fighters to move their bases outside American territory and, for some time, continued to provide some assistance to the exiles through friendly Latin American governments.

Between 1963 and 1965, in effect, the United States apparently pursued a dual policy with respect to Cuba: While the CIA continued to support several anti-Castro organizations that staged raids against the Communist island, the Justice Department grew more testy with Cuban freedom fighters. During that confusing period, the freedom fighters often had to contend with FBI and Cuban agents who infiltrated the anti-Castro organizations to learn their plans.[11]

Adding insult to injury, the Justice Department then began to prosecute the freedom fighters for organizing missions against Castro using the same weapons that the CIA had earlier provided to them; they were charged, ironically, with violating the U.S. Neutrality Act. The Cuban exiles did not know that the reversal in U.S. policy resulted from a secret agreement with the Soviets, but they had guessed as much all along. What they did know was that, without the help of the CIA, they would not stand a chance against the Cuban regime, whose military might increased steadily as the Soviet Union took Castro under its protective wing.

This was perhaps the darkest hour of the Cuban exile experience. The exiles saw themselves falling from the official grace of the United States, their trusted ally; and yesterday's prized freedom fighters were now regarded as a losing band of renegades, an inconvenience to the United States. From then on, the CIA became concerned with the "disposal problem" the exiles it had trained now represented. Although some freedom fighters continued to launch small independent actions, they had to overcome the vigilance of both Cuba and the CIA. The rules of the game had been drastically changed, and the Cubans now faced what would indeed prove to be a long exile. Actually, they were witnessing the dawn of a new era.

NOTES

1. Fidel Castro's speech during his trial in October 1953 for leading an attack against Batista's military barracks on July 26, 1953.

2. Carlos Franqui, *Retrato de familia con Fidel* (Barcelona: Editorial Seix Barral, 1981), 39–41.

3. Hugh Thomas, *Cuba: The Pursuit of Freedom* (New York: Harper, 1971), 1037.

4. Ibid., 1239.

5. Franqui, *Retrato de Familia*, 153.

6. Ibid., 149.

7. Since the nineteenth century, the United States had invoked the Monroe Doctrine to keep the European powers out of the American continent.

8. The first stage of the trade embargo against Cuba was imposed on October 13, 1960. In February 1962, the embargo was further tightened.

9. President Eisenhower authorized the Central Intelligence Agency to organize an army to invade Cuba in March 1960.

10. More than one hundred exiles were killed during the invasion; the rest were captured, tried, and sentenced to thirty years in prison. Twenty-one months later, however, the Cuban government ransomed the bulk of the prisoners, exchanging them for U.S.-supplied medical and agricultural equipment. The brigade members returned to Miami, where they were welcomed as heroes.

11. For a detailed and well-documented narrative of the anti-Castro effort, see Enrique Encinosa, *Cuba en guerra* (Miami: The Endowment for Cuban American Studies of the Cuban American National Foundation, 1994).

3

Development of the Cuban Exile Country

By now there is an entrenched, comfortable [exile] mainstream. It runs through the heart of Cuban Miami like a familiar boulevard, like *Calle Ocho*, a corridor of confidence and composure. It feels as if things have always been this way, this inclusive, and open and tolerant.

—*Liz Balmaseda*[1]

Since Cubans first began to flee their nation following the 1959 revolutionary takeover, the lost homeland has endured as the only constant throughout their diaspora—their common bond, the obligatory historical reference that lingers in their memory like bitter sugar on a child's palate. Cuba is, indeed, the shared past to which, whenever they left, wherever they settled, the emigrés could always relate. Not surprisingly, the Cuban Exile Country continues to be linked to its place of origin. Whether Cuban Americans or Cubans residing in other nations, nearly all Cuban emigrés tend to define themselves in terms of Cuba. It remains their collective homeland.

Over the years, most Cuban emigrés have insisted that they are political exiles even if their actual behavior in the United States partially contradicts the transient connotation of that definition. Exiles, for example, rarely take up a different citizenship or grow permanent roots in their new surroundings, as the Cubans have certainly done. Much has changed in the internal dynamics of *el exilio* since 1959 and, evidently, this long-held sense of identity has begun to relent under the weight of time. But the emergence of a Cuban American identity represents a new phenomenon; until very recently, the overwhelming majority considered themselves political exiles and, as such, reluctant emigrés. Among the older generation, most still do.[2]

From its onset, the political genesis of the Cuban exodus nurtured many self-defining characteristics that appear to set these emigrés somewhat apart from other Latin Americans coming to the United States. Unlike true immigrants, the early Cuban emigrés were well aware that they would lose in exile the socioeconomic status most of them had enjoyed in Cuba. Whereas immigrants are usually motivated by the "pull" this proverbial "land of opportunity" exerts upon them, the initial two waves of Cuban emigrés felt "pushed" by political conditions prevailing in Cuba at the time they left.[3] Truth be told, those Cubans did not come to the United States searching for the economic fortunes inherently promised by the American Dream; their exodus was a direct response to the impact of Fidel Castro's revolution, and, once they settled abroad, they adamantly rejected being classified as immigrants. By the time other Cubans with somewhat different motivations and socioeconomic backgrounds later joined them in America, that initial exodus had already given their collective experience its lasting political imprint.

Through almost four decades, Cuban exiles have tried obsessively to stay abreast of developments back in their homeland—so much so that the emigrés, particularly those in South Florida, have continued to be influenced as much by the course of events on the island as by what transpires in their adopted surroundings. Not only have ensuing revolutionary measures triggered the exodus of additional waves, but each successive emigration has had an impact on the orientation of those already here. Unfortunately, this obvious connection between Cubans on both sides of the Straits of Florida has often been neglected because current academic specialization tends to separate "Cubans studies" into two distinct fields: Cubans in exile and Cubans on the island. Their linkage, nevertheless, is remarkable: Time and again actions taking place in Cuba precipitate corresponding reactions among the exiles in the United States.

The connection is so strong that it characterizes the stages of development of the Cuban exile experience: survival (1959–1962), transition (1962–1965), adjustment (1965–1973), economic miracle (1973–1980), diversification (1980–1990), and post-Soviet era (1990 to the present).[4] These are not merely successive chronological periods; rather, they constitute true stages, for each has brought about a clear shift in the internal dynamics of the exile community and a new sense of collective direction.

THE SURVIVAL STAGE (1959–1962)

Following the coming to power of the revolution, the Cuban diaspora begins. Although some early exiles refer to members of that initial exodus as the "historic exiles" (implying that successive waves have come mostly for economic, not political reasons), such a distinction seems unfounded.

The Initial Exodus (1959–1961)

Cubans began their Castro-era emigration the moment General Fulgencio Batista fled the island on New Year's morning of 1959 and a "provisional" revolutionary government took over the reins of the politically troubled nation. The first exiles were hundreds of Batista's closest collaborators who feared reprisals from the regime that had ousted them. Soon after, they were joined in the United States by a massive exodus that originated within the nation's business establishment and professional class but quickly enough included early defectors from Castro's own ranks as well. That initial exodus, therefore, embraced three distinct exile "vintages," the largest of which was the island's nonpolitical elite.[5]

The upper and middle classes were disproportionately represented in that initial wave. Because of political circumstances, the emigrés were mostly destitute upon arrival, but many of them were familiar with the United States, having often visited it for business or pleasure before the revolution. Some also had old schoolmates, friends, and business contacts throughout the nation. In addition, because Cuban culture was highly Americanized, the members of this particular vintage were not complete strangers to America's way of life: To them, the United States was not terra incognita. Precisely because of their familiarity with the United States, they "were the least given to believe that the American government would permit the consolidation of a socialist regime in the island."[6]

> These were people who had it all in Cuba. They were living comfortable lives, they were professionals, they were well-adjusted, and they gave it all up because they wanted their children to live in an environment of freedom. They wanted to free Cuba; they came to this country with the idea that this was the place from where to organize the struggle for Cuba's freedom, where their children could grow and develop their full potential—something they couldn't do in Cuba. (Author's interview with attorney Rafael Peñalver)

The demographic profile of the exiles who arrived between 1959 and 1962 confirms other characteristics associated with their high socioeconomic status in prerevolutionary Cuba. Most may have left empty handed but not without human capital. Their educational and professional backgrounds, in fact, placed them near the top echelons of society—in Cuba and in America as well. This wave constituted the island's "cream of the crop"—those who had studied English at Havana's private schools or had learned it at American summer camps, high schools, and colleges. They were also older than most immigrants; hence, their cultural identity was rather defined by the time they left their homeland, a crucial factor in understanding how this group was able to resist becoming acculturated in America.

The role that their identity as exiles has played on their American dynamics defies quantification; so do other defining traits displayed by this initial wave, such as pride, enterprising drive, adaptability, and a host of other psychosocial aspects that served them well in their new environment. Neither can the cultural "baggage" they brought be accurately measured by statistics. The same is true of their political idiosyncrasies. Perhaps there is something unique in the mind-set of all exiles that acts as a special incentive to do well.[7] In any event, the initial wave of Cuban emigrés had it in abundance. They were also heirs to an enterprising tradition honed by centuries of commercial contact with the outside world, which may account for the self-confident attitude generally found among the winners—and these Cubans were definitely not wanting in the determination to succeed.

The Anti-Castro Struggle among Early Exiles

Upon their arrival in the United States, the initial wave was driven by one all-consuming objective: to return to Cuba after toppling Castro's revolutionary government. They expected that, with the support of their powerful American ally, such an objective would be accomplished within a short period of time. This expectation was not the result of wishful thinking; rather, it was a most natural assumption. Indeed, given the geopolitical interest Americans had historically shown in its Cuban neighbors, it seemed inconceivable that a Communist regime would be allowed to take hold within the U.S. sphere of influence.

Those first exiles reasoned that Castro did not stand a chance of remaining in power for long. Truly, the odds against the survival of the revolutionary regime seemed formidable. By the summer of 1960, guerilla groups linked to an incipient underground network had already surfaced in the Cuban mountains ("armed bandits," Castro called them). More ominously, the U.S. government had begun to recruit and train exiles for paramilitary actions against Castro. Such internal and external threats, the exiles inferred, could not be effectively countered by the nascent regime.

By early 1961, right after the inauguration of President Kennedy, the emigrés' confidence in the liberation of their homeland reached a feverish pitch, as scores of Cuban exiles were being recruited by the Central Intelligence Agency (CIA) and sent to training bases in Guatemala and other secret locations.[8] This was supposed to be a covert operation, but pictures of the training camps were prominently displayed in the weekly tabloids (*periodiquitos*) published in the United States by exiles as well as in *The New York Times*. Despite President Kennedy's repeated denials, everyone was well aware that a U.S.-sponsored invasion of the island would soon be launched. That prospect, certainly, was viewed as the coup de grâce for the fledgling revolutionary government.

The invasion fever sweeping the Cuban exile community became obsessive. A coalition of anti-Castro groups had been brought together under the auspices of "The Company"—the term used by the personnel of the CIA. The new umbrella organization, Consejo Revolucionario Cubano (Cuban Revolutionary Council), came under the political and military control of the CIA, making the exiles nothing more than willing instruments of the United States. Although the relinquishing of total authority to the CIA caused some friction among exile leaders, they were persuaded that this was an "unavoidable cost." The plans for the invasion continued at full speed.

The Need for Survival

Although their attention remained focused on the liberation of Cuba, the exiles still needed to find the means to survive during what they assumed would be a temporary stay in America. Since many did not speak fluent English, finding that first job represented a formidable challenge; an ever-expanding pool of exiles competed for limited local jobs. South Florida was clearly a buyers' market.

> It was Halloween night when I arrived in Miami with my wife and my one-year-old son. I saw the kids "trick-or-treating" and only $40 in my pocket. . . . We found a room to live in a house with an old lady—$5 a week was our room, one bed, all three of us slept in the one bed. But at last we were in the land of freedom and democracy and opportunity. (Author's interview with banker Carlos Arboleya)

For the exiles in those days, making ends meet meant accepting the first job that was offered. Since South Florida's strong unions maintained firm restrictions against the newcomers, Cubans were forced to take any jobs, even those traditionally held by Miami's African Americans. Former Cuban entrepreneurs and professionals parked cars, washed dishes, drove taxis, waited on tables, delivered newspapers, and performed a variety of menial tasks for which they were undoubtedly overqualified. Unlicensed Cuban doctors and dentists, ever so careful not to be discovered by the authorities, saw patients in their own homes. Housewives who had never held a job in Cuba found employment as waitresses, maids, seamstresses, factory workers, and vegetable pickers in the fields. Thousands of exiles were able to go on the generous payroll of the CIA, which during the Survival Stage may have been one of Dade County's larger employers.

The challenge of survival was met with a strong sense of solidarity. In South Florida, where the bulk of the emigrés waited for Castro's overthrow, those who arrived earlier tried to ease the shock of the newly arrived by offering them advice on how to obtain a social security card, to enroll their children in school, to look for housing, and to enlist in the federally funded Cuban Refugee Program, where they could get free medical attention and bags of groceries.[9] The few fortunate enough to afford a car drove their Cuban neighbors to work, to the doctor, and to supermarkets. Typically, they helped each other find jobs, and once hired, they recommended friends and relatives to their employers.

> Grass roots organization started practically in the beginning in the 60's. People didn't lose track of where they came from or their families and friends, and that facilitated the creation of an economic and social network that was going to contribute greatly to the Cuban success. (Author's interview with anthropologist Mercedes Sandoval)

Whether in the South Florida area or in other American cities, Cubans in those days seldom made a move outside their closely knit circle of family and lifelong acquaintances. The spirit of community that characterized the Survival Stage was to prevail until today, as each new wave went through a similar process upon arriving in America. Survival, indeed, became the shared rite of passage into exile.

Settling in South Florida

Given their expectations for a quick return to their homeland, the initial exodus settled primarily in and around Miami. That was understandable. Throughout the island's brief history as an independent nation, South Florida's proximity to Cuba had made it the haven of choice whenever political troubles forced Cubans into exile. Moreover, Miami's quasi-tropical climate resembled Cuba's.

Those who had come in the past as exiles belonged to the more politically active segments of Cuban society—for example, the opposition to Gerardo Machado in the early 1930s and to Batista in the 1950s—but not this time. This was a different type of exodus, far greater in numbers and consisting of the well-educated upper and middle classes and their families; unlike their predecessors, they had left everything behind. More significantly, their concentration in Miami, then a resort town catering mainly to winter tourists, would eventually offer them the opportunity to lay the foundations of a thriving Cuban enclave.[10]

> My arrival, November 11, 1960, alone, was probably one of the saddest moments of my life. I had $210 in a check hidden in my coat. My wife and my child arrived the next day. I was lucky that I was hired as a clerk—I was a lawyer and a CPA in Cuba. I was hired as a clerk at Washington Federal Savings and Loan. (Author's interview with banker Bernardo Benes)

As more and more exiles came, they tended to settle in the then-depressed areas of Miami's southwest section, where rents were low. South Florida, a racially segregated community, had never witnessed such an incursion of often destitute ethnics moving into "Anglo"[11] neighborhoods; these foreigners were very different from the free-spending Latin American tourists who stayed in Miami Beach's hotels. Their sudden impact on the community was greeted with mixed emotions by the established residents, who perceived the newcomers as clannish and loud. Like most immigrants who come to America, the Cuban exiles met with some resentment.

> Some people resented our presence here because we speak a different language, we were talking too loud, we didn't have enough money and, when we rented an apartment, a two-room apartment, maybe seven or eight relatives would move in. So, they had signs saying: "No Cubans, no pets, and no children." (Author's interview with banker Luis Botifoll)

The exiles, in fact, *were* clannish and loud. In those days, several nuclear families often pooled their resources and crammed into small apartments until each family was able to afford a place of its own. And they were also conspicuous. During the day, hundreds gathered downtown to share the latest news from Cuba and to exchange information about available jobs; at night, they visited with friends and sat on their porches seeking relief from

Miami's heat. From the very start, the emigrés showed an all-consuming desire to stay in touch with each other and, to the extent they could afford it, keep alive their traditional way of life. By the end of the Survival Stage, an embryonic exile community was already emerging within Miami.

THE TRANSITION STAGE (1962–1965)

The 1961 Bay of Pigs fiasco and the internationalization of the "Cuban Issue" following the 1962 missile crisis shattered the exiles' hopes for a quick return. The Cuban Exile Country then began to undergo a series of changes that characterize the Transition Stage. During this period, a new mind-set emerged, and the exiles started to redirect their focus from the anti-Communist struggle to the economic arena.

A Period of Hopelessness

Events involving Cuba—the Bay of Pigs Invasion and the missile crisis—jolted *el exilio*, leaving it in disarray. Deep within their psyches, the exiles felt defeated in their cause and lost in a new land. In the Transition Stage, the militant anti-Castro spirit that had so far lent coherence to the exile experience did not wane all of a sudden, but it certainly began giving way to painful introspection. During this period, commercial flights between Cuba and the United States were discontinued, leaving many of the relatives of the initial exodus stranded on the island.

Hopelessness about returning to Cuba was hard to accept. The invasion fiasco and the Soviet Union's involvement in the affairs of the Caribbean island had effectively consolidated Castro's regime; the United States had failed the exiles, not once, but twice. It was time for the emigrés, albeit reluctantly, to come to terms with the prospects of a long stay in America. It was a demoralizing transition for the proud Cubans; to make matters worse, they were forced to recognize that Castro's international image had grown to mythical proportions as a result of his victories against American "imperialism." Castro's regime, indeed, had been strengthened, while the Cuban exiles, abandoned by their American ally and denigrated by the world press, had suffered a lasting defeat.

That harsh realization could well have shamed the exiles into becoming an obscure curiosity, a meaningless footnote in the history of Cuba, or they could have followed the same fate as other immigrant groups and disappeared into America's melting pot. Instead, after a period of soul searching, they emerged determined to endure. Thus challenged, the exiles needed to find a new cause consistent with their battered convictions. Given the political nature of their exodus, the reluctant emigrés felt they could regain their collective self-worth only by somehow assigning a subliminal ideological justification to their commonplace struggle in America.

> The Cubans, the first, at least, and I think the rest, too, who came into exile, did not come here looking for a job or because of hunger. . . . And they brought a sort of desire to prove that Castro was wrong. Castro was calling us "worms," and the "scum of the earth," [and saying that] we were of no value whatsoever. And there was a sort of silent code or effort to say, wherever I am—and I have heard this from many mechanics, professors, writers, lawyers—wherever I am, I am going to demonstrate that I am a Cuban and that I am very good at what I do. (Author's interview with Georgetown University professor emeritus Luis Aguilar León)

The End of the War against Castro

For all intents and purposes, the exiles' struggle to liberate Cuba by force all but ceased during the Transition Stage. They lacked the resources to contend with Castro's growing military power, and without U.S. support, they knew any future action carried out by Cuban freedom fighters was doomed. There was no getting around this painful conclusion.

> It was like a trap for us. Castro had managed to internationalize the Cuban issue and he had all the support of Russia. Against that, a group of youngsters simply couldn't contend . . . we couldn't find a way out of that trap. And at the same time, there was a personal problem; we were already married—I had three children. That was an important reality in my life, and I had to face that responsibility. I could not continue living the life of a revolutionary. . . . We were not a bunch of professional revolutionaries; we had just become involved in that process because Cuba needed us. (Translation of author's interview with publisher Manuel Salvat, who was active in the anti-Castro struggle)

Responding to a new set of national priorities, Washington had abandoned the cause of Cuban freedom in favor of a policy of peaceful coexistence with the Soviet empire. The suddenness with which the United States implemented its turnabout left Cuban exiles in shock. In rapid succession, the CIA cut off the support it had been providing to Cuban freedom fighters since the summer of 1960, and the U.S. government began to persecute and prosecute exiles who tried to launch independent raids against Castro's regime. It was a sad finale to a struggle for which thousands of their comrades in arms had given their lives and tens of thousands more languished in Cuba's jails.

By December 1962, when negotiations with the Cuban government for the return of the prisoners from the Bay of Pigs Invasion concluded and President Kennedy arrived in Miami to welcome the invasion veterans as heroes, the active struggle symbolically came to an end. From then on, group after group of militant exiles were forced to accept that theirs was a lost cause, and many of their members joined the U.S. Army or reluctantly reoriented their lives in exile. They had no other alternative. After four turbulent years of diplomatic and military confrontations, Castro's revolution had triumphed against the Cuban exiles and the United States.

> It was sad. . . . When I emotionally turned the page, was after the Bay of Pigs. When those men came back, namely the father of my children and my brother who was nineteen at the time, I said: "This is it; we have done what was expected of us to recover Cuba." And then I thought: "I don't want to suffer anymore; I don't want to go through this anymore." So, at that point, I said to myself: "I think this country has a lot to offer. I'm not going to forget my country of origin, but I'm here and I'm gonna represent Cuba and act in the most dignified and in the most successful way that I can to represent my country of origin." (Author's interview with businesswoman María Elena Toraño)

Shortly thereafter, dozens of front companies, through which the CIA had funneled funds to its covert activities, disappeared into thin air just as quickly as they had materialized a few years earlier. Others went legitimate after the CIA stopped funding them. It was a telling sign. The time had come for Cuban exiles to relegate the cause that had sustained them so far and to begin to reconstruct their lives in America.

Resettlement Policy of the Cuban Refugee Program

From the moment the Cuban exiles began arriving in the United States, the official intention of the American government had been to relocate the newcomers throughout the country. That policy encountered much initial resistance, because most Cubans preferred to stay in South Florida in the hope that their exile would be a short-lived one. During the Transition Stage, however, thousands of exiles began to resettle in other communities across the nation.

My father could not get a job in Miami, because if you were Cuban in the early 1960s, you could not get a job here, you could not rent a house, you could hardly get a telephone without a substantial deposit. So, for lack of opportunities for my father, we left Miami and ended up in Long Island, New York, and that's where I grew up. (Author's interview with businesswoman Cruz Hernández Otazo)

The stated rationale of the resettlement efforts of the Cuban Refugee Program was to lighten the financial burden that the exiles represented to South Florida's strained social institutions. While the validity of this argument cannot be disputed, the U.S. government may have also feared the social and political implications of a growing and increasingly frustrated (and well-armed) exile population concentrated in Miami. In any case, once the exiles realized that a quick return to a free Cuba would not be forthcoming, some began to take advantage of the resettlement assistance offered through the Cuban Refugee Program.[12]

For nearly all of those who left Miami during the Transition Stage, their decision involved a tacit reordering of their personal priorities; the well-being of their family would now take precedence over the struggle to liberate their homeland. That recognition did not mean that the exiles were turning their backs on the cause of Cuban freedom, but rather that their war against Castro would be largely reduced to a rhetorical exercise. The fact was that most violent anti-Castro activities had all but stopped after the 1962 missile crisis; and South Florida's job market was saturated with hard-working, non-English-speaking applicants. Given those realities, the decision to relocate seemed a practical alternative.[13]

Among those leaving were thousands of Cuban professionals, particularly lawyers and educators for whom secure employment as Spanish teachers in other states seemed to offer better prospects than hard-to-secure, dead-end jobs in South Florida. They were joined by former managers of American companies that had operated in Cuba until confiscated by Castro, blue-collar workers attracted by higher paying union jobs in the frigid north, and disillusioned freedom fighters who joined the U.S. Army in the faint hope that a twist of fate might send them to fight Castro under the American flag. They all left Miami with mixed feelings but with the resolve to carve out a new life in the "land of opportunity."

They offered us the opportunity to enroll in the U.S. Army, which we saw as an opportunity to get additional training and be ready to try again. But what happened was that, once we enrolled in the U.S. Army, Miami's anti-Castro movement came apart. Our leaving Miami, in effect, disjoints the militant groups, which was probably what the United States wanted. (Translation of author's interview with José Basulto, a freedom fighter who joined the U.S. Army)

Everywhere the exiles went, they carried with them an undying anticommunist spirit. They formed small colonies in New Jersey,[14] New York, Chicago, Boston, Washington, D.C., and other urban centers of the northeast as well as in dozens of cities in the Midwest and as far west as California. They went wherever jobs were available and, once there, they spread their largely conservative political gospel by founding cultural and patriotic organizations, holding meetings, and writing letters to the editors of the local newspapers in their newly adopted communities.

Emergence of Little Havana

While some exiles were relocating throughout the nation, a countertrend also ensued; a four-square-mile area in Miami's southwest section continued to attract new Cubans during the Transition Stage. It was during this period that the first Cuban businesses made their appearance on Flagler and Eighth streets, the area's main commercial thoroughfares. Although difficult to anticipate, in a few years Miami's *la saguesera*—as the early exiles mispronounced "southwest"—would grow from a quaint ethnic neighborhood with specialized ethnic shops to become the heart of the economically viable exile enclave in South Florida; it would come to be known as "Little Havana."

The new Cubans settling in Little Havana were not coming directly from the island, since flights between the United States and Cuba were discontinued after the missile crisis. Once Miami became identified as the capital of the Cuban Exile Country, it acted as a magnet to Cubans who had first gone to Spain and Latin America. The process was self-reinforcing. No matter where they had settled initially, when the scant resources with which they had left Cuba were depleted, the exiles wanted to come to Miami. They wanted to share life with their fellow Cubans, for inaccessible as the island actually was, it felt a lot closer from Little Havana. Similar feelings of nostalgia also brought back to Miami some exiles who had earlier been resettled elsewhere in the United States. Where else but in Miami could they find friendly restaurants that served Cuban bread, *café con leche*, and an assortment of other culinary favorites?

They would find a job in the northern or western states, but as soon as they were able to find a job here in Miami and bring their families back, they did so. The official U.S. policy might have been a policy of resettlement, but the heart called otherwise—it was the love of traditions, of foods. It became obvious after Miami started to be the focal point of the exile community that Cubans, regardless of where they were settled, slowly trickled back to Miami. Hence, Miami became the capital of the exile community. (Author's interview with attorney Rafael Peñalver)

During the Transition Stage, hundreds of Cuban-owned establishments, frequently named after their Cuban precursors, dotted Little Havana's emerging landscape; and each opening was celebrated by the exiles as a collective victory. Home-made signs often distinguished the gas stations, grocery stores, cafeterias, bakeries, and a variety of mom-and-pop shops that catered almost exclusively to an exile clientele. A rudimentary service network, partly underground, was also developing within the fledgling enclave. Doctors, dentists, and accountants saw their Cuban clients in their own apartments; electricians, roofers, plumbers, and other technicians offered cut-rate prices to fellow exiles. None needed to advertise; the exiles could always find them through word of mouth.

Hialeah also attracted thousands of exiles, and, although on a smaller scale than Little Havana, a Cuban enclave developed in this working-class community during the period. The exiles settling in Hialeah found employment at nearby Miami International Airport and in the textile and garment industries. Northern companies began to move their garment and textile factories to Hialeah to take advantage of the pool of hard-working exiled women. The fact that these were nonunion workers made for a thriving industrial district, and the city of Hialeah eventually emerged as the second-largest exile community in the United States.

Toward the conclusion of the Transition Stage, Cuban emigrants were feeling torn between loyalty to their Cuban past and concern over their American future. Despite overwhelming evidence that the emigrés were putting down tenuous roots in their newly adopted American communities, Cubans were not yet psychologically prepared to admit that exile was anything other than a transitory experience; most, in fact, still rejected the idea of forming permanent attachments to this country—an attitude that sharply contradicted their actual behavior. Their obsessive desire to reunite, albeit on the *American* side of the Straits of Florida, with family members who were stranded on the island spoke louder than the stale harangue of exile rhetoric.

THE ADJUSTMENT STAGE (1965–1973)

Castro's opening of the Cuban port of Camarioca to the exiles signaled a new exodus. This event triggered two interrelated developments: the Cuban Adjustment Act and the freedom flights. During the period, Cuban exiles finally accepted the fact that their stay in the United States would be extended, perhaps indefinitely, and they rededicated themselves to building their lives in America.

Beginnings of the Second Exodus: The Camarioca Boatlift

The Transition Stage came to an abrupt conclusion in September 1965, when Castro surprised the exiles with the announcement that any Cuban with family residing in the United States would be allowed to leave through Camarioca, a port located on the northern coast of Cuba, a hundred miles from the Florida Keys. The Cuban leader also invited the exiles to come by sea to Camarioca to pick up their relatives who were left stranded in Cuba since commercial flights between the two countries had been discontinued during the 1962 missile crisis.

Castro probably intended, by this action, to rid the island of political malcontents with close ties to the exiles. In one clean sweep, he would release the internal pressure of "closet counterrevolutionaries" who stood ready to undermine his Communist regime. By unleashing this demographic bomb, Castro also wanted to show Washington how easily he could disrupt U.S. immigration policy. The opening of Camarioca, therefore, carried a thinly veiled warning to the United States: Havana, not Washington, exercised de facto control over Cubans entering Florida's seacoast borders.[15] Castro's gambit proved to be an effective one, for his invitation triggered a frenzy among family-oriented exiles who could not pass up this unexpected opportunity to retrieve their loved ones from the island. Predictably, thousands of exiles responded by sailing toward Cuba, much to the chagrin of U.S. immigration authorities. Blood, indeed, would prove thicker than ideological water. In just a few weeks about 5,000 Cubans made the trip to freedom before the United States halted the boatlift.

Although most Cubans who left from Camarioca—as well as those who followed in the freedom flights—belonged to the middle class that had supported Castro's initial revolutionary promises, a not-insignificant number of peasants and blue-collar workers also left during this second emigration wave. By the time they had become disenchanted with the totalitarian nature of the revolution, it was too late to leave the island because flights between the two countries had ceased. In contrast to their relatives who had left earlier and hoped for a quick return to a free Cuba, this new wave did not entertain such illusions; they just wanted to get away from the Communist regime, not plot its destruction from across the Straits of Florida.

The Freedom Flights and the 1966 Cuban Adjustment Act

Soon after the beginning of the Camarioca boatlift, the administration of President Lyndon B. Johnson reacted to the illegal flow of Cubans into South Florida. Standing before the Statue of Liberty in October 1965, the American president announced that the United States would continue to welcome Cubans seeking freedom—as long as they sought it in an orderly, lawful fashion. The following month, the Johnson administration disclosed it had negotiated a "Memorandum of Understanding" with the Cuban government whereby close relatives of Cubans already in the United States would be allowed to emigrate into this country. In December, the freedom flights were inaugurated.

President Johnson also took the necessary steps to enact legislation designed to implement his open-arms policy toward Cubans fleeing the communist island. Almost one year to the day of his first announcement, the American president signed the Cuban Adjustment Act into law. With its passage, Cubans already in the United States were given the opportunity to "adjust" their legal status so that they could become American residents or naturalized citizens without having to go through the cumbersome process required for refugees from other countries. Coming during the height of the Cold War, the Cuban Adjustment Act resonated with the prevalent anticommunist rhetoric of the time, even as it set a policy for treating Cubans differently from other immigrants, creating in effect a double standard.[16]

By the time the Cuban Adjustment Act was proposed, reality, in a way, had sunk in. The Cuban Adjustment Act changed the concept of the exile mission. Cubans "adjusted" their status, they became citizens. But the burning desire for Cuba's freedom didn't change. That has always remained in the heart of the exile community. (Author's interview with Rafael Peñalver)

For the next eight years, planes loaded with Cubans would make the short daily trip from Varadero, Cuba, to Miami. About 300,000 Cubans had come to the United States by the time Castro unilaterally discontinued the freedom flights in 1973.[17] By then, most of the immediate relatives of the initial emigration wave were in the United States, a development that facilitated the redirection of the exiles' attention to the task of rebuilding their lives in this country. Much like those who left right after the revolutionary takeover, the second wave was predominantly white, attesting to the fact that most were the relatives of those in the initial exodus. Because the revolutionary regime restricted the emigration of men of military age, females and older men were vastly overrepresented in this second wave. From a socioeconomic perspective, however, there were other marked differences. Whereas about a third of the earlier exiles had come from the professional and managerial ranks, less than a fifth of those coming between 1965 and 1973 were categorized as professionals and managers.[18]

Although the majority of those arriving in the freedom flights were initially resettled, many began returning to South Florida toward the conclusion of the Adjustment Stage, much like the exiles who had relocated earlier. This trickle-back phenomenon added critical mass to the development of the Miami enclave, the Cuban population of which increased in absolute numbers during this period at the expense of all other geographical areas. The trend toward concentration in South Florida would continue unabated throughout the 1970s.

Cuban Exiles Turn to the Economic Arena

Cubans did not overcome the shock of losing their country all at once. Rather, it was a gradual, uneven, and certainly, painful process. For some, it began earlier, right after the Bay of Pigs Invasion and the Cuban missile crisis. It was during the Adjustment Stage, however, that most exiles actually came to terms with the reality of a long stay in the United States.

This recognition did not mean that they forgot the cause that had brought them here; instead, by summoning their most creative talent, the exiles were able to reconcile apparently clashing demands: the practical requirements of their new life and the devotion to their old political agenda. Cubans managed this convoluted adjustment by subliminally elevating their ordinary ambitions in the United States to the realm of an ideological quest; they planned to demonstrate the superiority of the capitalist system—of which they considered themselves self-appointed representatives—over Cuban socialism. Finding a new direction consistent with their old ideological cause was an unconscious yet masterful stroke that allowed them to change behavior without dismantling their essential political values.

I know my father was very proud of the fact his children had retained not only the love for Cuba, but had also taken over the torch in the struggle for

Cuba's freedom. This was something that one generation passed to the next, and even though we are now professionals and have adjusted well to this country . . . I still feel that we have a mission to accomplish, that we owe it to them—I owe it to my father—to carry on that torch, to contribute in any way that I can to the liberation and future development of my homeland. (Author's interview with Rafael Peñalver)

But their new quest was not simply a matter of realism plus ideology; it was also motivated by a much deeper individual need to prove their self-worth. After losing the social position and economic status many of them had enjoyed in prerevolutionary Cuba, the exiles desperately yearned to reclaim their rightful place in society. How else but by excelling economically in their new land could the exiles demonstrate they were really not "the scum of the Earth and worthless worms" that Castro called them? The disgrace and humiliation of their political defeat became the psychological impetus that fueled their efforts to prevail in the economic arena. Since they belonged to the classes most able to meet the challenge of succeeding economically, they set out to accomplish precisely that.

Indeed, throughout the Adjustment Stage, much as their political exile identity shielded them from the pressures to melt into America's society, the exiles' marginality helped them carve out a territory of their own in South Florida. They did it with characteristic conviction, as their practical quest took on the attributes of a political crusade to demonstrate what Cubans could achieve in a free, democratic society. Anticommunist ideals, practical imperatives, and psychological motivations were three elements that coincided at that difficult juncture; they produced a winning economic formula. A tacit covenant came into play at this dark hour of the Cuban exile experience—an unspoken determination, if not to overcome their political fate, at least to bolster their wounded collective pride; and, in a capitalist society, that could only mean prevailing in the economic arena. So, instead of becoming a tragic, downcast, and forgotten community, they were driven by their predicament to work harder.

Let me give you a personal example. I was determined that my children would be middle class even if I had to have two jobs—which I did for fourteen years. I was determined that I was going to make good, that my children were going to be part of the tradition of being a professional family. That was something that a lot of Cubans in here experienced; they were more than willing to overwork themselves to death to give a chance to the young, and also to make sure that the young felt proud of their Cuban heritage. In other words they were more than willing to do anything to take away the stigma of being *gusanos* [worms] and so forth. (Author's interview with Mercedes Sandoval)

This spirit paid off handsomely. Toward the end of the Adjustment Stage, booming Cuban communities were emerging in South Florida and in Union City, New Jersey, and smaller but thriving exile colonies flourished throughout the United States. By then Little Havana could boast of being second only to Havana in terms of Cuban population—and its economic power already surpassed that of the entire communist island.

Self-Employment in the Informal Private Sector Economy

Despite their determination to adjust to life in America, the Cubans' insistence in considering themselves to be political exiles carried one costly implication: They were to remain estranged from American politics and consequently the public sector. For a while, this attitude kept the obstinate exiles from using their potential voting power to their advantage. The acquisition of American citizenship, in fact, became sort of a litmus test, a line of demarcation between "true exiles," who rejected becoming Americans, and "opportunistic turncoats," who embraced it.

Until the 1970s, therefore, the exiles' progress was driven by economic gains derived from the private sector. Many Cubans, of course, felt forced to accept help from the federally funded Cuban Refugee Program right after they arrived, but that was rationalized strictly as a matter of survival. After the emigrés found jobs in South Florida or in other states, the elderly and the infirm remained the only beneficiaries of public largesse. Besides, the conviction that they were political exiles, rather than an immigrant minority, may have kept them from identifying with the civil rights demands of the 1960s; as a result, they did not feel morally entitled to government assistance. The exiles were too proud to accept public charity and too anticommunist to benefit from an American welfare state that reminded them of Castro's socialist programs. How could they demand public jobs and other services targeted to minorities if most still considered the very idea of becoming American citizens a betrayal of their patriotism?

This self-imposed exclusion from the public sector, in combination with a lack of English language proficiency and the discriminatory barriers of organized labor, left few employment opportunities available for Cubans in Miami. During most of the Adjustment Stage, consequently, many exiles gravitated toward the informal fringes of the private sector—a variety of professional, technical, and personal services rendered to other Cubans; a narrow range of marginal business activities requiring minimum startup capital; and nonunionized garment and construction jobs. Paradoxically, those low-paying jobs in the apparel factories and the building trades of Miami and Hialeah turned out to be a blessing in disguise; they would give thousands of exiles an opportunity to demonstrate that what they lacked in experience and language proficiency was more than compensated for by a positive disposition and good work habits.

Cubans were also able to show that they were ambitious. As soon as the enterprising exiles mastered entry level jobs, they began to talk their employers into restructuring hiring practices in the form of subcontracts. A new arrangement, which became prevalent in the garment industry, proved to be mutually advantageous: For the same amount of money, Cuban subcontractors took on the responsibility of hiring and accommodating workers in their living rooms and garages and delivering the finished goods on time. That rudimentary mode of self-employment often meant working longer hours, but they could enjoy the satisfaction of being their own bosses—even if their "workers" were actually relatives or friends. Although it was not far from the ground floor, subcontracting nonetheless represented a first step up the business ladder; countless small companies were started this way.

Self-employment also became widespread in the Cuban service sector. This was the case particularly in the construction trades, where Cuban laborers could work out of the back of their beat-up trucks. It is easy today to sneer at the underground network of "independent" tradesmen, unlicensed doctors, dentists and electricians, clandestine beauty shops, and door-to-door service workers that made their appearance in the Transition Stage and would become increasingly prevalent in the Adjustment Stage, but that network provided much-needed income to thousands of uprooted professionals and technicians while rendering inexpensive benefits to the ever-expanding Cuban population in South Florida. Since the exiles were willing to work long hours and often extended credit to their satisfied clients, their service network enjoyed advantages over the American counterpart.

We created a network of services that was not available to other communities, ethnic or otherwise. This was beneficial in two directions: It permitted the advancement of some people in the service industry that would have been discarded because they had no license; at the same time, it provided very cheap services to the majority of the exile population. (Author's interview with Mercedes Sandoval)

Understandably, from the very onset of the Transition Stage, self-employment was also the preferred mode for the entrepreneurial class, which had been overrepresented in the initial exodus, as well as for industrious Cubans whose lack of marketable skills severely limited other job opportunities. These aspiring businessmen and businesswomen pooled their family resources to set up the first mom-and-pop stores along Eighth Street and Flagler Street. Those boarded-up storefronts in what was then an economically depressed section of Miami could be leased cheaply, and with hardly any need for capital to buy equipment and inventory, the exiles were able to open up grocery stores and cafeterias that offered culturally differentiated products and services not available outside the Cuban enclave. They served a distinct market of fellow exiles.

The minimal risks of going into business were worth taking in those days when the freedom flights continued to bring an endless flow of Cubans from the island. To the exile entrepreneur, the newcomers provided two critical ingredients that fueled their developing businesses: a growing captive market and a source of cheap labor. The third ingredient, availability of financing, was the only bottleneck that kept the Cuban enclave from experiencing a true economic takeoff.

Personal Style of Doing Business

The lack of investment capital with which to finance the growth of their small businesses was largely overcome by relying upon personal contacts. This style of conducting business was really an extension of a time-tested tradition brought from Cuba. Since their arrival, Cubans rarely made an important decision without consulting friends and relatives, and only as a last resort did they venture outside the closely knit circle of acquaintances they had known and trusted all their lives. Whether they needed to buy a used car, see a doctor, fix a refrigerator, or build an addition to their home, the exiles depended on personal contacts and references.

A friend of mine, which I had known from Cuba, bought the Republic National Bank and asked me to be a member of its Board of Directors. At that time, I told him that I could not accept the appointment because I was not a citizen. But when I became a citizen about a year later, he insisted that I join his Board of Directors, and that's when I joined the bank. And I did work as a member of the board until they appointed me first, Vice-Chairman, and then, Chairman of the Board. (Author's interview with Luis Botifoll)

When looking for a loan to start up or expand a business, it seemed only natural that the exiles would rely upon their characteristic personal style. That usually meant finding, or being recommended to, a handful of Cubans already working for Miami's banks. It was their only option. The exiles had neither the track record in the Anglo community nor the collateral to secure conventional financing. In this way the practice of lending based "on moral character" became instituted, particularly at Republic Bank, a newly established financial institution that attracted a Cuban management team around 1970.

> At the time, Republic probably was the only Hispanic bank in Miami, and of course, we knew the people, we knew who was who, and we started giving loans based on character and not on [financial] statements. These people that we know from Cuba were able people, capable people, but they didn't have statements. They came—all of us came—without a cent, so when they wanted to start a business, they could not offer collateral or anything to secure a loan. But since we knew them, we took a chance . . . and gave them loans to get started. And that's how the Cuban community started many businesses—and I am very proud that we were able to help. (Author's interview with Luis Botifoll)

> We had banks like the Republic National Bank . . . They looked at the person, if they knew you from before, if they knew that the person was going to make it, they took you on as a customer. . . . That's how a lot of us got started. (Author's interview with restauranteur Felipe Valls)

Those "character loans" proved effective in attracting and maintaining a loyal Cuban clientele for Republic Bank. Taking advantage of such a practice, the enterprising exiles were able to expand the business base of their economic enclave, and Republic Bank was on its way to becoming the largest Miami-based bank some years later.

The personal style of doing business also proved effective in Latin America. The exiles' old contacts with business associates and executives of American companies operating in that region offered Cubans a quick entry into the largely untapped import-export field. It was a perfect fit for the Spanish-speaking exiles—so much so that they packed their bags with samples and catalogues and headed south of the border by the hundreds. These international traveling salesmen returned to Miami with lucrative orders and contracts. Within a few years, they managed to establish countless small import-export businesses operating out of their homes and apartments. They constituted the incipient foundation of a thriving international market that would lead South Florida's economic development during the 1970s.

> You had Cubans traveling all over Central and South America, selling everything you could think of—from spare parts to new machinery, to industrial equipment, to whatever you can imagine. They sold everything. That's why Miami later became "the Gateway of the Americas." (Author's interview with international lawyer Raúl Valdés-Fauli, mayor of Coral Gables, Florida)

Barely a decade after fleeing their country, the adaptable exiles, albeit reluctantly at first, had finally come to accept their lot and proceeded to carve out a prosperous niche that extended from Little Havana to most Latin American capitals. By then, Miami was already positioned to become an international center, and the enterprising energy of the newcomers was its driving force.

Diehard Exiles, Militant Students, and Terrorists

While by the mid-1960s most Cubans had actively abandoned the war against Castro to dedicate themselves to rebuilding their lives wherever they had settled, others tried to keep that struggle alive. In addition to the obvious economic imperatives and the hindrance of U.S. officials, diehard exiles faced another major obstacle: The movement was so divided by the proliferation of anti-Castro groups that any concerted effort on behalf of the exile community seemed impossible.

In 1964 the need to unite the exiles behind a leadership of their own choosing had persuaded Bacardi Rum's millionaire Pepín Bosch to underwrite a massive referendum throughout the Cuban Exile Country; over 75,000 emigrés polled selected their representatives, which formed a new super-front, the Representación Cubana del Exilio (RECE). RECE's leadership, among whom Jorge Mas Canosa figured prominently, received the endorsement of scores of exile groups, raised funds for propaganda and paramilitary operations, and financed some commando raids against Castro's regime on the island. Like other efforts of this period, however, RECE was ultimately infiltrated by the FBI, and, by the end of the Adjustment Stage, its ambitious role as a unifying representation of Cuban exiles had slowly waned.

During the 1970s, only a minority of die-hard exiles continued their full-time involvement in the anti-Castro movement. Lack of significant support from a largely disenchanted emigré community, internal strife among the militant leadership, and questions about some of their extremist tactics undermined several well-intentioned initiatives, and others were exposed as ill-conceived efforts or simple frauds.[19] The most bizarre of these initiatives was led by José Elías de la Torriente. His so-called *Plan Torriente* counted on the symbolic endorsement of some anti-Castro organizations and supposedly raised considerable funding throughout the Cuban Exile Country. In February 1970, *Plan Torriente* organized a major rally at a baseball stadium that was attended by about 40,000 Miami Cubans; shortly thereafter, a paramilitary commando operation on the island was staged under its auspices, but neither event succeeded in reviving the war against Castro. Doubts and confusion over its tactics and finances ultimately derailed *Plan Torriente*. From then on, most militant exiles turned to other types of activities; the violent era had essentially concluded.

> Until then the exiles had concentrated on taking the war to the island and in providing support to the guerilla movement within Cuba. But toward the mid-sixties, I think they had to recognize that the violent stage was over, and the exiles started a new phase in which their objectives were to stage actions in the United States that called attention to the crimes committed by Fidel Castro's Communist regime. (Translation of author's interview with Ninoshka Pérez, spokeswoman for the Cuban American National Foundation)

During this period, the younger emigrés tried to keep the spirit of the anti-Castro struggle alive by involving themselves in protests designed to bring international attention to the Cuban issue. They founded the Federation of Cuban Students (FEC), an organization that soon had chapters in the United States, Puerto Rico, and Costa Rica. The FEC published a monthly newspaper, *Antorcha*, and organized two student congresses. At the same time, another group of students founded Abdala in New York. Although it initially constituted a small study group, by the early 1970s Abdala had attracted about fifty students from the northeastern states. In 1971, in a symbolic act of protest, sixteen Abdala members chained themselves to the United Nations building. In the wake of this incident, Abdala's membership soared, and new chapters were formed in Washington, D.C., Chicago, Miami, and Puerto Rico. In the early 1970s, this student group became bolder, and its members staged dozens of civil disobedience actions, the most spectacular of which may have been the protest held at the Statue of Liberty. After 1972 the group broadened its scope to include nonstudents and, for the next few years, served as the cradle for a new generation of militancy in exile.

During the Adjustment Stage, terrorist tactics also gathered new momentum, leading to what the exiles referred to as *la guerra por los caminos del mundo* (the war through the roads of the world). Terrorism on an international scale, of course, was not an untried tactic for the exiles; in the 1960s, a few violent actions had been staged, such as the attempt against the life of Che Guevara during his 1964 visit to the United Nations and several attacks against Communist vessels in Canada and the United States. But in the 1970s, frustrated die-hard militants formed such secret groups as the Frente de Liberación Nacional (National Liberation Front), Acción Cubana (Cuban Action), Omega Siete (Omega Seven), Gobierno Cubano Secreto (Secret Cuban Government), and Jóven Cuba (Young Cuba), which revived those violent tactics. Some of them carried out legitimate operations against figureheads in the Castro government and against Castro's installations. These ''legitimate'' operations were nevertheless illegal, but that did not deter militant exiles from carrying out their violent war against pro-Castro targets throughout the world; hundreds of explosions rocked Cuban embassies in Europe, Canada, Latin America, and the United States, and attacks against the Cuban regime's personnel abroad became commonplace. While most of the established exile organizations disavowed their participation, it was clear that some of them secretly helped to raise funds for terrorist activities. By 1974 the wave of terror reached its peak, and those allegedly linked to such activities—Orlando Bosch, Guillermo Novo, Humberto López, and Luis Crespo—became heroes to many exiles.

By the end of the Adjustment Stage, terrorism was becoming more indiscriminate, as its targets also included exiles considered traitors to the anti-Castro cause; José Elías de la Torriente was the first of a series of exile victims. *La guerra por los caminos del mundo* was entering into a new violent phase.

THE ECONOMIC MIRACLE STAGE (1973–1980)

Castro's 1973 cancellation of the freedom flights signaled the beginning of the Economic Miracle Stage. During this period, the consolidation of Miami's enclave became an economic, social, and political reality; on a smaller scale, other exile colonies thrived as well. Interest in the Cuban issue waned, as older exiles resigned themselves to living in the United States and a new Cuban American consciousness emerged in the younger generation.

La Guerra por los Caminos del Mundo

The new wave of terrorism that resumed in around 1970 reached its peak in the middle of the decade. By then, the attacks were not limited exclusively to pro-Castro targets such as Cuban embassies and consulates; among its victims were now several exile leaders who supported dialogue with the Cuban regime as well as others such as radio personality Emilio Milián who had publicly criticized these radical tactics.

In the three-year period between 1973 and 1976, more than 100 bombs exploded in South Florida. Debate over the appropriateness of these extreme tactics divided the exile community as well as the terrorists themselves. Despite an intense investigation by the FBI and other intelligence agencies that resulted in the conviction of dozens of militant exiles, terrorism continued to claim more victims. In 1976 the exile terrorists grew even bolder: In Washington, D.C., they killed Orlando Letelier, a former minister of Chile who was allegedly linked to Castro's regime; far more brutal was the blowing up of a Cubana de Aviación airplane off the coast of Barbados killing seventy-three passengers. Although Venezuelan authorities charged controversial exile leader Orlando Bosch with blowing up the Cubana plane, the courts never found him guilty.

From then on, popular opinion throughout the Cuban Exile Country turned against the indiscriminate spread of violence. The consensus at the time was that random terrorism had tarnished the image of the exiles' cause and had actually strengthened Castro's regime. By then, moreover, there was increasing evidence that Castro's agents in the United States were behind some of the terrorist actions that were blamed on militant exiles. The violent "war through the roads of the world" had finally reached a dead end.

Expansion of Miami's Cuban Enclave

In the years that followed Castro's suspension of the freedom flights, the once-displaced exiles put down roots in South Florida. Although the process had actually started earlier, it was continually sidetracked by the constant influx of relatives from the island. As soon as Cubans on both sides of the Straits of Florida effectively lost touch with each other, the exiles sui generis integration into their host society could no longer be delayed. The result soon became evident, as their economic prosperity led the way to their involvement in the entire political and social fabric of the community.

In Miami, the Economic Miracle Stage was fueled primarily by the business boom that began within the Cuban enclave. Ironically, the 1973 economic recession, which severely hurt the local Anglo business sector, may have actually helped the smaller Cuban entrepreneurs gain a lasting advantage, since the exile firms tended to fill the vacuum left by their more entrenched competitors. During this period, the shops in Little Havana flourished, leading to the establishment of countless restaurants and cafeterias; supermarkets; gas stations; book, record, and hardware stores; private schools; appliance and furniture outlets; dry cleaners; pharmacies, clinics, and doctors' offices; theaters and radio stations; funeral homes; and a whole gamut of services that could well support the population of a medium-sized city. It was said at the time that from cradle to grave Cubans could spend their entire lives without having to emerge from their enclave. Although indeed possible, that was not what the exiles had in mind.

The fact is they did come out, in droves, expanding the borders of their enclave into the middle-class neighborhoods of Westchester and the residential districts of Coral Gables and Kendall. Everywhere they went, their business and informal service network followed. Typically, the sections of Greater Miami to which they moved could be distinguished by the opening of new Cuban shops and the large number of cars parked outside their homes—clear evidence that the traditional concept of the extended family still prevailed among the exiles. Another telling sign of the times was the coming and going of pickup trucks and vans carrying construction supplies to convert garages into family rooms or to build new additions to accommodate grandparents and uncles who had arrived from Cuba or serve as business offices. During the Economic Miracle Stage, the small construction companies the exiles had started from the backs of their trucks grew into aggressive firms. The exiles founded the Latin Builders Association, which was their very first attempt to use the political system to advance their economic interests. The Latin Builders made significant contributions to the consolidation of the exile community and ultimately emerged as a formidable power broker.

The proliferation of the small-business sector and service network, as well as the boom linked to international trade, continued to drive the economic fortunes of the Cuban Exile Country. Its prosperity was reinforced by three distinct developments: the entry of a younger generation into the professional ranks, the licensing of older Cuban professionals, and the return to Miami of many relocated exiles. These constituencies, although dissimilar in age and background, were lured by the desire to put down roots among their fellow exiles and share in their affluence. Their decision was a significant one, for the exiles now had other choices available outside South Florida; in fact, the colonies they had established in other parts of the nation were also thriving.

The attraction of the expanding Miami enclave nonetheless proved irresistible to thousands of Cubans who had earlier gone elsewhere in search of better economic opportunities. Estimates of the number of resettled exiles returning to South Florida vary, but by the end of the 1970s as many as 40 percent of the Cuban population in Greater Miami may have settled previously in other American cities.[20] After years of hard work in cold weather, the returning exiles brought their savings, which they quickly invested within the enclave, as well as a variety of new experiences that proved invaluable to South Florida. From a comparative historical perspective, it is interesting to note that even though Little Havana may have then resembled earlier German, Norwegian, and Greek insular communities, their similarities were superficial; whereas those European enclaves had traditionally performed the role of facilitating the immigrants' gradual adjustment to U.S. society, the exiles' cocoon attracted other Cubans who had *already* adjusted to living in America. Arguably, the scale and efficiency of the Cuban enclave were such that they pushed Little Havana to a different qualitative dimension.

The New Professional Class

Because the initial wave of Cubans had come disproportionately from the well-educated elite, the early exiles placed a high value on education. That belief was brought from Cuba, but its worth was fully confirmed during their diaspora. Everywhere they settled, it became a practical credo: "You can lose your house, your farm, your business or even your homeland, but a good education is something no one can take away from you."

> Education is a critical value in Cuban society. As with most Cubans, the value of education was ingrained in me at a very early age. My mother always told me that education was the only portable asset that would always go with me wherever I went. The journey in search of an excellent education took me to MIT, then to Harvard, then to Stanford, and then to Florida International University, where I now serve as President. (Author's interview with Modesto Maidique)

Upon their arrival in America, the first generation of exiles had to face all sorts of hardships, but they always insisted that their children learn English, graduate from high school, and attend college. Hence, the youngsters went to school in record proportions while their parents, lacking valid U.S. credentials, were forced to put on hold their professional careers or to practice underground. In the Economic Miracle Stage, however, those youngsters were completing their university education, and many of their parents were returning to school to obtain professional licenses. The gradual entrance of both generations into the professional ranks further boosted their prospects wherever they settled.

From the beginning, the parents' road to earning professional licenses in the United States was fraught with frustration, and not just because of their lack of English proficiency. Florida's politically entrenched professional associations, for example, fought them every inch of the way. Even after the Florida Legislature enacted laws to facilitate the validation of Cuban educational credentials, the state's regulatory boards continued to deny licensing to Cuban-trained professionals. Not until the exiles flexed their economic and political muscles were they able to compel the state's Department of Professional Regulation to take positive action. Only then, did former doctors, architects, lawyers, and other Cuban professionals see their dream of practicing in America become, at long last, a reality.

For the younger generation, on the other hand, the educational path was much smoother.[21] Taking advantage of the federal government's Cuban Student Loan Program, they had flocked to universities throughout the country. Upon graduation, many of them returned to work in Greater Miami, or other areas of exile concentration. The young professionals were as eager to prosper as their parents, but they were clearly better prepared to compete for high-paying executive positions in mainstream businesses, take over and expand their parents' small shops, and challenge the Anglo establishment on its own turf. This bilingual generation, raised and educated in the United States, became known as "Cuban Americans." Their involvement in every facet of the economic, social, and political life of South Florida raised the illusory capital of the Cuban Exile Country to new levels.

Miami Emerges as the Gateway to Latin America

Several decades before the arrival of the initial Cuban exodus, Miamians often wondered why their city was not taking full advantage of its geographic location to tap markets south of the border. Although they knew such a development would have been natural given Miami's proximity to Latin America, other cities like New Orleans, Houston, and New York continued to dominate the import-export trade with America's southern neighbors. A report commissioned at the time by the city's civic leaders offered one drastic recommendation: South Floridians needed to learn to speak Spanish.

It was many years before Miami would realize this potential. Even then, it happened in a most unpredictable fashion. Miami suddenly acquired its bilingual capability as a by-product of the Cuban diaspora. The influx into South Florida of thousands of Spanish-speaking exiles confirmed the validity of the earlier recommendation, as the embryonic import-export network started by the Cubans in the 1960s flourished during the Economic Miracle Stage. The expansion of Cuban firms involved in international markets triggered an unprecedented surge of related activities that broadened Miami's commercial base and bestowed a new economic identity on the city. It became the gateway to Latin America.

The boom in international trade lured a growing number of multinational corporations, initiating a trend of moving their Latin American headquarters from New York, New Orleans, Mexico City, or Caracas to Coral Gables and later to Miami. This development, in turn, attracted freight forwarders and insurance companies as well as out-of-state institutions specializing in financing import-export transactions. Under the Edge Act, bank agencies operated as if they were branches of the head offices, except they were not allowed to accept deposits from U.S. residents.

> At that point, I think, there were several interrelated developments . . . but the dominant sector may have been the international field; you had banking, you had import-export, you had communications, you had medical centers, all of which brought us closer to Latin America. (Interview with Raúl Valdés-Fauli)

As a result of the spectacular growth in international banking, Miami attained high visibility, which unquestionably affected foreign investment decisions in its favor. To cap the internationalization of South Florida, many wealthy Latin Americans, fearing their own country's political instability, brought large amounts of capital.[22] The Cuban exiles, of course, took full advantage of the economic opportunities afforded by the growing Latin American market—after all, they had been the first to open it for South Florida a decade earlier.

Ethnic Politics in the South Florida Enclave

Since settling in South Florida the exiles had steadfastly chosen to remain isolated from the political life of their adopted community. During this decade-long estrangement from politics, taking out U.S. citizenship, not to mention actually registering to vote, was often deemed a betrayal to the homeland. That attitude, however, began to change with the emergence of a new Cuban American consciousness in the 1970s. Still, before breaking away from their self-imposed political marginality, Cubans needed to find a justification that would make sense in terms of their old exile mind-set. That rationale was finally provided by the argument that, as voters, they would be able to influence U.S. foreign policy toward Cuba.

When we first came here, we really did not want to become American citizens. We were only involved in the process of liberating Cuba from Castro's communism, and we thought it was almost treason to become an American citizen and be active in American politics. . . . But that changed around the year of 1970, when we realized that our community was growing and there were a lot of things that were of importance to our families and to our children born here. We were not being adequately served by the government to which we were paying taxes and doing everything that American citizens were doing. So, it was in '68, '69, that you started to see a new kind of activism. (Author's interview with political activist Alfredo Durán)

During the Economic Miracle Stage, when Cubans still lacked the voting power to elect their own representatives, prominent exiles like Manolo Reboso and Alfredo Durán, who enjoyed impeccable anti-Castro credentials because of their participation in the Bay of Pigs Invasion, escorted Anglo politicians who were courting votes to Little Havana, Westchester, and Hialeah. At the time, English-speaking politicians had to learn only enough Spanish to yell ¡Viva Cuba Libre! at political rallies in order to throw Cuban crowds into a frenzy. It was American ethnic politics as it had been traditionally practiced by first-generation immigrants. The Cuban American surrogates soon developed political machines capable of delivering sufficient votes within the enclave to provide the margin of victory for their favorite candidates; in turn, they were rewarded with political patronage, access, and influence.

In the early 1970s, Reboso and Durán were able to leverage their own political power among Cuban Americans into appointments for themselves to the City of Miami Commission and the Dade County School Board, respectively, thus becoming the first exile incumbents. Reboso was elected to the nonpartisan City of Miami Commission at the conclusion of his term. Durán, on the other hand, could not win the Democratic party's nomination to the school board; his failure attests to the bias of registered Democrats against Cuban American candidates. That rejection, if anything, spurred the exiles to register, but as Republicans. Truth be told, since Cubans had not forgotten that the Democratic administration of President Kennedy had let them down during the Bay of Pigs Invasion and the missile crisis, the majority of them had developed a strong aversion to the Democratic party and leaned toward the more conservative Republican party.

We first set our eyes on the city of Miami. We had Manolo Reboso and Durán. And slowly we kind of started taking over and exercising some influence and power in the City of Miami and in the School Board. After that it was Metro-

Dade and, of course, Sweetwater and Hialeah. We were then focusing on municipalities and smaller centers of power. (Author's interview with María Elena Toraño)

By the latter part of the 1970s, the old dilemma between competing allegiances to Cuba and the United States was finally overcome, opening the way to massive American citizenship and voter registration drives. To commemorate America's bicentennial, for instance, Cubans for American Citizenship was created to encourage the exiles to become U.S. citizens.

One important project was the "Votaton," which for the very first time promoted voter registration among our television audience. Thousands of Cuban Americans did register, but more significant was the consciousness that such campaigns created. (Translation of author's interview with José Cancela, then general manager of Miami's Channel 23)

During the decade, the number of Cubans who became American citizens more than doubled.[23] It would be misleading, however, to assume that all those who adopted U.S. citizenship had actually replaced their sense of identity as Cuban exiles for that of ethnic immigrants. Becoming American, in most cases, involved a rather pragmatic consideration. Since they were not about to return to their homeland, they wanted to take advantage of their full rights as citizens of the United States, a nation with which they shared political ideals, if not cultural idiosyncrasies.

I remember the day I went to the Miami courthouse and took my oath. I was proud to be a U.S. citizen and, at the same time, very proud of my Cuban origin, very proud of my Cuban roots. It was an emotional day—different emotions ran through me. I was very grateful to this country, and yet very proud to be a Cuban and of my Cuban origin. (Author's interview with Rafael Peñalver)

Summary: The First Twenty Years

After just two decades in America, the Cubans' impressive performance was a much-celebrated reality. Arguably, their path from a largely penniless, displaced group of political exiles to thriving Cuban Americans had been paved by a variety of interrelated developments whose common origins must be traced, at least in part, to the sense of identity fostered by their shared political fate. In the late 1960s, the enterprising exiles moved into the economic sphere, and, during the next decade, they made inroads into every facet of their host community.[24]

In retrospect, it seems obvious that Cuban exiles made the best of a limited number of opportunities; some came as a result of their entrepreneurial and their Spanish-language skills; others just happened, almost by accident. For the most part, ironically, taking advantage of those opportunities was somewhat related to their political idiosyncrasies. Had those early emigrés given up their exile identity, they would probably have lost the unique bond that lent coherence to their experience. Had they become assimilated into America's melting pot, they never might have mustered the critical mass to carve out self-sustaining enclaves in South Florida and Union City. Had they initially depended on the public sector, they might have channeled their energies away from their own business development. Had they not been rejected by local unions, they might not have gone on to establish their informal service network. Had they settled somewhere else, they would not have become the prime motor of Miami's emergence as the gateway to Latin America. The adversity and discrimination they initially faced, in other words, often proved a blessing in disguise, strengthening their shared solidarity and making them more determined to succeed and to be less dependent on others.

The Cuban success story has too often been explained as only an economic phenomenon. Beneath the prosperous surface of their business achievements, however, lies a host of cultural, social, and political considerations that played significant roles in the early progress of the exiles. Although at first look they appeared unprepared to meet the challenge of a new life in America, Cubans had in fact brought rich traditions that had nurtured their national character for centuries. For example, their characteristic enterprising spirit, which was part of the rich legacy they brought from their homeland, served them well in America. Unlike typical immigrants who rely mostly on the blood, sweat, and tears of their labor, Cubans tended to use their creative and entrepreneurial skills to control their own destinies.

Not all Cubans were economically successful; however, as a community, the achievements seem remarkable after such a short period. By the end of two decades, their aggregate income had reached as high as $2.5 billion, and over 60 percent of all Cuban families owned their own homes. More than one-third of Miami's businesses, including 80 percent of all gas stations and 500 local supermarkets, were owned or operated by Cubans. In the construction industry, the dominance was even greater: Approximately half of the companies in the Greater Miami area were Cuban, controlling about 90 percent of the residential and commercial construction within the enclave itself. At that time, there was one exile business for every twenty-seven Cubans.[25]

By 1980 the Anglo establishment had finally taken notice of the Cubans' aggressive advancement, and "white flight" from the exiles' expanding sphere of influence had become a familiar trend. The exiles' adamant refusal to follow the *traditional pattern of ethnic immigrants and assimilate at the bottom of society was daunting to the host community, which often perceived Cubans as rude and ungrateful. Language became a divisive local issue, and the exiles were severely criticized for speaking Spanish among themselves in front of mixed company. It was obvious that such a reaction was motivated, at least in part, by economic defensiveness on the part of longtime residents who resented the newcomers for "taking over" Miami, as much as for the exiles' arrogant behavior. But if the Cubans came across as insensitive or cocky they admittedly did not care. Largely ignoring the polarization of the community along ethnic lines, the Cubans merely pressed on.*

By the end of the Economic Miracle Stage, Cubans had become involved in every aspect of South Florida's economic, social, and political life. They had created dozens of community-based organizations, such as the Spanish American League Against Discrimination (SALAD), to advocate for their civil rights; the Latin Chamber of Commerce (CAMACOL), to defend their business interests; and the Latin Builders Association, to leverage economic influence into social and political gains. These power brokers were instrumental in placing Cubans on the City of Miami Commission and the Dade County School Board.

Similar gains, though less dramatic, were also achieved by exile colonies across the nation. By then, indeed, the Cuban Exile Country had given a resounding answer to that initial challenge of the early 1960s, when political fortunes turned against the emigrés: They showed what Cubans could accomplish in a free and democratic society.

THE DIVERSIFICATION STAGE (1980–1990)

Late in 1978, the Cuban regime invited a group of exiles from throughout the world to attend a series of meetings to be held in Havana. This unprecedented dialogue set in motion momentous events within the island, leading to the exodus of 125,000 more refugees from the Cuban port of Mariel. The arrival of the Marielitos *thrust the exiles into a new phase. The Diversification Stage is characterized by often contradictory developments that exposed bitter cracks beneath the surface of the monolithic appearance of the Cuban Exile Country.*

The Controversial *Diálogo*

Once again, shock waves originating from within the island impacted the lives of Cubans living in the United States. The fuse that triggered it was set in November 1978, when Castro invited a group of exiles to meet with him in Havana. The unforeseen consequences of that event changed Cubans on both sides of the Straits of Florida. Arguably, in the wake of this dialogue, the prosperous Cuban American community was stunned into the Diversification Stage.

The initial event itself was dramatic enough. After nearly two decades during which Cubans in the United States could not even dream of visiting their homeland, the *Diálogo* stunned the Cuban Exile Country like no other event since the 1961 Bay of Pigs fiasco. The meeting between Castro and the exiles was supposed to follow a strictly humanitarian agenda, but its political implications soon overshadowed the professed goals of negotiating the release of political prisoners and the lifting of travel restrictions to the island. Upon returning home from their meeting with Castro, the dialogue's seventy-five participants were denounced as traitors by a majority of their fellow exiles. Threats soon escalated into terrorist attacks against some of the exiles who had participated in the controversial talks.[26]

Since then, the rift between supporters and opponents of the *Diálogo* has dominated the political debate among Cuban exiles. Moderate exiles hold a more favorable view of the 1978 event and its consequences.

> Although at the time I had no faith in that dialogue, I do recognize today that it had positive aspects. I believe that it created, for the first time, a link between the island and the exile, and that, in turn, it generated great disaffection toward the regime inside Cuba. . . . Ultimately, it represented a setback for Castro. (Author's interview with writer Uva de Aragón)

> The irony was that, despite a very vocal opposition to the dialogue by the exiles' political establishment, thousands went back. The impact of those visits created tremendous political dissatisfaction within the island . . . and many turned against the government. (Author's interview with New York businessman Marcelino Miyares)

The consequences of the agreement negotiated between Castro and the exiles were not any less significant on the communist island. As a result of the dialogue, the Cuban regime for the first time opened its doors to emigrés who wanted to visit their families back home. Thousands of Miami Cubans, bearing generous gifts for relatives and friends, defied threats from hard-line exiles and descended in droves upon the island. The impact of the visitors— and their gifts—shook the communist regime to its ideological core. The exiles, whom Castro had repeatedly called *gusanos* (worms), were now welcomed as beneficent *mariposas* (butterflies) by their countrymen. To be sure, the Cuban population, tired of years of the severe hardships and shortages caused by the system's economic failures, were amazed at the contrast between their own ordeal and the exiles' success in America.

> That first contact between Cubans on both sides, that meeting in *La Habana*, that *Diálogo*, evidently opened new prospects and, inside the island, it created a favorable atmosphere toward the exiles. To us [in the human rights movement] this meeting was very encouraging. . . . Among those of us inside Cuba, the exile visits also created a different vision of what transpired in Miami. Another positive aspect resulting from *el Diálogo* was the amnesty of political prisoners. . . . When those thousands of prisoners reached the United States, they paved the way to denunciations of human rights violations in Castro's jails. (Author's interview with human rights' activist Ricardo Bofill)

The ensuing internal turmoil rekindled the Cubans' desire to join the exiles already in the United States. Some went so far as to risk their lives trying to cross the Straits of Florida in small boats and fragile rafts; others felt their only way out of the island was to seek diplomatic asylum at foreign embassies, obviously a risky proposition, since the communist regime kept a strong police presence around all embassies to prevent just that possibility. By the spring of 1980, just over one year after the *Diálogo* was held, the stage was set for the first of many of the shockwaves that had been triggered by that milestone event.

The Peruvian Embassy Incident

Given the widespread dissatisfaction with conditions on the island, Cubans attempted to leave by whatever means they could. After one daring episode, in which a bus crashed through the gates of the Peruvian embassy in Havana and a Cuban guard was killed, the government of Peru lodged an official protest against the communist regime's heavy handling of the incident. An angry Castro retaliated by announcing he was retiring the security forces that surrounded the Peruvian embassy.

In making this impulsive move, however, Castro underestimated the intensity of his subjects' determination to escape. Within a few days, over 10,000 Cubans crowded the embassy compound. The resulting spectacle embarrassed the *Máximo Líder* to no end, for the massive defections represented an obvious rejection of his regime—by a generation raised under Marxist slogans, no less. The Peruvian embassy incident was widely covered by international television and news agencies, adding to Castro's public embarrassment. The communist regime did what it could to discredit those inside the embassy grounds, calling them delinquents and social deviants whom the revolution would be all too glad to see leave the country. Trying to end such a damning display of disaffection, the regime offered safe conduct to the refugees so that they could return to their homes while it negotiated their emigration. Peru, however, agreed to accept only one thousand refugees.

It was then that Castro resorted once again to his old ploy—the demographic bomb. It made sense. In the aftermath of exile visits and the Peruvian embassy crisis, mounting discontent among the island's population had reached such menacing levels that the Cuban leader was persuaded that the time had come to open the safety valve once more. In one bold sweep, he hoped to release internal pressures and defuse the volatile political situation on the island, while resolving the problem of the Peruvian embassy refugees.

In April 1980, just as he had done in 1965, Castro invited the exiles to come by sea and pick up, not only the refugees who had originally sought asylum at the embassy, but anyone who wanted to leave. What followed was a reprise, albeit in a much larger scale, of the earlier opening of the port of Camarioca, although this time Mariel was designated the port of exit. As on the previous occasion, Cuban Americans sailed south to retrieve their loved ones. The Mariel Boatlift was under way.[27]

The Third Exodus: The Mariel Boatlift

The Diversification Stage may have actually started that moment in May 1980 when the first exiles sailed to the port of Mariel, and it certainly started off with a bang. About five months later, when this chaotic exodus finally concluded, approximately 125,000 Cubans had been brought into the United States in vessels owned or chartered by their fellow Cubans in exile. By then, the new refugees[28] had also managed to sink Miami into a deep crisis and to stigmatize the exiles who had brought them to America. Admittedly, the Mariel boatlift cast a dark shadow over the image of the established exile community. Thereafter, *el exilio* would never be the same.

Demographically and ideologically, the refugees who arrived during the Mariel boatlift appeared very different from the Cubans already in the United States. Whereas the two earlier waves were made up of older, mostly white, and upper and middle class people, the *Marielitos* were younger and represented a mix of races more typical of the island's multiracial population. Brought up under Cuba's socialist regime, the newcomers lacked their predecessors' business and professional experiences as well as their familiarity with free market economies.[29] To these differences in racial background and socioeconomic status, it is important to add the obvious contrast between the revolutionary political upbringing of the new arrivals and that of the established exiles. Moreover, unlike those who came in the first two waves, this new group was completely unfamiliar with Miami; they were clearly of a different vintage.

Before they reached Key West, the *Marielitos* had already gone through a traumatic nightmare. As tens of thousands of them flocked toward the port of Mariel, mobs of Castro's supporters, with full encouragement and participation by the police, chanted insulting slogans, hurled stones, and unleashed guard dogs at them. Cuban authorities had set the tone for such excesses, as radio and newspapers resorted to revolutionary invectives reserved, until then, for counterrevolutionary enemies. The *Máximo Líder* himself called them "antisocial, homosexuals, drug addicts and gamblers whom the revolution welcomed being rid of." While they waited at Mariel to be claimed by the exiles, the Cubans endured their countrymen's full wrath; countless of them also suffered physical assault. The exiles who went to Mariel did not fare much better.

> We sailed as the first shipload of *Marielitos* was arriving in Key West. When we got to Mariel, about a dozen exile boats were already there. It was then that we were told that we had to bring three strangers for each family member—imagine our frustration! As hundreds of ships kept arriving in the next few days, the situation deteriorated into complete chaos. . . . Finally, more than two weeks later, we were able to locate our family and return with them to Key West. (Translation of author's interview with businessman Rafael Palacios)

On the exile vessels, gathered inside the port, they waited for days or weeks to locate relatives. When they ran out of fuel, water, and supplies, many actually had to return to Key West empty handed. Other exiles, however, decided to weather the chaotic situation and stayed on hoping to retrieve their families. The Cuban regime, however, had a different agenda. It forced the exiles to take on board individuals selected by the government, so the exiles often came back with a full load of strangers instead of family members. Among those thrust on the unsuspecting exiles were scores of convicts and mental patients ushered straight from the country's hospitals and correctional institutions to the waiting boats.

At first, Cuban Americans had reacted with enthusiasm to the incident at the Peruvian embassy and the ensuing boatlift. The fact that these mostly young men, raised by the revolutionary regime, had turned their backs on communism was certainly cause for great celebration in Miami and the other exile colonies.

When we saw about 11,000 Cubans in the Peruvian embassy compound, it was a feeling of ecstasy and great exhilaration. Cubans in the U.S. were very happy to see that young people who had been brought up by the revolution—many of them black—were rejecting the system. So practically everybody in the U.S. started manifesting the desire to help bring them to this country. (Author's interview with Mercedes Sandoval)

But the festive mood lasted only a short while. As boat upon boat load of racially mixed *Marielitos* made their way across the Straits of Florida, the euphoria gave way to apprehension. After it was revealed that Castro had sprinkled the exodus with thousands of criminals and the mentally ill, the exiles' mood turned to rancor. Even Miami's Puerto Rican mayor, Maurice Ferré, a staunch ally of the exiles, charged that Castro "had flushed these people on us." Everyone agreed.

The Post-Mariel Crisis

Within a few weeks of its onset, the adverse repercussions of the boatlift had already reached crisis levels. The housing shortage, unemployment, and the crime wave unleashed by the newcomers upon South Florida prompted President Jimmy Carter to declare a state of emergency and to release $10 million to help local governments cope with the crisis.[30] But that was hardly enough. By then, community leaders were up in arms, and Cuban Americans were rightfully blamed for bringing in the refugees. The positive image the exiles had worked so hard to achieve appeared irrevocably tarnished.

For a while, it seemed as if the Cuban success story would be eclipsed by the *Marielitos'* penchant for getting themselves into trouble. A grim tent city appeared within the heart of once-quaint Little Havana, homeless peddlers roamed the streets, and violent crime engulfed South Florida. When police arrested the offenders, federal authorities confined them to prisons in other states, where they were to languish without hope of ever being released, even after serving their full sentences. Given the refugees' uncertain immigration status, these so-called excludables, whom the Cuban regime had forced into the boatlift, were to remain in prison indefinitely, unless they could be deported to Cuba. And Castro, of course, did not want to take them back. Facing such a dreadful legal limbo, the *Marielitos* confined at Fort Chaffee rioted, injuring scores of guards and setting fire to several buildings. Those housed at other federal penitentiaries soon followed suit.

A few years from now, when this country looks back at the 1980s, we are going to ask ourselves as a nation, "How could this have happened in the

U.S.? How could we have kept thousands of individuals locked up in indefinite detention year after year, warehousing them without any kind of civil rights . . . locking them up, throwing away the key, under the legal fiction that, although they are physically present in the United States, they haven't really entered our borders, therefore, they have no rights." That has to be one of the darkest pages in the history of American justice. . . . It goes against the grain of everything that America stands for. (Author's interview with Rafael Peñalver)

As the crisis escalated, America's backlash could be matched only by the exiles' own outrage; some Cuban Americans turned their backs on the refugees, while others joined voluntary agencies trying to ease the refugees' lot. Because there was no end to the boatlift in sight, the still-arriving *Marielitos* were no longer being released into the community. They desperately awaited family members and sponsors. Every available facility in South Florida, from National Guard armories to the Orange Bowl stadium, was used to house, care for, and process the refugees. The unremitting boatlift, however, overwhelmed all efforts. Miami, used to frequent hurricanes, seemed to have been hit by a destructive force far worse than any natural disaster, and the boatlift continued for weeks and months.

U.S. officials had initially attempted to control the boatlift, but later they changed their position when President Carter himself reaffirmed this country's open-arms policy to Cubans seeking freedom. Aware of the grave implications the uncontrollable boatlift could have on domestic politics, however, the administration was losing its patience with the exiles who kept going back for more refugees, as well as with the Cuban regime for its role in encouraging them. After appeals and moral suasion failed, the United States again changed its posture; it threatened the exiles with heavy fines and the confiscation of their vessels if they continued to bring refugees from the island. This did not deter them, however. Next, the United States turned to Castro for cooperation, but the Cuban regime rejected an American proposal for the orderly emigration of the remaining refugees.

Because the peak of the refugee crisis occurred during the presidential campaign, President Carter's own reelection prospects absorbed the full brunt of voter indignation. The president was blamed for being inept in handling the boatlift and for indecisive leadership. Not unlike the biblical David, Castro scored an improbable bull's-eye on the American Goliath and, arguably, contributed to the president's eventual defeat at the polls. It must have been sweet revenge for the Cuban dictator, who had been riled by the Carter administration's strong emphasis on human rights.

Toward the end of the summer of 1980, as the boatlift began to slacken, the Cuban regime finally closed the port of Mariel to the exiles, which effectively concluded this bizarre episode. Despite the damage that sensationalist reports had caused to South Florida's image, and in particular to Cuban Americans, the worst was finally over; the troublemakers among the Mariel refugees, in reality, represented only a small minority, perhaps as low as 5 percent of the total. After authorities had rounded them up, the post-Mariel crisis slowly faded away, but the damage had been done. The American press, and even the exiles themselves, echoed Castro's characterization of the entire batch of refugees as "worms and scum."

In time, the bulk of the *Marielitos*, with help from established exiles, were integrated into the Cuban American communities throughout the nation. Perhaps their most visible influence was in the artistic and cultural spheres, which experienced a veritable revival thanks to the substantial number of writers, artists, and musicians present in the group. To counter negative publicity, Cuban Americans founded Facts about Cuban Exiles (FACE), an organization that disseminates information about the exiles' positive achievements in the United States. The stigma cast on the *Marielitos*, however, still lingers.[31]

The Cuban Exile Country Matures and Diversifies

After a fleeting but chaotic interlude, the post-Mariel period was characterized by a consolidation of earlier trends toward a more diversified exile community, as evidenced by the appearance of new and often contradictory developments: demographic shock, renewed leadership, political mobilization, economic maturity, and controversy over exile trips to the island. Despite the hard-liners' staunch opposition, thousands of Cuban Americans defied political pressure and continued to visit their relatives on the island. This opening of communications restored the umbilical tie between Cubans on both sides of the Straits of Florida and renewed the exiles' interest in their historical roots.

Up to the Diversification Stage, the major thrust of Cuban business development in Miami had taken place within the ever-expanding boundaries of the enclave economy, where the exiles enjoyed definite sociocultural advantages. Although by 1980 there were already over a dozen bank presidents and more than a hundred vice presidents born in Cuba, and the new U.S.-trained bilingual generation was being recruited by local enterprises as well as by multinational corporations, it was outside the mainstream economy where the exiles had concentrated their business efforts. That was to change drastically. In the 1980s, Cuban enterprises expanded beyond the enclave and began to challenge the Anglo business establishment on its own turf.

The growth of exile business outside the enclave proved rather successful in attracting the patronage of younger Cuban Americans (and even some Anglo customers) to a new breed of Cuban-owned supermarket chains, car dealerships, appliance stores, and health maintenance organizations. They managed to accomplish this feat by combining the traditional personal practices that had served them so well within the informal enclave economy with the aggressive advertising and price discounting that were generally associated with large mainstream businesses. It was a winning strategy that combined the best of both cultures.

Cuban construction companies and developers, now proficient in taking advantage of minority opportunities, began to vie with the biggest established enterprises for their share of government contracts and multimillion-dollar projects. By the time South Florida's entrenched businesses realized the full potential of the exile economy, it was too late to stop the exile advance; by then, Cubans not only enjoyed an almost exclusive control of their thriving enclave, but were also making significant inroads into the rest of the South Florida market.

The influx of many Nicaraguans and many Central American refugees, as well as a new wave of South American immigrants, contributed to the further expansion of the geographical and ethnic boundaries of the enclave economy. Their integration into South Florida was eased by the emergence of Spanish as a marketable skill much in demand. The Nicaraguans, who had left their country under political conditions somewhat similar to the Cubans, followed the trail traveled earlier by the Cuban exiles. The Latinization of Greater Miami had become a reality by then, and the Cubans remained in a position of leadership—or as author David Rieff recently put it, they had taken control of Miami's "atmosphere."[32]

Cuban Americans Become a Political Force in South Florida

During the 1980s, the exiles fully discarded their earlier reservations about participating in American politics. When that barrier had been surmounted, the political enfranchisement of thousands of newly registered Cuban American voters, as well as the reapportionment of new Hispanic districts, gave additional clout to the exiles. Cuban Americans quickly became adept at the art of using a political base to serve economic interests. As a result, Miami, Hialeah, and other municipalities where the Cuban population was concentrated emerged as strongholds for the conservative brand of politics overwhelmingly favored by the exiles.

That combination of economic and political power proved very effective in furthering the aspirations of the Cuban Exile Country. During the Diversification Stage, in fact, the exiles mustered sufficient political power to realize a goal that only a decade before had seemed highly implausible—influencing U.S. foreign policy toward Cuba. The creation of the Cuban American National Foundation (CANF) in the early 1980s stands as the best example of how the exiles managed to combine political and economic power, and in so doing, avail themselves of a sophisticated political lobby in Washington.[33]

> *La Fundación* (Cuban American National Foundation) was created in 1981. By then we had prospered—over 30,000 businesses in South Florida, banks, we got all kinds of institutions. . . . But politically we were behind . . . [we were] being perceived as a bunch of terrorists, right wingers incapable to govern ourselves, . . . a bunch of fanatics that saw communists all around. So I went to those guys who like me had some success in business and said: "Look, I think we owe it to our country . . . [to bring] into the political arena, into the civic Cuban arena, the talent, the experience that we have gained in this country." And that's how the Foundation was created. It didn't take me that long to do it; most people were ready. (Author's interview with Jorge Mas Canosa, chairman of the Cuban American National Foundation)

Although primarily a politically oriented group that advocates Cuban freedom, *la Fundación* has helped articulate a sense of collective pride in what Cuban Americans have achieved. By reviving and refining the crusading spirit that had driven the exiles in the 1960s, the CANF and its chairman, Jorge Mas Canosa, have attracted considerable popular support and have emerged as formidable forces in the Cuban Exile Country. Everywhere Cubans had settled, successful exiles wanted to join *la Fundación*.

> I am one of the directors of the Cuban American National Foundation. A director has to pay $10,000, a trustee $5,000, and after that, it costs you all year. Our leader is Jorge Mas Canosa, who is a businessman . . . very dedicated, because he thinks that us [*sic*] Cubans have to free Cuba of Fidel and Raúl Castro. (Author's interview with Felipe Valls)

The CANF has also attracted scores of critics. Although no one appears to question its effectiveness, some perceive its political tactics as heavy-handed.

The Foundation has been very successful, but they do not speak for the entire exile community, as they like to represent. CANF may be powerful in Washington, but in Latin America, in Europe and, of course, inside Cuba, the moderate approach has more credibility. . . . We all feel passionate about the freedom of Cuba, but that does not justify the intolerance that the Cuban American National Foundation and other hard-line groups often demonstrate. (Author's interview with Marcelino Miyares)

In South Florida, not surprisingly, the exiles have demonstrated tremendous strength in the political arena. Their bloc voting has lead to the election of Cuban Americans as well as Anglo candidates identified with anticommunism. Since the platform of the Republican party appeals to most Cuban Americans, they have overwhelmingly registered and voted Republican, breaking the hold traditionally enjoyed by Democrats in South Florida since Reconstruction days.

THE POST-SOVIET STAGE (1990–)

The Post-Soviet Stage began with the Cuban regime's economic collapse following the suspension of Soviet assistance to the island. It may be premature to suggest that el exilio *is entering its final phase, but a hopeful attitude certainly prevails in the Cuban community in the United States. The perceived imminence of a transition to a free Cuba is prodding many exiles into making plans for the reconstruction of the impoverished island in the post-Castro era.*

Renewed Hopes after the Soviet Collapse (1990)

After the disintegration of the Soviet Union and the suspension of the massive economic assistance it had been providing to the Cuban communist regime since the 1960s, Cuban society suffered a dramatic deterioration. Hope for the demise of the regime revived among the exiles, however, who became once again convinced that Castro's days were numbered. Those expectations drove Cuban Americans to recommit themselves to the struggle to liberate Cuba. They did so with novel strategies, but with the same passion of old.

With its patriotic spirit aroused, the Cuban Exile Country recaptured the anti-Castro zeal that had been waning since the Transition Stage. Wherever they were settled, the exiles began making plans for the post-Castro reconstruction of the impoverished island, and scores of new organizations sprouted in New York, Washington, Madrid, London, and, of course, Miami. The strategies often embraced by these groups were somewhat different from those of the early 1960s: Cuban Americans now recognized that for political change to take place in Cuba, it would have to be initiated by the opposition movement inside the island. Within that strategic context, the role of the exiles would be reduced to providing economic, diplomatic, and moral support to the incipient internal opposition in order to pressure Castro into a transition. Admittedly, this younger generation that is taking over the political agenda of *el exilio* has been more moderate than its predecessors and is more inclined to consider a wider range of approaches—a development that has revived the bitter political debate between moderate and hard-line exiles.

The first among the new breed of organizations was the Plataforma Democratica Cubana (Cuban Democratic Platform), a pluralistic coalition founded in Madrid by Cuban writer Carlos Alberto Montaner in the summer of 1991.[34] The *Plataforma* attempted to break away from the exiles' historical dependence on Washington by concentrating its energies on an international effort to pressure Castro toward a peaceful transition. For hard-line exiles, however, this approach was suspect, since its success was predicated on Castro's willingness to undertake democratic reforms. Despite the credibility that the Cuban Democratic Platform gained among European and Latin American governments, its failure to attract the support of the exile mainstream has limited its ultimate effectiveness.

> Ironically, the *Plataforma* gained more prestige and support in Latin America and Europe than among the exiles in the U.S. The idea that Castro could be forced into a peaceful, democratic transition was never accepted by a majority of Cuban Americans. What's more, I would tell you that here in Miami, the proposal of the *Plataforma* was not understood. (Translation of author's interview with Uva de Aragón, a founder of the Cuban Democratic Platform)

While the *Plataforma* urged foreign governments to persuade the Cuban regime to undertake democratic reforms, the CANF continued to lobby in Washington to tighten the thirty-year-old U.S. embargo on Cuba.[35] Although the efforts of these two organizations were really complementary, their tendency to perceive each other as rivals alienated both from less partisan Cuban Americans. By contrast, other groups that surfaced during the Post-Soviet Stage, like the humanitarian-oriented Brothers to the Rescue and the civic-minded *Democracia* movement, have been characterized by a more open, all-inclusive attitude, and precisely because of that reason, they have attracted a substantial following from the ranks of previously uncommitted Cuban Americans. It is worth noting the deep involvement of Cuban American women in patriotic efforts during the Post-Soviet Stage. Recent exile initiatives, such as Brothers to the Rescue, the *Democracia* movement, Mothers against Repression, and the *Concilio*'s Support Group, have drawn the active support of scores of successful business and professional women.

In the 1990s, the involvement of the "last generation" of Cubans, who came as youngsters and rebuilt their lives in America, surprised most observers. It had been generally assumed that this generation of successful Cuban Americans had lost all interest in Cuba's political future. It is still too early to ascertain whether this constituency will demonstrate the same enduring commitment of its militant predecessors, but the new consciousness that younger Cuban Americans have introduced in the anti-Castro movement seems to be spreading throughout the Cuban Exile Country.

The Fourth Exodus: The Rafters (1994)

In the early 1990s, the number of Cubans leaving the island began to increase noticeably. Their exodus seemed to follow the carrot-and-stick effects of two powerful forces: hope for a better life among exiles in the United States and despair about worsening conditions on the island. But it is the latter, the near-collapse that Cuban society suffered after the disintegration of the Soviet Union, that appeared to be the determining factor in this new exodus.

From the perspective of the exiles, the latest exodus of refugees seeking to escape Cuba's miserable conditions suggested that the Castro regime could be reaching its final phase. To be sure, economic activity in Cuba had dropped by about 40 percent since the collapse of the Soviet Union, a predicament that forced the communist regime to impose draconian measures that clearly undermined its popular support. It was no coincidence that human rights and dissident groups opposing Castro proliferated throughout the island and, for the very first time, established working alliances with moderate exile political organizations.[36] The emergence of these loose coalitions linking opponents on both sides of the Straits of Florida began to nurture a new kinship between Cubans who, although very dissimilar in backgrounds, experiences, and even ideological visions of Cuba's future, shared a commitment to rid the island of communism. Obviously, this tactical alliance represented a portentous development of concern to the Cuban regime.

Coupled with the continuing downward spiral of the Cuban economy, the emboldened internal opposition added instability to the political climate on the island. Before conditions could reach a flash point, however, Castro again resorted to his time-tested ploy—the demographic bomb. In the spring

of 1994, the communist regime reversed its three-decade-old policy of ar-
resting anyone who tried to escape the island by sea; from then on, Castro
announced that Cubans would be allowed to leave in small vessels and make-
shift rafts if they wished to embark for the United States.

> The absolute failure of Cuba's communist regime generated deep disappoint-
> ment among Cubans in the island. This caused the exodus of more than
> 50,000 Cubans who took to sea in search of a better future. Hermanos al
> Rescate [Brothers to the Rescue] was founded with the idea of saving those
> who, risking their lives, boarded fragile rafts and vessels. (Translation of au-
> thor's interview with José Basulto, founder of Brothers to the Rescue)

To the Cuban dictator, the dramatic spectacle of Cubans openly boarding
anything that could float in order to escape was probably a bitter pill to
swallow, but Castro must have felt confident that, as a result of this new
exodus, the U.S. government would be forced into negotiating an immigration agreement, or even relaxing the U.S. embargo on Cuba.

The End of Open-Arms U.S. Immigration Policy
toward Cubans

Castro's ploy once again worked to perfection. By the summer of 1994,
as tens of thousands of *balseros* (rafters) took to the sea with the regime's
overt encouragement, the Clinton administration negotiated an agreement
with Cuba to put a stop to this new exodus. The accord between the United
States and Cuba suspended the preferential treatment that had been accorded
to Cubans for three decades. Naturally, the new immigration agreement
provoked angry reactions among the exiles, who interpreted the de facto
suspension of the open-arms policy toward Cubans fleeing the island as a
first step toward normalization of relations between the two countries. The
secrecy with which the accord was negotiated further fueled those fears. In
protest, exiles staged civil disobedience demonstrations throughout South
Florida. Most of them could not bear the thought of U.S. Coast Guard vessels
working side by side with their Cuban counterparts in a joint effort to stop
the flow of rafters and return them to the communist island.

The 1994 immigration agreement provided for the detention of those
rafters who managed to reach American soil; from then on, all *balseros* were
to be sent to the U.S. Navy Base in Guantanamo,[37] where they would have
to stay indefinitely, unless they agreed to go back to the island from which
they had risked their lives to escape. In a matter of weeks, the detainee

population at Guantanamo reached 32,000 men, women, and children. Critics, as well as supporters of the shift in immigration policy, saw this development as a tacit recognition that *el exilio* was entering a new stage, since Cubans would no longer automatically be allowed into the United States. For the first time since the enactment of the 1965 Cuban Adjustment Act, Cubans would presumably be treated the same as immigrants of any other nationality.

Six months later, the Clinton administration again shifted its position, allowing the Guantanamo detainees to qualify for entrance into this country. By then, nevertheless, the United States had made its point: Cubans wishing to leave the island had to follow a normal application process in order to qualify for immigrant visas, 20,000 of which would be issued every year through the U.S. Interest Section in Havana. It is likely, however, that political pressure exerted by Cuban Americans will keep succeeding administrations from a strict implementation of the 1994 immigration agreement— at least as long as Castro stays in power.

The 1996 Crisis and the Tightening of the Embargo

The 1994 immigration accord gave credence to the notion that *el exilio*, as such, could be approaching its final phase. Although for different reasons, both Washington and Havana were under intense pressure to end the thirty-year-old U.S. trade embargo on Cuba and to normalize diplomatic and commercial relations. These speculations, however, soon proved premature. What derailed the fledgling rapprochement was Cuba's shooting down over international waters two unarmed American airplanes belonging to Brothers to the Rescue. Four Cuban Americans lost their lives in the incident, which dragged U.S.-Cuba relations to a confrontation level reminiscent of the bygone Cold War days.

In many ways, the genesis of this tragedy was somewhat predictable. Since the beginning of the recent *balsero* wave, Brothers to the Rescue planes had been engaged in humanitarian missions, carrying out thousands of rescue flights near or inside Cuban airspace in search of rafters adrift in the Straits of Florida. In 1995, however, the exile organization deviated from its original life-saving objective, and twice their unarmed airplanes actually intruded over Cuban territory to drop leaflets encouraging nonviolent rebellion. They seemed intent on provoking Castro, though peacefully. Finally, on February 24, 1996, Castro retaliated with a vengeance. He ordered the Cuban air force to shoot down two exile planes flying close to the island, thereby triggering an international crisis. President Clinton forcefully denounced the Cuban government for its criminal aggression and, reversing his personal opposition to the pending Helms-Burton Bill, promptly signed it into law. Enacted under the name of the Cuban Liberty and Democratic Solidarity Act, this piece of legislation tightened the U.S. embargo on Cuba even further—too much, according to its critics; just enough to force Castro out, according to its supporters. Its most controversial feature imposes sanctions on international companies doing business in Cuba. This provision has already created a division between the United States and its Canadian and European allies.

What will happen in the wake of these developments is yet to be seen. In the short term, the once-hopeful prospect of forcing Castro into initiating a democratic transition has all but disappeared, which is not to suggest in any way that the *Máximo Líder* had shown the slightest inclination to amend his totalitarian ways. Ironically, the hard-liners' position appeared to be validated by the belligerence of their nemesis, who at the same time cracked down against dissidents on the island with renewed ruthlessness. Given Castro's obstinate hold on power, *el exilio* can be expected to go on as long as the aging dictator continues to extend his thirty-nine–year-old rule. When his regime will actually end may depend on the outcome of the deep crisis faced by Cuba as it struggles toward the next century.

NOTES

1. Liz Balmaseda, "Exiles Become Establishment," *The Miami Herald*, 18 January 1995, first ed., 1B.

2. The Cuban population in the United States exceeded the one million mark in 1990. Only 6 percent of those had arrived before 1960; about 33 percent arrived in the 1960s, 13 percent in the 1970s, and 20 percent in the 1980s. The remaining 28 percent were born in the United States but identify themselves as Cubans. See The Cuban American Policy Center, *A Demographic Profile of Cuban Americans* (Miami: Cuban American National Council, 1994b).

3. The distinction between immigrants and refugees has been noted before. See Everett S. Lee, "A Theory of Migration," *Demography* 3 (1966): 47–57.

4. These stages of development were first published by the author in 1996. See Miguel Gonzalez-Pando, "Doing Business," in *Greater Miami: Spirit of Cuban Enterprise*, ed. Miguel Gonzalez-Pando (Fort Lauderdale, Fla.: Cooperfield, 1996), 40–69.

5. E. F. Kunz, "The Refugee in Flight: Kinetic Models and Forms of Displacement," *International Migration Review* 7 (Summer 1973), 137.

6. Nelson Amaro and Alejandro Portes. "Una sociologia del Exilio: Situación de los grupos cubanos en los Estados Unidos," *Aportes* 23 (January 1972): 10.

7. That much has been suggested by Joel Kotkin in *Tribes: How Race, Religion and Identity Determine Success in the New Global Economy* (New York: Random House, 1992).

8. Several authors have documented the Cuban exiles' anti-Castro war. See for example, Hugh Thomas, *Cuba: The Pursuit of Freedom* (Harper, 1971); Juan M. Clark, *Cuba: Mito y realidad* Miami-Caracas: (Saeta Ediciones, 1990); Enrique Encinosa, *Cuba en guerra* (Miami: The Endowment for Cuban American Studies of the Cuban American National Foundation, 1994).

9. In December 1960, the Eisenhower administration created the Cuban Refugee Emergency Center to coordinate the relief efforts of voluntary agencies and to oversee resettlement. Some months later, President Kennedy created the more generous Cuban Refugee Program.

10. Portes and Bach define the term "enclave" as "a distinctive economic formation, characterized by the spatial concentration of immigrants who organize a variety of enterprises to serve their own ethnic market and the general population." Alejandro Portes and R. L. Bach, *Latin Journey: Cuban and Mexican Immigrants in the United States* (Berkeley: University of California Press, 1985).

11. For lack of a better term, "Anglo" and "American" are used interchangeably throughout this volume to refer to the white, non-Cuban, English-speaking U.S. population. Obviously it is a misnomer, for it includes Jews, Italian-Americans, and other ethnics who, although American, are not Anglo.

12. According to the Cuban Refugee Program's 1978 Fact Sheet, more than 300,000 Cubans resettled outside of Miami between 1961 and 1978—about 64 percent of all the exiles who had come to the United States during that period.

13. As a means to encourage unemployed refugees to resettle around the country, the Cuban Refugee Program threatened to cut off benefits to those who remained in South Florida.

14. Exiles established a Cuban enclave in Union City, New Jersey, and much like Little Havana, it thrived. Small Cuban-owned businesses eventually dominated the commercial district of this so-called Havana on the Hudson.

15. Since Camarioca, one of Castro's most effective tools has been the periodic encouragement of emigration. He has adroitly played this hand whenever he wanted to retaliate against the United States or relieve internal political pressures. Castro would use the demographic bomb again during the 1980 Mariel boatlift and the 1994 rafter exodus.

16. This preferential treatment lasted until the summer of 1994, when the Clinton administration placed a de facto hold on the open-arms policy toward Cuban refugees.

17. U.S. agencies persuaded about half of the newly arrived Cubans to resettle outside of Miami.

18. Researchers often disagree on the precise socioeconomic extraction of the second wave. See Silvia Pedraza-Bailey, "Cuba's Exiles: Portrait of a Refugee Migra-

tion," *International Migration Review* 19 (1985): 4–34; Clark, "The Exodus from Revolutionary Cuba."

19. For a unique insider's account of the anti-Castro war, see Encinosa, *Cuba en guerra*.

20. According to a recent survey conducted by *The Miami Herald*.

21. The author has long referred to this group as "the last generation." They are the *last generation* of Cubans old enough to remember pre-Castro Cuba.

22. The flow of billions of dollars from Latin America to Miami included both legitimately earned funds and drug monies. This capital provided further impetus to the economic Latinization of South Florida. Drug laundering schemes flourished during the period, and some Cubans became involved in illegal financial operations.

23. Whereas in 1970 only 25 percent of the Cuban exiles were American citizens, by 1980 a majority (55 percent) was.

24. An insightful analysis of the exiles' metamorphosis from "political militants to ethnic entrepreneurs" can be found in Alejandro Portes and Alex Stepick, *City on the Edge: The Transformation of Miami* (Berkeley: University of California Press, 1993).

25. Alejandro Portes, "Social Origins of the Cuban Enclave Economy," *Sociological Perspectives* 30 (1987).

26. Bombs were exploded in Miami at the Continental Bank and at Padrón Cigars. Their respective owners, Bernardo Benes and Orlando Padrón, had participated in the dialogue. *Dialogueros* were also victims of terrorist attacks in Jersey City and Puerto Rico.

27. In 1965 the Cuban government opened the port of Camarioca to exiles. Although only 5,000 refugees left with exiles at that time, the event led to the freedom flights which brought 300,000 Cubans to the United States between 1965 and 1973.

28. To observe the prevailing terminology, Cubans who came in the first two emigration waves are referred to as "exiles" in this volume; those who left during the 1980 Mariel boatlift and the 1994 exodus are referred to as "refugees."

29. It was estimated that only 8.7 percent of the new arrivals, compared to 22.2 percent of the early exiles, had a managerial background.

30. At first, the *Marielitos* were processed by exile volunteers. That practice changed, however, after the federal government took charge and sent thousands to camps around the country: Eglin Air Force Base in Florida, Fort Chaffee in Arkansas, Fort Indian Gap in Pennsylvania, and Fort McCoy in Wisconsin.

31. South Floridians' anger at the Mariel crisis was one factor in the success of the referendum that repealed the 1973 Bilingual-Bicultural Ordinance.

32. David Rieff, *The Exile: Cuba in the Heart of Miami* (New York: Simon & Schuster, 1993).

33. The most dramatic accomplishment of the Cuban American National Foundation (CANF) was its lobbying effort in favor of creating the U.S.-sponsored Radio Martí which broadcasts news and commentaries to Cubans on the island.

34. Three ideologically differentiated groups—liberals, social democrats, and Christian democrats—founded the *Plataforma*. The Committee for Human Rights, the first dissident group on the island, was also a signatory to the Madrid Declaration.

35. In 1992, largely as a result of the lobbying efforts of the CANF, the U.S. Congress passed the Cuban Democracy Act, a controversial bill that tightens the embargo against Cuba.

36. In 1996 more than one hundred "free" independent unions and dissident groups came together in Cuba under an umbrella organization called Concilio Cubano, which is currently the most recognized anti-Castro movement on the island.

37. The Guantanamo Navy Base has operated on Cuban territory since it was ceded to the United States following Cuban independence in 1902. This last vestige of American imperialism on the island has remained a vexing presence often denounced by Castro.

Chairman of Republic Bank Luis Botifoll, the author, and Manuel Jorge Cutillas, Chairman of Bacardi–Martini Rosi, during a meeting of the "Amigos" of the Cuban Living History Project, an initiative dedicated to documenting the Cuban exile experience. Courtesy of Pedro Portal.

Panoramic view of the 1997 Calle Ocho Street Festival. Since 1978, over a million people attend this yearly event, which is organized by the Kiwanis of Little Havana. Courtesy of Pedro Portal.

Cuban Americans marching in front of the White House to protest deportation of Cuban rafters. Courtesy of Pedro Portal.

Cuban Americans commemorating their nation's independence day, May 20, 1902. The exiles continue to celebrate Cuba's patriotic holidays. Courtesy of Pedro Portal.

Cuban Americans hold a special place in their heart for fallen heroes in the struggle to free their country from communism. This special edition of *El Nuevo Herald* shows the four pilots who were shot down by Cuba's air force on February 24, 1996. Courtesy of Pedro Portal.

Many among the new Cuban American generation continue the patriotic traditions of their parents and grandparents. Courtesy of Pedro Portal.

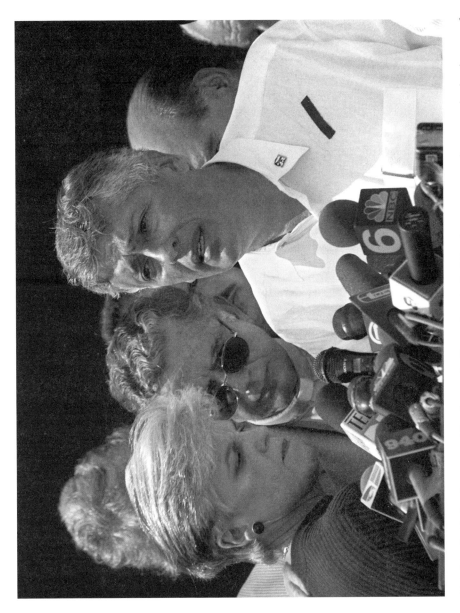

Silvia Iriondo, Father Santana, and Brothers to the Rescue founder José Basulto at a press conference on the day that two of the Brothers planes were shot down by Castro's air force. Courtesy of Pedro Portal.

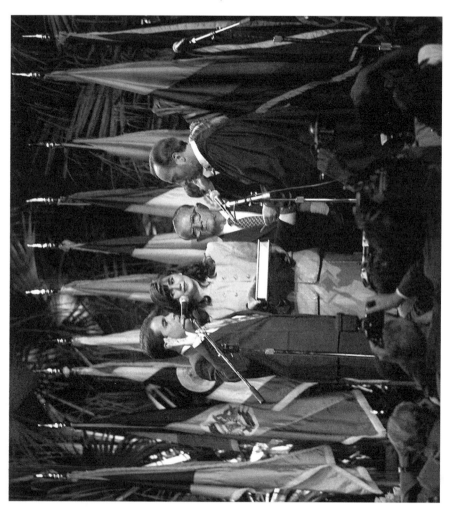

Alex Penelas, Dade County's first "strong" mayor, during his 1996 swearing-in ceremony. Courtesy of Pedro Portal.

Cuban Americans observing Cuba's patron saint, the Virgin of Charity. Courtesy of Pedro Portal.

The three Cuban American representatives in the U.S. Congress, Lincoln Díaz Balart, Bob Menendez, and Iliana Ros Lehtinen, attending a massive exile demonstration at the Orange Bowl Stadium. Courtesy of Pedro Portal.

Cuban exiles have periodically run into conflict with coverage of the island's political situation by the American press. This 1994 campaign against *The Miami Herald* was organized by the powerful Cuban American National Foundation. Courtesy of Pedro Portal.

Cuban rafters enjoy their first meal in freedom. Courtesy of Pedro Portal.

Willy Chirino in concert. The Cuban singer-composer established the Chirino Foundation to help needy children throughout Latin America. Courtesy of Pedro Portal.

Three Cuban exile celebrities at the 1994 Miami Film Festival: Grammy-winning musician Israel Lopez "Cachao," Oscar-nominee Andy García, and Guillermo Cabrera Infante, arguably the best-known Cuban writer anywhere. Courtesy of Pedro Portal.

The Stars and Stripes often decorate South Florida's Cuban-American businesses. Courtesy of Pedro Portal.

Cuban exiles are best known for their enterprising spirit and their political passion. Courtesy of Pedro Portal.

4

Identity, Culture, and Exile Life

I find this effort to recreate yesterday's Cuba in today's America both heroic and pathetic. Heroic because it tries to rise above history and geography. Pathetic because it is doomed to fail.
                                        —*Gustavo Pérez Firmat*[1]

IDENTITY OF THE CUBAN EMIGRÉS

The emigrés sense of identity as political exiles is at the heart of who they are and what they have accomplished during their diaspora. It may truly be said that their identity represents the mortar used in building the Cuban Exile Country. Indeed, beyond the singularity of each emigré's prior background or individual experience in America, beyond their particular wave or vintage, they have all shared a collective identity—ambiguous, unmeasurable, ever-changing as it may be. Arguably, the role that identity has played in their dynamics is yet to be fully addressed. Its significance, however, remains crucial to understanding them. Upon close examination, one finds persuasive arguments in support of considering the role of the exiles' identity among the major explanations of their success in the United States.

Defining the Identity of Cuban Emigrés

The Cuban post-Castro diaspora continues to puzzle academicians, many of whom have approached the emigrés from the diverse perspectives of cultural anthropology, social history, psychology, ethnic studies, and sociology.[2] Following their respective conceptual frameworks, every researcher has encountered varying degrees of success in documenting the details of the Cuban exodus and describing the behavior of the emigrés in America. Excellent analyses of the motivations for leaving of each of the four main waves that has formed this emigration and their demographic characteristics are also found in the academic literature. But time and again, most researchers have run into the same obstinate challenge: defining the identity of the subjects of their inquiry.

Who are these Cubans, really? The elusiveness of the answer to this crucial question may lie in the eye of the beholder; that is, in the particular theoretical lens through which distinct researchers struggle to make sense of the identity of the emigrés. But beyond the limitations inherent in disciplinary biases and methodological reliance on statistics, there is also another problem: Cuban emigrés certainly do not lend themselves to unequivocal, abiding labels. They may appear to be old-fashioned Cubans, fanatical political exiles, struggling ethnic minorities, successful Cuban Americans, or proud Americans—and all these façades can be displayed by the same individual, alternatively or even simultaneously. And these are not progressive acculturation stages through which Cubans travel in linear succession over time while incorporating characteristics from their adopted surroundings.[3] Paradoxically, the emigrés, individually and collectively, can go back and forth with relative ease, defining and redefining their identities according to their ever-changing relationship to the homeland and their adopted land as well as the situational context in which they may find themselves at any given moment. Indeed, theirs has been a highly adaptable breed.

> I consider myself Cuban. I consider myself black. And by virtue of the opportunities given to me here and by virtue of my naturalization, I also consider myself an American. . . . I was born in Cuba; that makes me Cuban—nobody can take that away. I was born black because my parents are black—and nobody can take that away either. So I consider myself all of the above. . . . I do not feel an identity conflict between being Cuban, being black, and being an American citizen. I just don't. (Author's interview with Gerardo Simms, a Miami attorney)

> I consider myself 150% American. But I'm also 150% Cuban. That's not a mutually exclusive thing. You can feel them both and you can love them both and you can be loyal to both. (Author's interview with Florida State Senator Mario Díaz Balart)

For all its lack of academic rigor, defining these emigrés as Cuban "political exiles" appears to be the best option. That was the identity first chosen by the initial exodus upon arriving in the United States, and regardless of contrasting experiences in America or the time that elapsed since then, this definition is consistent with the fact that their shared predicament was irrefutably forced upon them by political events in Cuba: They were clearly "pushed" out of their homeland. Once so designated, most have overtly or intimately remained Cuban political exiles, although no longer exclusively.

To complicate the definition issue further, the emigrés encompass four major "waves," but in terms of their attitudes at the time of leaving, each wave also may have included different "vintages," to use the nomenclature coined by E. F. Kunz.[4] These vintages, as Silvia Pedraza points out, are "alike only in their final rejection of Cuba."[5] The initial emigration wave (1959–1962), for example, was made up of at least three diverse vintages: the *batistianos*, the socioeconomic elite of the island, and the earliest defectors from the fledgling revolutionary regime.

> To me Cuba was a bit of a nightmare. I could not go to school like any other kid. I had to go to school with a lot of guards and a lot of protection because of the civil war that was basically going on and the fact that our dad was a prominent person in the Batista government and also, the fact that he was very verbal against Fidel Castro, because he had known him very well. So, we had been singled out. I was eight years old [when we left], and I remember my parents always seemed very unhappy about not being in their homeland. And that was something that was very evident from day one in exile, and that made me become very aware of what Cuba meant to them and, over time as I grew up, I also developed that love. (Author's interview with Miami banker Rafael Díaz Balart, who was part of the *batistiano* vintage)

> I remember the day I left Havana on National Airlines. . . . I was told that it would be for two to three months. I only packed my winter clothes. I was coming back! In Cuba I lived in a very nice world. It was very secure and privileged, and for me to come here and to have no resources, have no friends, to actually come to a hostile place, because Miami in 1960 was a hostile place . . . then, we became exiles. (Author's interview with businesswoman Cruz Hernández Otazo, who was part of the elite vintage)

> When the revolution came to power, while Fidel Castro was making his January 8th speech with the pigeon perched on his shoulder, my father said to me, "This is a repetition of what I saw when I was a young boy in Russia; this is over with: Let's prepare to leave." This was just eight days after Castro came to power. The three of us, my brother, my sister and I, we had a big fight with him—that he was wrong, that Cuba was different. But at the end,

he [my father] was right. (Author's interview with Jewish banker Bernardo
Benes, who was part of the early disaffected revolutionary vintage)

Defining the emigrés as Cuban political exiles, however, seemed much
more fitting in the case of those who left their country right after Castro's
revolutionary takeover. That initial wave most closely conformed to the standard definition of "exiles" as people politically coerced to flee their country
with the expectation of returning. Admittedly, that has not been the con-
dition under which later waves of Cubans left their homeland. Although in
all cases political events were responsible for the entire emigration, the historic circumstances, as well as the motivations for leaving, have certainly kept
changing over the nearly four decades during which Castro has remained in
power. Whereas the initial wave (1959–1962) clearly left expecting Castro's
imminent overthrow, the second wave that came in the freedom flights
(1965–1973) wanted to escape from the communist dictatorship; the *Marielitos* (1980) wanted to escape from communist misery; and the recent rafters
(1994) just wanted to escape.

The precise historical juncture impelling these four emigrations notwithstanding, the members of each succeeding wave sought to join their countrymen already living in *el exilio*. Like those who had preceded them, the
newcomers also chose to identify themselves as Cuban exiles. Cuban emigrés
may speak English with a heavy accent, fluently, or no English at all; they
may have become Americanized, refused to acculturate altogether, or adopted
a dual cultural identity; however, to this day, their overarching leitmotif
continues to revolve around their fate as political exiles. Their sense of identity, in other words, "uses Cubaness or *cubanía* as point of reference within
the communities in which they settled."[6] Once in the United States, however, each emigration wave has met somewhat differing social experiences.

We settled in New York with the family—my aunts and uncles and my grandparents. . . . We were in the Upper West Side in Manhattan and we landed
across the street from a welfare hotel. And because of the drugs and the pros-
titution in the area I wasn't allowed to play downstairs. . . . Eventually, we
moved to Union City, New Jersey, because my parents, again, felt they hadn't
left the island to bring up their children in an area that was crime infested and
so on. We settled in Union City, a very Cuban enclave—besides Miami,
Union City has the highest concentration [of Cubans] in the U.S. . . . Every
summer we came to Miami because we had relatives here. . . . Miami was very
much the hotbed of the Cuban community, in a different way than Union
City was. You couldn't escape Cuban politics here. (Author's interview with
journalist Bárbara Gutierrez, editor of *El Nuevo Herald*)

Exile Identity, Language, and Culture

Largely intuitively, like many other psychosocial processes that guided their collective behavior in exile, the first Cuban emigrés retained the Spanish language to protect their identity from the contextual forces compelling them to surrender their *cubanía* in America. That belief, whether clearly or tacitly expressed, found justification in the shared expectation of an eventual return to Cuba.

> We were going to conserve the culture because we were going back. After it became evident that there was no going back . . . that changed to, "Let's pre-serve our culture so that our children are proud of us." That's a psychological ingredient of great importance. The older parents, the grandparents, were instrumental in trying to conserve among the young generation the language as well as the Cuban music, the taste for Cuban culture and so forth. (Author's interview with cultural anthropologist Mercedes Sandoval, a professor at Mi-ami Dade Community College)

The extended-family structure prevalent among the early exiles provided a constant reinforcement of the Cuban mind-set. In addition to its obvious economic advantages, the three-generation family acquired cultural viability as a repository of popular tales, folklore, rituals, and myths, lending coherence to the collective actions of *el exilio*.

> They always brought me up with the Cuban tradition. My father and my mother always used to tell us to speak Spanish at home. They had a rule that when you walked in the door, they wanted us to speak Spanish. My mother would say to me, "Don't talk English with your brothers"—because we used to speak English with one another when we were living in the United States. (Author's interview with Alberto de la Cruz, a young Cuban American busi-nessman).

The young quickly learned English, of course. Among the elderly, how-ever, learning a new language was far from a priority. To them, in fact, English represented more than just a practical obstacle; it subconsciously challenged the affective and symbolic underpinnings of a past they so obses-sively revered. English also threatened to estrange them from the world of their grandchildren. The fear of losing the young to the American culture caused grandparents to "push" Spanish on the grandchildren; consequently, the mother tongue—the grandmother's tongue, in this case—remains the language predominantly spoken at home to this day.[7] With similar zeal, the exiles insisted that their children not forget the homeland to which they hoped to return. Thus intertwined, psychocultural motivations and patriotism were critical in preserving the Spanish language. This triad became the means for the daily reaffirmation of the Cuban political exile identity.

The collective need for cultural self-preservation, along with the ambition to get ahead, explains much of the Cuban exiles' intimate dynamics in the United States since the Transition Stage (1962–1965). From its outset circa 1960, the emigrés' language and national identity always constituted the first line of defense against becoming diluted in American society as had other immigrant groups.

> We were not immigrants. We were exiles. There is a big difference between an exile and an immigrant. An immigrant is somebody who tries to get out of his country and get to another place where he can earn a better life. Now, an exile is a different person. An exile is somebody who doesn't want to leave his country . . . [and has to] only for political reasons—expecting to come back. (Author's interview with retired banker Luis Botifoll, dean of the Cuban American community)

Until very recently, indeed, most emigrés considered themselves political exiles, not immigrants—a denomination that to them implied a set of motivations different from their own. Immigrants, in contrast to exiles, generally want to come to this country; that is, they react to the seductive "pull" of America's society. Cubans, on the other hand, largely feel they were reluctantly "pushed" out of their homeland. Hence, as exiles, they always rejected for themselves the immigrants' mythical concept of the "melting pot." To them, the process of melting ultimately would have led to the disappearance of their group's unique identity.

That identification as political exiles was considered a badge of honor, an explicit and unyielding commitment to the struggle to liberate their homeland, no matter how long they had to live outside of it. But more than just an outward posture, this identity reflected an intimate conviction shared by the first Cuban exiles and, to some extent, passed on to their American-born children and to succeeding waves of emigrants.

> I think that Fidel is not good. . . . People go away from Cuba because they want liberties, they want freedom, they want the right to say what they want to say, to express themselves. . . . [In Cuba] they take you to jail or . . . *a cortar caña*—this means they make you cut sugar cane. And my Mom once had to go to a sugar cane camp. . . . Well, I would like to be born in Cuba but, you know, unfortunately, I was born here. Although maybe if I was born in Cuba

I would have come here. . . . I think I have Cuban DNA, and my roots are Cuban and the most important thing, I like *frijoles negros*. I was born here but I consider myself Cuban. I feel like I am Cuban. I am Cuban! Spanish is the language of my country, my parents, my great-great-great ancestors. (Author's interview with ten-year-old Aurelio García)

In every facet of their experience in exile, Cubans obsessively have held on to that sense of political identity; it characterizes them, it sets them apart from other Hispanics, and it provides the strength for their quest in America. To them, being political exiles has meant reaffirming the notion that although they were defeated in the struggle against Castro, they have never given up. Despite mounting evidence that most exiles may never go back to the home they once left—at least not to the Cuba they still yearn for—their mostly rhetorical war to liberate Cuba continues. They accept that they are Cuban Americans, but they still see themselves as Cubans.

Ironically, the practical implications of this willful stance may have helped Cubans survive, endure, and ultimately prevail through almost two generations in America. Their refusal to forego their language and to acculturate, as well as their initial decision to remain isolated in somewhat segregated sociocultural cocoons, has allowed them to carve out enclaves of their own within the larger society. In Little Havana, Hialeah, New Jersey, and other exile colonies, they have managed to keep alive much of their language, cultural traditions, and way of life, as well as their political idiosyncrasies and sense of identity.[8] Even when these insular exile communities across the United States were later diluted, many Cuban emigrés still turned their backs on the cultural dimensions of the traditional American Dream as understood by mainstream society.

But how then did they understand the American Dream? Since the Transition Stage (1962–1965), most Cubans have hoped to do well in America while, at the same time, they have refused to give up their exile identity. What they did not consider was how seeking these apparently conflicting goals would affect them; they really had no forethought about what they would eventually become in their newly adopted country. At first they were too busy surviving and adjusting, and then they were too determined to change, not themselves, but their cultural milieu to fit their nostalgic memories. In so doing, they were largely improvising most of the time.[9]

That made the Cuban group completely different—much more traditional, much more conservative. And, of course, it also created a lot of stress between

the younger members of the family and the older members of the family.
(Author's interview with Mercedes Sandoval)

Toward the conclusion of the Economic Miracle Stage (1973–1980), after
just two decades of being subjected to the opposing effects of assimilation
and isolation, actual evidence that the exiles had reached a compromise surfaced for the first time. By then, they had begun to integrate structurally into
the host society while forging, at the same time, a uniquely functional identity, one that ranged over varying degrees of the acculturation spectrum without casting off their identity as Cuban exiles. During the 1970s and beyond,
in other words, Cuban Americans seemed to be having the proverbial cake
and eating it too.

That has been one of the more remarkable paradoxes revealed by the
unique fashion in which Cubans have progressed in America: Their self-
imposed cultural marginality, rather than a weakness, was turned into a
source of strength. This could be seen in how they managed to integrate the
pursuit of competing economic and sociocultural needs. For instance, although from the very beginning most Cubans in South Florida actually
worked in the mainstream economy, they preferred to live close to Little
Havana and patronize its informal business and service network. Such an
attitude allowed their development to start within their South Florida enclave. Much as their relative isolation served to fend off acculturation in the
formative period of el exilio, their voluntary segregation facilitated the defense
of their economic self-interest within the geographical boundaries of Little
Havana. Only as this cultural base acquired economic, social, and political
viability did its entrepreneurs and professionals venture into the larger community.

Another factor that assisted the initial emigrés in negotiating[10] with the
American culture was their prior familiarity with it. The differences between
Cuba and the United States have been so overemphasized that there is a
pervasive impression that the two were entirely different societies. That could
never have been the case given the closeness of Cuba to the United States
and the geopolitical relationship between the nations. Yes, the society that
the first exiles found upon arriving in America was essentially different from
Cuba's, but it was not entirely foreign to the Americanized upper and middle
classes who came in the initial wave right after the revolution. Although that
vintage of emigrés obviously did not share the same cultural values of mainstream America, most of them were not completely new to the American
way. After all, since only ninety miles separated them from the United States,

the Cuban elite had been exposed to American cultural influences before they crossed the Straits of Florida.

Once here, a number of contextual factors inherent to American society combined to allow, if not to actually promote, the cultural isolation of the incipient exile communities. This politically more tolerant society permitted the newcomers to enjoy the freedoms they often lacked in their own country; more significantly, it was more socially segregated and thus more inclined to leave the Cubans alone. These characteristics allowed the newcomers to "circle their wagons" around a territory of their own, particularly in South Florida. As their Miami enclave developed, its relative self-sufficiency reinforced the exiles' cultural isolation and retarded, or at least conditioned, the process of cultural negotiation. That suited the exiles' reluctance to become Americanized and to continue indulging in their early expectations-later-turned-myth of an eventual return to Cuba.[11]

The periodic arrival of fresh emigration waves from the island kept the enclave's affective links with the homeland culture from becoming stale. Each additional newcomer served to recharge the *cubanía* on this side of the Straits of Florida. Moreover, the success attained by the early exiles provided the new arrivals with appropriate role models for rebuilding their lives in America without losing their cultural identity and, in many instances, even learning English. The constant influx of Cubans assisted in the preservation of an exile cultural cocoon in Miami somewhat impervious to outside contextual forces. Thus, it was mostly the young and the upwardly mobile professionals who actually came to embody the original agents of cultural change among the exiles, a development that naturally triggered the earliest intergenerational gaps within the Cuban Exile Country.

In time, of course, the exiles could not completely escape the pressures to acculturate. But even as they negotiated their cultural adjustment with the host environment, they did so on their own terms; they adopted a dual sense of cultural identity. This functional biculturalism, which seemed the perfect compromise for dealing with different situations, allowed them to assume a Cuban American identity when among non-Cubans, yet remain essentially Cuban among themselves.

We like to deny it, but we have changed more than we think we have. I think this has happened in a greater sense to younger Cubans. I came when I was twenty-seven, and I don't really think that I've changed that much in terms of my Cuban identity. I consider myself Cuban American when I have to participate, which I do, in American society processes: I vote, I pay taxes, I am a homeowner, I have neighbors, I speak English, I work in an American institution, I deal with a lot of Americans. In that sense, I have an advantage; I am as American as I can be, or need to be, but I keep being very Cuban. (Author's interview with María Cristina Herrera, professor at Miami-Dade Community College)

The new generation, brought up and educated in this country, at first followed a bicultural path similar to the one their parents had already blazed ahead of them. As they later came of age, Cuban Americans developed an "affinity"—which is not as deeply rooted as an identity—for the cultural values of their American peers. To be sure, the unique brand of success attained by both generations has so far been accomplished without forsaking a sense of pride in their identity.

Intercultural Conflict

From the perspective of the early exiles, the world as they had known it certainly appeared to be coming to an end; they had fled Fidel Castro's revolution only to settle in a society about to undergo its own revolutionary convulsions. Beginning in the mid-1960s, the United States underwent deep transformations in cultural and political values, as evidenced by the civil rights movement, the antiwar protests, and the advent of a new generation that seemed intent on challenging everything Americans—and Cuban exiles themselves—held sacred about the established social order.

In the Cuban case, the acculturation was probably harder, because we came at a time when America was experiencing a great number of changes. . . . The schools were not giving directives, the society at large was not giving clear directives. . . . The Cuban parents and the grandparents were alarmed by all these changes that go against the thread of traditional society. . . . I remember many Cuban parents telling me, "If I would have known that my children were going to be exposed to this, I would have stayed in Cuba." (Author's interview with Mercedes Sandoval)

The exiles were not psychologically prepared to cope with the dawning of the Age of Aquarius and the ensuing sexual and drug revolutions; given their recent political trauma, they often suspected such developments were linked to an international communist conspiracy to undermine the last remaining bulwark of law and order in the free world. In the view of many, Castro surely had something to do with the cataclysms of the 1960s. Those up-heavals threatened the exiles and may have actually hastened their retrench-ment into the security provided by their increasing numbers within their incipient sociocultural communities, where they created dozens of organizations to keep their traditions alive and to instill their values and ideals in the young. And they did so while attaching a political meaning to the urgency with which they defended their identity and cultural heritage. Exile organizations sponsored all kinds of cultural events where their political counterparts frequently collected funds for the anti-Castro movement; culture and patriotism were indeed inseparable—and to a large extent, they still are among Cubans in the United States.

If exile life in their American cultural cocoons reinforced *cubanía*, its effect among a large segment of die-hard exiles was to "freeze" them circa 1959.[12] Charter members of this "frozen" subculture concocted an idealized perception of what prerevolutionary Cuba had been like and what they themselves had been like before, glorifying the past in order to rationalize their own unwillingness, or inability, to adapt to American society. In a sense, theirs was a backlash reaction to the trauma of seeing their world turned upside down by revolution in Cuba and by the social upheaval occurring in their adopted land. Because anything new provoked this defensive reaction, the frozen group, composed mostly of the influential elite vintage, kept the Cuban Exile Country somewhat out of touch with reality. Although that attitude certainly allowed Cubans to cling stubbornly to their *cubanía*, which on balance proved to be positive, it also fostered a climate of collective denial.

Under such conditions, the Miami and Union City enclaves were able to thrive economically and to consolidate culturally. From the perspective of interethnic understanding, however, Little Havana's relative self-sufficiency posed hard challenges to the community at large, for Miami's increasing cultural diversity often acted as a barrier distancing its residents along ethnic lines. The Miami Cubans must accept some responsibility for this, as well as for the ensuing tensions that developed in the community's social fabric.[13] But the emigrés were on a mission; they could not care for anything except getting ahead and protecting their own way of life. Truth be told, most early exiles were not particularly interested in integrating into American society. Instead, they sported a deliberate attitude that voluntarily kept them detached from their Anglo and African American neighbors—a stance that, as could be expected, did not play well with the rest of the community.

Toward the end of the 1970s, the emergence of a dual cultural identity among the *yucas* (an acronym for young, upwardly mobile Cuban Americans) began to wear away the once-impregnable cultural barriers of their expanding Miami enclave. Many of the so-called *yucas* belonged to what this author has referred to as the "last generation"—the last one, that is, that remembers pre-Castro Cuba.[14] They had left their homeland as teenagers, still too young to have internalized typically Cuban values, but old enough to identify fully with the values of their American peers. This generation also fits into the "no-culture" group identified by Fernando González-Reigosa in the mid-1970s[15] and later popularized as the "1.5 generation" by Rubén G. Rumbaut.[16] Their sense of personal orientation was characterized by rather individualistic behaviors, which may help explain how they used their conspicuous self-reliance and opportunistic performance to compensate for their rootlessness and psychocultural insecurity while growing up in America. Rumbaut finds that "although it is true that the "1.5 generation is *marginal* to both its native and its adopted culture, the inverse is equally true: only the 1.5 generation is marginal to neither culture."[17] More than any other factor, it may have been their economic success that eventually led to their involvement in mainstream society.

The *yucas'* newly gained prosperity allowed them to move from Little Havana to suburbia, where this young Cuban American generation of professionals and entrepreneurs ultimately put down roots. In time, they increased their social interactions with their contemporary yuppie and Anglo colleagues through civic groups, professional associations, parent-teacher associations, and so on. But even then, they overwhelmingly continued to speak Spanish or "Spanglish" at home and to socialize with their Cuban American friends. Interestingly, many among that Cuban American generation have later shown a surprising inclination to return to their parents' old-fashioned orientation in two important areas: in their child-rearing practices and in their political beliefs. This unfolding reveals how deeply imbedded in their makeup are the values instilled in them by their parents and grandparents.

> A great majority of Cubans were in the business of making a living, and their kids were into becoming Americans, because after all that's what they heard in the schools—"you should speak English." In junior high schools, Cubans rebelled against the Cuban identity; when they were older, they tried to go back to their Cuban roots. (Author's interview with Mercedes Sandoval)

> The Cuban exile has never lost the love for their music, for their language, there's a passion . . . They keep preserving at home all the traditional customs. Like they teach the children the language; it's so incredible that a person born here in Miami, when people ask "Where are you from?" they say, "I'm Cuban." I can't believe it! This is something unique. (Author's interview with Norma Niurka, arts and entertainment critic with *El Nuevo Herald*)

That is not to suggest that young Cuban Americans have remained rigid and oblivious to change. On the contrary, in the United States, this "last generation" made good use of that uncanny adaptability that has been part of the Cuban national character for centuries. As time went by, they obviously changed, yet very selectively; in areas associated with improving their material lot, changes took place with particular ease; changes that implied a deeper transformation in their cultural identity were largely resisted.

In the end, through almost four decades of exile, the emigrés, young and old, have definitely evolved, adapted, and conformed to circumstances while remaining essentially loyal to past idiosyncrasies.

> The fact is that Cuban culture is highly syncretic and eclectic, and it's able to borrow from any other culture or configuration without any feeling of discomfort or ambiguity . . . but with a lot of efficiency. (Author's interview with Mercedes Sandoval)

This improvised high-wire act, suspended between psychosocial impetus and contextual influences, aptly describes the exiles' process of cultural negotiation. Indeed, they may have incorporated electronic instruments into their music, but they keep dancing it with the gusto of old; they may take their *cafecitos* in styrofoam containers rather than in the traditional porcelain demitasse, yet they still insist on drinking their black nectar at every coffee break; and they, particularly the young, may speak English fluently, but they turn to Spanish when they are at home. That ability to compromise behavior, but not essential values, is part of the cultural baggage brought from Cuba by the initial exodus.

ARTS AND CULTURE IN THE CUBAN EXILE COUNTRY

> Cuban Culture is shamelessly materialistic and resolutely lowbrow. As a fascinating mixture of class and crass, *kitsch* and *caché*, it honors consumers over creators; or rather, it treats consumption like a creative art. You will find Cuban America not only in museums, concerts, and bookfairs, but also, and primarily, in shopping malls, restaurants, and discotheques.
>   —*Gustavo Pérez Firmat*[18]

In the late 1950s, South Florida may have been a frequent shopping and tourist destination just a short hop away from Havana, but to most of those upper and middle class vintage of Cubans who first came into exile it resembled a cultural desert—a "country town," they often called it with unconcealed disdain. Certainly, there was no mistaking that winter resort largely dependent upon out-of-town shows and entertainers catering mostly to visitors and retirees for a cultural mecca; Lenny Bruce's comment that "Miami is where neon goes to die" cleverly satirized the area's pre-Cuban image. But even after the Cubans came, it would take South Florida several years to overcome its geriatric image and to explode into a fast-paced international center whose unique cultural and artistic dimensions ultimately reshaped present-day Miamians' own sense of identity.

> The economic and political importance, the prosperity of the Cubans in Miami, has not been matched in the arts and culture. Even if there are many Spanish and Cuban nightclubs, a very vibrant nightlife in Spanish, and many advancements in the arts that show the importance of what has been done . . . I think there's no match between the prosperity in economics and politics, and in the arts and culture. (Author's interview with Norma Niurka)

> Exile art in Miami is certainly uneven. You have great artists who left Cuba in the early sixties who have continued to do good work in exile. . . . Of course, an exile community is not the ideal community to support a cultural program and an artistic group or creation. But certainly there is an awareness, there is a desire to protect our culture, there is a need to identify with our cultural roots and, in that sense, there is a willingness to do more as economic conditions allow it. (Author's interview with art collector Ramón Cernuda)

There are historical reasons that explain why the exiles' creative endeavors have lagged so far behind their economic performance: Those emigrés who arrived in the first two emigration waves largely belonged to the more economically productive layers of Cuban society; as such, they were able to lay the business and professional foundations of their South Florida enclave and other exile colonies almost from the start. Among that socioeconomic class, however, artists and intellectuals were vastly underrepresented. In fact, given the revolution's enthusiastic support for arts and culture, much of the island's best creative talent was seduced into staying and joining the regime's impressive cultural offensive. The Cuban intelligentsia's love affair with the revolution did not start to wane until the late 1970s; that turnabout was confirmed by the strong contingent of artists and intellectuals among the refugees who left by means of the 1980 Mariel boatlift. Until then, rather than the quality of the cultural life of the Cuban Exile Country, what stood out was the loyalty of its audiences and the persistence of their somewhat amateurish artists.

The First Decade: The Culture of Nostalgia in the 1960s

The earliest cultural activities of Cuban emigrés resulted from their compulsive need to protect their *cubanía* from the effects of the acculturation forces of American society. From the beginning, exiles gathered in the cramped apartments of yet-to-be-named Little Havana and other emigrant colonies to play the music they had brought from the homeland; aspiring actors met in back rooms and garages to rehearse plays they had once enjoyed; youngsters mastered at home the basic steps of the same mambos, cha-cha-chas, rumbas, and *danzones* their parents had danced in happier times. What drove them all were the memories that had turned into a consuming nostalgia the instant they crossed the Straits of Florida.

Their earliest cultural manifestations simply reaffirmed the emigrés' sense of national identity in a foreign land. No dreams of stardom lit their eyes during the initial years of exile; no hopes of rising to fame compelled that first generation of artists. Instead, a deep sense of nostalgia was their driving motivation. In the Transition Stage (1962–1965), when they first managed to rent modest halls in which to hold their performances, only friends and relatives driven by the same longings for the past were in attendance. Naturally, that first generation of exile artists started by replicating on a smaller scale what they remembered from Cuba for audiences who shared similar feelings of nostalgia.

> The development of the Cuban culture in South Florida is based on the desire of preserving their language and their roots, the nostalgia—the effort to try to maintain and recuperate all the good things in art and culture that Cubans had in the island. . . . That's why Gratelli [Pro Arte], which was the exiles' first significant effort in the arts . . . played *zarzuelas*, the traditional lyrical music, and tried to capture that time that was past. (Author's interview with Norma Niurka)

In those early days, shows such as *Añorada Cuba* (Yearning for Cuba) and *La Cuba de Ayer* (Yesterday's Cuba), the very titles of which reflected the nostalgia typical of exile, were performed for enthralled Cuban audiences; parents and grandparents brought the children to enable the youngsters to grow up appreciating their rich legacy and be prepared for their eventual return home. Those struggling performers could not have anticipated that they were the shaky cornerstone of Greater Miami's future cultural awakening. Had it not been for the homegrown talent of Cuban exiles and the faithfulness of exile audiences, Miami could well have remained the third-class cultural community the Cubans found upon their arrival.

The need to keep alive their *cubanía* caused the exiles also to hold free Cuban history and literature classes for their children at the University of Miami's Koubek Center and at various parochial schools and to organize

concerts and dances in the 1960s. During those first years, when their access
to radio and television was limited, their live shows and performances depended on acquaintances and a closely knit network of exile organizations
that publicized their presentations. Celebrations of Cuban patriotic holidays
and religious festivities honoring patron saints of the cities and towns where
they grew up provided the ideal venue for the exiles' modest cultural offer-
ings; top billing was always reserved for such stars as singers Celia Cruz and
Olga Guillot who had achieved wide recognition in pre-Castro days. It was
that combination of nostalgia and patriotic fervor that brought together performers and audiences alike; indeed, the arts were an extension of the political
crusade against Castro's regime.

> Culture comes second or third [but] that's not the main problem. . . . Because
> of the concentration of the exile community in this country, politics is the
> number one, not only occupation, but also the number one entertainment.
> (Author's interview with London-based writer Guillermo Cabrera Infante)

> Here in Miami, plays have been canceled because of this kind of terrorism
> that Cubans, at the beginning, wanted to implant. Some of the Cubans; not
> all the Cubans. But there was a kind of censorship and auto-censorship that
> undermines the culture and the arts here. That has been very negative. (Au-
> thor's interview with Norma Niurka)

> The exile community looks at artistic and cultural activities with suspicion.
> Because in arts and in culture you normally present new ideas and try to
> generate discussion, debate, flow of concepts. And yes, we have had difficulties
> precisely because of this tendency . . . [and] the predominant forces of the
> Cuban exile political atmosphere. (Author's interview with Ramón Cernuda)

Precisely because of that extreme anticommunist militancy, many emigrés
tried to pursue their creative endeavors away from Miami's charged political
atmosphere. By the late 1960s, for example, a pioneer literary journal, *Exilio*,
was being published in New York; journalist Carlos Alberto Montaner, perhaps the most influential intellectual among Cuban emigrés, moved to Madrid, where he founded *Editorial Playor*; and Guillermo Cabrera Infante
revived his writing career in London. That trend would continue to sap South
Florida of much of the brightest Cuban talent. But even in the cities where
they settled, the fascination Castro's revolution inspired among American,
Latin American, and European intellectual circles, a climate that undermined
the success of Cuban exile writers, as well as the lack of universality of their

themes, condemned most emigrés to little more than marginal literary careers.[19]

As the first decade in exile was coming to an end, the emigrés' intelligentsia split into two groups: the older generation who grew up on the island and considered themselves Cubans living in America; and the younger thinkers who were becoming Cuban Americans. While their differences seemed subtle in such fields as painting, in which words are not used as a means of expression, the new writers whose literary language was English were emerging for the first time.

The Second Decade: The Cuban American Culture in the 1970s

Their economic penury overcome, the exiles began to support the cultural and artistic efforts of their fellow exiles more generously. Early in the 1970s, the emigrés' creative endeavors still fitted into the category of Cuban culture in America—as opposed to the Cuban American culture that was just starting to emerge among the younger exiles.

Small schools like Ballet Concerto, Rosita Segovia, and Lily Batet taught children ballet, traditional Spanish dances, guitar, and piano; plays and *zarzuelas*, a type of Spanish-language opera, were performed regularly by the Pro Arte Gratelli, a company subscribed to by thousands of loyal, elderly patrons; Las Máscaras and other groups popularized the vernacular theater which featured light comedies that usually ridiculed Castro to the delight of Cuban audiences; a small publishing house, Librería Universal, reprinted classic Cuban texts and published its own literary magazine, *El Alacrán Azul* (The Blue Scorpion); and such art galleries as Argosi catered to an almost exclusively Cuban clientele interested in the works of Cuban painters, including Rafael Soriano, José María Mijares, and later, Humberto Calzada.

The first years that I painted, like from 1972 to 1981 or 1982, is what I call my anecdotical period. In that period I was painting exactly what I remembered from the houses in Cuba, from my childhood. I would use black and white tile floors, my tile roofs, the stained glass arches, the railings—all those things. But in the context of Cuban, colonial, or neo-classical architecture; I was trying to reconstruct a physical past that I felt we didn't have. I felt that in Miami we had all our friends and family, we had the food, we had the music, but visually what we saw was very different. So, my idea was to try to reconstruct that for myself. (Author's interview with Cuban American painter Humberto Calzada)

But certainly the most telling symbol of the exiles' obsession with their past was the creation of the Cuban Museum of Arts and Culture, which for years operated without a permanent facility. This "museum without walls," as its founders euphemistically described their fledgling initial effort, was spearheaded by a few exiles who kept lobbying local politicians until the early 1980s, when the city of Miami finally assigned them a building in the heart of Little Havana.

Whereas the Cuban Museum's patrons often came from the more conservative ranks of the exile community, another group of emigrés from around the world coalesced around the International Congress of Cuban Intellectuals, which held its first meeting in Paris in 1979. International heavyweights of different ideological hues, such as Madrid's Carlos Alberto Montaner, Puerto Rico's Carlos Franqui, London's Cabrera Infante, and Paris' Eduardo Manet, lent intellectual credibility to this effort which continued to meet in other cities for several years.

By their second decade in exile, an incipient media industry was also developing among the South Florida emigrés. This network included the only local Spanish-language newspaper in town, the *Diario Las Americas*, founded earlier by Nicaraguan exile Horacio Aguirre, as well as exile radio and television broadcasts and dozens of weekly tabloids that were distributed for free in the neighborhoods of Little Havana, Hialeah, and Westchester. In other exile colonies across the United States, similar publications also proliferated.

> Cuban newspapers and radio stations played a very significant role in keeping alive the anti-Castro sentiment—fighting for our freedom. . . . These small publications we call *periodiquitos* [tabloids] and the Spanish radio gave the exiles a sense of community . . . we were sending at the time a message to Cuba. That was, in my opinion, very important to our fight for freedom. (Author's interview with radio journalist Emilio Milián)

By playing heavily upon the intense political passions of the exiles, South Florida's Spanish media developed a winning formula that focused on news from the island and hard-line political commentary. Noteworthy among the radio stations was the amazing success of WQBA, La Cubanísima (the most Cuban), which quickly rose in the ratings battle to lead all area stations. Clearly, a self-contained cultural industry was well under way in the enclave, and the Spanish media promoted it by dispensing critical acclaim indiscriminately to good, as well as to obviously mediocre, cultural activities.

The radio stations have had perhaps the most impact on maintaining the "Cubanization" . . . because they have kept alive traditions, customs, even the traditional *chistes* [jokes], and common, everyday words. A lot of this responsibility goes back to the radio stations; they've kept that alive. But they also kept alive an interest in knowing what was happening in Cuba. (Author's interview with radio personality Margarita Ruiz)

In the 1970s, the arts and entertainment fields continued to experience some steady, if unspectacular, progress thanks to the increasing economic prosperity of the exiles and the sponsorship of small, Cuban-owned businesses. That was also the period during which a first generation of Cuban artists who grew up in the United States began gaining recognition alongside the established stars of prerevolutionary Cuba. In theater, for example, the group Prometeo, founded at Miami Dade Community College by Teresa María Rojas, became the cradle for young actors who later organized their own companies and fed such emerging Spanish television productions as the bilingual comedy "Que Pasa USA!," which centered upon the travails of a Cuban family coping with life in America.

Given the Cubans' legendary passion for music, it was natural for that artistic expression to lead the creative talents of Cuban Americans in the 1970s. Young musicians such as Willy Chirino made their appearance in the local entertainment circuit. Likewise, Emilio Estefan's Miami Sound Machine band, in which sang a then-unknown teenager named Gloria (whom Emilio later married), stepped up from entertaining at school proms and wedding receptions to being featured in local recordings and concerts. In contrast to the traditional musicians who preceded them, this new crop developed a unique style that kept the unmistakable rhythmical essence of Cuban music while it borrowed elements from American popular music—a concession to the fact that younger artists were developing a dual Cuban American identity after two decades outside their native country.

The creation of that new exile sound in Miami coincided with the popularization in New York, Puerto Rico, and the Latin Caribbean of salsa, a term still derided by most Cuban musicians. London-based Guillermo Cabrera Infante, arguably the best known Cuban writer alive and an insightful music connoisseur himself, maintains that salsa is just the traditional Cuban rhythm known as *son* when it is poorly played by non-Cubans. Be that as it may, the commercial success of salsa did open new markets for Chirino, the Estefans' Miami Sound Machine, Los Sobrinos del Juez (The Judge's Nephews), Carlos Oliva, and scores of other emerging groups.

Like the Cuban American musicians, emigré intellectuals raised in the

United States were influenced by the contextual forces of their adopted land. In contrast to the earlier generation of Gastón Baquero, Eugenio Florit, Hilda Perera, and Cabrera Infante, most of these young writers tended to show a preference for writing in English about themes that, although rooted in the alienation of the exile experience, dwelled on the issue of identity and the trauma of the acculturation process that had molded their own lives outside of the island. Typical of this Cuban American crop were playwrights Dolores Prida and María Irene Fornés, as well as writers Gustavo Pérez Firmat and Roberto G. Fernández. Others, like Uva de Aragón and José Kozer, however, became poets in exile but write primarily in Spanish.

> In my poetry and my writings, Cuba is a constant presence in my literary work. Sometimes explicitly, sometimes very softly, sometimes in symbols, sometimes in the presence of the sea, in the remembering the way the sun used to shine, and sometimes, of course, in more profound ways. I think it's something common of my generation of Cuban writers and also common to generations before ours. I think the most obvious example is José Martí, who lived in the United States for many years, who left Cuba when he was nineteen, and who is the most Cuban of all Cuban poets. (Author's interview with poet Uva de Aragón)

Much of the intellectual production of Cuban Americans, consciously or not, has attempted to provide a bridge between the two distinct cultures to which their authors had been exposed. Unfortunately, their works often proved too Americanized or too liberal for die-hard emigré readers, and too Cubanized for the larger American public. One notable exception was Iván Acosta's play *El Super*, which was made into a film in 1979 by León Ichazo and Orlando Jiménez-Leal. This jewel of a movie captured the intimate struggles of an exile who could not come to terms with his life as an apartment-building superintendent in New York. To this day, the popularity and critical acclaim attained by Acosta's *El Super* has not been matched by any other exile work.

An offshoot of this generation of intellectuals includes several Cuban American scholars, such as sociologists Alejandro Portes and Silvia Pedraza-Bailey, political scientist Jorge Domínguez, and economist Carmelo Mesa Lago, most of whom have specialized in Cuban studies and have risen to prominence within American academic circles. The mainspring of many of these Cubanists was the Instituto de Estudios Cubanos, founded by María Cristina Herrera in the early 1970s.

While many young exiles who belonged to the "last generation" were gradually becoming Cuban Americans after two decades in the United States, it is undeniable that Miami was also becoming Cubanized during this period. Nowhere was that development more noticeable than in the Spanish language's impact upon English-speaking residents, many of whom had mixed feelings about the rapid transformation that "their" community was experiencing and decided to leave town. Frankly, the old Anglo establishment felt threatened about the Cubans' growing political, economic, and cultural influences. That reaction notwithstanding, Miami's bicultural imprint was already an entrenched reality by 1976, when *The Miami Herald* launched a Spanish edition that quickly gained the favor of Cuban American and Latin American readers as well as advertisers. Bilingualism, in other words, had become good business in the South Florida market—and the daily publication of *El Herald* proclaimed that fact.

Again, it was the growing economic power of the exile market, as well as the influx of thousands of Latin American immigrants attracted by that market to South Florida, that sustained the bilingual and bicultural life of the community. By the 1970s, for example, Editorial America, the giant Spanish-language magazine publisher, had moved its headquarters to Miami; *Miami Mensual*, a monthly publication designed for upscale Cuban readers, was about to hit the stands; and Ediciones Cubanas began reprinting classic Cuban books. Two other major intellectual efforts that occurred during this decade were Ramón Cernuda's *La Gran Enciclopedia Martiana* and Leví Marrero's monumental *Cuba: Economia y Sociedad*, arguably the most ambitious historical work attempted by a Cuban exile.

Several local television stations were also broadcasting exclusively in Spanish, and national advertisers were making South Florida the chosen location for the production of television commercials targeted to Hispanic markets throughout the country. For the exiles, this concentration of production activities in South Florida meant that Cubans would gain a leading position in the growing Spanish television industry—a dominance far exceeding what their relative strength in numbers otherwise justified.

The Miami market is considered to be much more upscale, much more demanding than any other Hispanic market in the country. And I think that due to that, we immediately realized, back in the days of Channel 23, that we needed to appeal to that educated, upscale, high income market. Especially if we wanted to bring in the younger audience to Channel 23. So, in order to do that we had to improve the product, we had to improve programming, we had to improve sports, we had to improve the editorial position of the station. And all those were elements that were absolutely crucial to the success of the station; I think that differentiated us from all other stations in the country. (Author's interview with media executive Alfredo Durán, Jr., president of *Exito!* magazine)

The higher production values to which national advertisers were accustomed stimulated improved levels of professionalism in the Spanish media; that, in turn, raised quality standards and prepared the way for Miami to become the headquarters of the Spanish International Network (now Univision), the first national Hispanic network in the United States. Hundreds of new job opportunities suddenly became available for Cuban and Latin American reporters, script writers, musicians, dancers, choreographers, makeup artists, set designers, and actors, as well as technical personnel and workers in other related occupations.

The influence Miami was gaining in the entertainment business attracted a number of established stars from Spain and Latin America. Most notable among these was Spaniard Julio Iglesias, who moved to South Florida to launch a new career in the lucrative American market. The amazing success attained by Iglesias triggered a trend that soon turned the area into the crossover capital of the Spanish entertainment world; such established Hispanic stars as Rafael, "El Puma," and Rocío Jurado made Miami their home. By this time, clearly, the exiles who had sustained the spectacular growth of Miami for twenty years were no longer the sole engine driving Miami's incipient cultural transformation.

The Third Decade: *Marielitos* and Big Festivals

As the decade of the 1980s was inaugurated, just when the twenty-year-old memories of Cuba were starting to fade throughout the Cuban Exile Country, a dramatic development on the island altered the cultural prospects of the Cuban community in the United States: the Mariel boatlift. Among the 125,000 new refugees who came in that exodus were significant numbers of artists and intellectuals who had been raised under a revolutionary regime that placed much emphasis on the promotion of cultural activities. That vintage included, among others, writers Reinaldo Arenas, Carlos Victoria, and Andrés Reynaldo; dancer-choreographers Juanita Baró and Pedro Pablo Peña; and painters Juan Abréu, Víctor Gómez, and Gilberto Ruiz Valdez. Their sudden arrival did more than inject a fresh dose of *cubanía* into the Cuban Exile Country; it added a rich cultural dimension to an emigrant community thus far characterized by the predominance of culturally apathetic upper and middle class entrepreneurs and professionals. The newly arrived refugees revived the traditional Cuban culture in America.

The *Marielitos* reattached the exiles' umbilical cord to the island, but even more significantly, their creative talent and artistic training generated a cultural awakening in the exile community throughout the United States. Arriving musicians formed their own groups or fed the established bands; theater and dance companies proliferated; and a new generation of painters and writers who had been raised on the communist island began to exhibit and to publish their works in America. The wave of creativity triggered by the Mariel exodus added vital force to Miami's cultural scene; it was not until then, for example, that Mara and Orlando Gonzalez Estevez presented their first of an ongoing series of traditional Cuban song festivals at the Dade County Auditorium. A new era, indeed, seemed to open, nurtured by the *Marielitos'* own contributions and the established exiles' rediscovery of the arts as an integral component of their own rich cultural heritage.

> In the eighties, the Mariel Boatlift was a very important influence in that explosion. . . . Exiles that had been here for years and that in their hearts and minds remembered Cuba, all of a sudden were shocked . . . by the arrival of people who had come from the same roots. . . . That's why there was an explosion of paintings and arts in general. (Author's interview with Norma Niurka)

One telling measure of this cultural boom was observed in the publication business. In the 1980s, exile publishers, such as Manuel Salvat's Librería Universal, began to print hundreds of new titles every year—an amazing feat considering the limited size of the exile market.

> By the eighties, the Spanish publication business was starting to decline [because] the elderly Cubans were dying and the new Cubans were really becoming more American. Then Mariel hits, and an important group of writers and many who had worked in the Instituto del Libro Cubano [Cuban Book Institute] came . . . creating a new revival in the literary field. . . . Adding to this phenomenon, many young Cubans coming out of [American] universities, whom I thought had lost their *cubanía*, were really bilingual and were concerned about Cuban things. It amazes me that these youngsters could . . . write about serious Cuban historical topics and that they handled it so well. (Translation of author's interview with Manuel Salvat, president of Librería Universal)

That atmosphere provided further impetus to the Calle Ocho Street Festival, which the Kiwanis of Little Havana had begun to organize in 1978. This yearly multifarious happening offered the *Marielitos* an opportunity to show off their creative zest. From then on, a continuous trickle of refugees from the island became commonplace; and the newcomers, particularly those with talent and formal training in the arts, were able to integrate easily into the growing cultural scene of *el exilio.*

By the 1980s, the early efforts of the Cuban emigrés to maintain their cultural traditions had truly materialized into hundreds of events that competed year-round for the attention of local residents, as well as a new breed of national and international visitors. The exiles, for instance, were largely responsible for the creation of the Miami Book Fair International, the Miami Film Festival, the International Hispanic Theater Festival, the Calle Ocho Street Festival, the Miami Carnival, and a host of other exciting events that confirmed South Florida's gradual emergence as a world-class hub for the arts and popular culture.

For all the recognition that such big events brought to Miami, it was behind that glittering surface where Cuban exiles arguably had the most influence; one full generation after they first settled into their Little Havana enclave, the established emigrants, aided by the arrival of the *Marielitos,* were finally succeeding in fostering a creative climate that kept many of their own artists in South Florida. Whereas before much of the local emigré talent had moved on to New York or Los Angeles in search of fame and fortune, by their third decade in exile, that trend had been reversed, and some of the most promising Cubans and Cuban Americans found South Florida's cultural life exciting enough to stay, or even to return to. Gloria and Emilio Estefan are notable examples of local artists who have remained and been successful. The cultural revival continued gaining steam throughout the 1980s, and the high-profile events organized by the exiles clearly transcended the boundaries of the Cuban enclave. First came the Miami International Film Festival, the brain child of Cuban exile Natalio Chediak, a movie enthusiast who for years had operated the Cinematheque, a small movie theater in Coral Gables that screened foreign films. The festival became an unqualified triumph when Chediak and a handful of determined Cuban American as well as Anglo supporters and sponsors managed to bring to South Florida a unique sampling of some of the best cinema produced worldwide. The film festival, housed at the grand old Gusman Center right in the heart of Miami's much-maligned downtown, has attracted such luminaries of the international screen as Spanish filmmakers Fernando Trueba and Pedro Almodovar, both of whom were introduced to America at this local venue.

For many Cubans, the film festival has also provided an opportunity to share a few days with some of the brightest stars of their own intelligentsia; exile artists and writers have traveled from New York, London, Rome, Madrid, and other cultural capitals to participate in what has become a yearly ritual of the Cuban diaspora. Indeed, beyond the enjoyment of the excellent program premiered by festival director Natalio Chediak every February in South Florida, the exile gatherings rival for excitement, the official events. After the movies, informal *tertulias* (gatherings), inviting stimulating discussions, are frequently convened with such festival habitues as exile filmmakers Jorge Ulla (*Nobody Listened, Guaguasi*), Orlando Jiménez-Leal (*El Super, 8-A: Ochoa*), and actor-director Andy García; enfant terrible writer Guillermo Cabrera Infante (*Mea Cuba, Tres Tristes Tigres*); and Latin jazz legends Chico O'Farrill, Paquito Hechavarría and Paquito d'Rivera. Admittedly, these celebrities are well known only to Cuban Americans, a sad realization that reflects the isolation that has plagued Miami's multiethnic community.

> The Miami Film Festival is an event that addresses itself to people that are not usually represented in this community. To the eyes of the outsider, it is an elitist event; to the eyes of those who produce it along with me, it is a popular, populist event . . . I certainly do not produce the Film Festival for the Cuban exile intelligentsia. To the degree that I have a successful Festival or not is to the degree that it addresses the complex community that it is. I approach it, certainly from an exile's perspective. But we're all exiles here; you know, the only true Americans are the Native Americans. (Author's interview with Natalio Chediak)

The film festival, nevertheless, made it clear for the first time that Miami had definitely outgrown its earlier image as a cultural wasteland, and that a segment of the area's multiethnic audience was ready to support events capable of achieving a measure of national and international stature. Hence, under the auspices of Miami Dade Community College and headed by Cuban American educator Eduardo Padrón, the Miami Book Fair International was established. Despite its brief history, the book fair has already grown into a year-round literary program in which some of the best-known contemporary writers participate. Once a year, the fair's main event features such famed international authors as Peruvian Mario Vargas Llosa, Chilean Isabel Allende, Mexican Octavio Paz, Spaniard Camilo Cela, and Cuban Guillermo Cabrera Infante, all favorites of Miami's Cuban and Latin American readers. The event also attracts scores of national publishers and local bookstores that peddle their latest books at bargain prices much to the appreciation of the large crowds. Perhaps more so than any other local cultural event organized by the exiles, the book fair's appeal reaches the entire community.

Events such as the book fair and the film festival have broadened the cultural horizons of the exile community and have introduced an intellectual and artistic ingredient that complements the achievement experienced by the enterprising Cubans in business. Nevertheless, the politically charged atmosphere that exile militants have infused in South Florida continues to represent the Achilles' heel of the cultural life of the capital of the Cuban Exile Country. Nowhere was this more evident than in the controversy concerning the Cuban Museum's showing of works by Cuban artists who had remained on the communist island.

> The people at the Cuban Museum had been people committed to freedom and to the respect for the rights of others, to the extent that we did not censor artists because of their political beliefs. But we have been labeled as communists by these extreme right-wing forces, these extremely intolerant forces in the community; we have been branded as enemies of Cuba and of freedom precisely for having exercised those freedoms and shown artists whose political ideas are not the same as ours, but whose work is good quality work. (Author's interview with Ramón Cernuda)

> The controversy of the Cuban Museum is certainly very unfortunate, very unfortunate. I think it exemplifies the worst of our culture: Our intolerance— and I'm talking about both sides—and our lack of ability to conciliate different points of view. And what concerns me most is that it's a symptom that we have not reached the kind of maturity needed to live within a democracy. That's certainly something to worry about. (Author's interview with Uva de Aragón)

The mass resignation of that institution's more conservative board members in 1989 triggered a wave of political charges that polarized the exile community. Words and threats soon escalated into terrorism, and several bombs were exploded at the museum's facilities.

Another cultural effort worth mentioning because of its sheer magnitude is the Endowment for Cuban American Studies established in 1981 by the Cuban American National Foundation (CANF). Although most of its projects have obvious political overtones, the endowment has sponsored the publication of dozens of works by Cuban and international writers and scholars. CANF also served as a launching pad for the Universidad Latino Americana de la Libertad Fredrick Hayek, a promising initiative that promotes the free exchange of ideas. Due to its parent organization's anticommunist bent, these two projects have been able to avoid the controversy that has periodically plagued other cultural activities within South Florida's exile community.

The Fourth Decade: South Florida's International Culture

During the 1990s, the line that for years separated the cultural efforts of the Cuban emigrés from the life of the community at large all but disappeared. It would certainly be difficult today to find a significant cultural event in which the exiles are not directly involved side by side with non-Cubans. Prominent Cuban Americans like businessman Carlos Manuel de la Cruz, arguably South Florida's preeminent art collector, and architect Raul Rodríguez serve on the boards of the area's major cultural institutions.

The emergence of Miami as a world-class cultural center in the 1990s has benefited from two mutually reinforcing developments: the establishment of a thriving television, film, and musical production industry, and the influx of yet more artists and intellectuals from Cuba. The first of these developments evolved from the momentum created earlier by the local Spanish-language television and recording industries. At present, two Hispanic international networks, Univision and Telemundo, regularly produce television programs and commercials for broadcast throughout American and Latin American markets; the movie industry has discovered South Florida; and the "Miami Sound" popularized around the world by Gloria Estefan has given the area a new musical identity. The consolidation of the entertainment business, in turn, is attracting big-name celebrities to South Florida.

The second component of the current cultural explosion had its origins in the alarming economic crisis experienced by communist Cuba following the collapse of the Soviet Union. As a result, hundreds of excellent artists and entertainers continue to abandon the island and settle in South Florida, enriching its cultural life. Such has been the case, for example, with singer Albita Rodríguez, whose songs have taken the Cuban Exile Country by storm. Likewise, the recent arrival of some of Cuba's best painters, including Tomás Sánchez and José Bedia, has furthered the already flourishing local arts industry, particularly around Coral Gables, where more than twenty galleries exhibit the newcomers' works alongside those of such established Cuban and Latin American masters as Wifredo Lam and Fernando Botero. The interest in Cuban art among exile collectors has also generated significant commercial activity; the works of painters like Tomás Sánchez now command fabulous prices around Miami and at such auction houses as New

York's famed Sotheby's and Christie's, both of which now have offices in South Florida.

To be sure, these two forces originated as unrelated developments. The consolidation of the local film, television, and music businesses had long been in gestation; however, nobody could have predicted the wealth of talent that would arrive from Cuba in the 1990s. The two developments together, however, created the synergy that is currently taking South Florida's cultural life to new heights. The exiles, indeed, have come a long way since the days when the Estefans, Miami's reigning first couple, were entertaining at birthday parties. This couple's career closely parallels the evolution of the cultural life of the exile community: First, they played the traditional songs that reminded them of Cuba; when they became Cuban Americans, their Miami Sound Machine began to incorporate elements and instruments from American music; after their marriage came the business period, when the enterprising Emilio left his job at Bacardi Imports to dedicate himself to managing their promising careers; finally came their spectacular crossover, but even then they never strayed too far from their Cuban roots—a fact recently corroborated by their nostalgic album, *Mi Tierra* (My Land).

The Estefans, obviously, cannot be considered an average exile family; nevertheless, they are representative. Moreover, the way in which they achieved their fame may serve as an apt metaphor for the progress experienced by the exiles in little over three decades. Like many of their countrymen, they have gone through the same stages that characterize the cultural development of the exile community: the early nostalgic period, the Cuban American adjustment, the experience in the business world, the remarkable crossover, and, finally, the return to their Cuban traditions. And like many exiles, they have always remained in Miami, where they enjoy the momentum they helped create.

EXILE LIFE AND FOLKLORE

Cuban American means that you have fun in Spanish, that you go to Cuban parties, that you dress like a Cuban, because Cubans like to dress in a spectacular fashion, that you dance like a Cuban, because nobody dances as well as a Cuban, that you put on perfume like a Cuban, because nobody smells as good as a Cuban; but at the same time, that you have the ability to take control of your life. (Author's interview with Mercedes Sandoval)

For all its human trauma and all its political drama, *el exilio* has never been a dreary, solemn experience; that would have been out of character for the Cuban emigrés. Known for their cheerful personality, Cubans in exile have continued to enjoy life even in the most troubled of times. Hence, as they went about transforming their adopted milieu to accommodate their own orientations, preferences, and culture, they cast their lively imprint upon their creation. As a result, Miami today is so profoundly unique that its atmosphere may appear surreal, but only to an outsider. For all its folkloric contrasts and exaggerations, this capital of the Cuban Exile Country is incredibly authentic.

What it does have is a character of its own; the sounds, the rhythms, the smells, the tastes, the colors, the architecture, everything the senses can perceive, reflect the deep imprint Cubans have made on this century-old city. The powerful cultural dynamics they have triggered since they first settled in Little Havana can mesmerize or confuse, fluster or threaten longtime Miami residents as well as visitors from mainstream America. To one and all who come to see for themselves this bilingual and bicultural experiment, life among Miami's Cuban exiles certainly offers an experience unlike that found in any other American city. Anything Cubans and Cuban Americans enjoy, they can find within their community. From the moment they wake up to the Spanish morning news and take their first shot of *café cubano* to the last evening *tabaco* they savor with nostalgia for their idealized past, their spare time—and for many their workday, too—may be spent inside the exile community. So diverse is the life within the ever-expanding boundaries of the enclave they control, that Cubans—and even Cuban Americans born in the United States, for that matter—continue to live as they assume they would have in their lost country had Castro not disrupted their history nearly two generations ago.

Cultural Folklore: Combining the Old and the New

Sharp cultural contrasts can be discovered everywhere around South Florida's Cuban community. Where else is there a religious temple like the Babalu-aye, which had to appeal its case all the way to the U.S. Supreme Court to establish its legal right to conduct animal sacrifices as part of its Afro-Cuban ceremonies? And what Ermita de la Caridad del Cobre, a church built by the exiles to honor their revered patron saint, which displays on its altar a mural depicting both religious figures and patriotic heroes of Cuba's past?

Cubans have attempted to re-create in Miami another Cuba, an exercise in nostalgia. And then, of course, we tend to exaggerate, sometimes we go overboard, and that has created tremendous contrasts which at times can be very funny—and also very sad. (Author's interview with Rosario Kennedy, the first Cuban American woman elected to the City of Miami Commission)

Another peculiar example of the exile lifestyle is found in their funeral services. The wakes generally turn into somewhat lively affairs that bring together dozens of friends and relatives of the deceased; after dutifully paying respect to the grieving circle of the intimate family, those in attendance usually move a few feet away from the open casket where the natural sadness of the occasion is combined with the excitement of meeting old acquaintances again. Cuban *velorios* (wakes) once continued throughout the night, a few close friends and relatives continued to sip *café cubano* and engaged in the customary political discussions until morning. Lately, however, these traditional vigils are giving way to the fast-paced schedule of the host society.

For folkloric kitsch, however, probably nothing matches the *Quinces*, the birthday parties some Cuban families organize for their fifteen-year-old debutante daughters. In Cuba, the *Quinces* was celebrated with a traditional formal ball hosted by the wealthy. In the early years of exile, however, even those from more humble backgrounds spared no expense and often went into debt to hold these pretentious affairs, which featured spectacular choreographies and live entertainment. The climax of the party featured a grand entrance by the honored girl and her court while their families wept tears of joy. By all accounts, these extravagant affairs once so popular among the working classes of *el exilio* have begun to lose their appeal.

That does not mean that Cubans have tempered their passion for partying. Any occasion, from the traditional observance of birthdays, anniversaries, christenings, and weddings, to the newer American rituals of watching football games on television, provides a good excuse for getting together with friends and family. Cubans appear to have embraced all the celebrations popular in their adopted country without giving up any of those they brought from the homeland; it is common, for instance, to commemorate such American holidays as Independence Day, Labor Day, and Thanksgiving, although the typical American turkey dinner is frequently replaced by the traditional Cuban *lechoncito* (roasted pig), *congrí* (rice and black beans), and *yuca* (a distant cousin of the potato). Regardless of the occasion that brings them together, Cubans always manage to end their parties with music and dancing. It is in their blood, they claim.

Resilient Cultural Legacy and Traditions

Much of the traditional rituals of Cuban exiles center around eating. Family and friends like to gather together and share a meal when celebrating a birthday, an anniversary, and other special occasions—and beef and pork still reign supreme in their menus. The *palomilla*, a thin cut of well-marinated beef, is the steak of choice among Cuban gourmands, who can engage in passionate discussions about where this Cuban delicacy is best prepared. Some claim the *palomilla* served by Lila's in Westchester, under a mountain of homemade (not frozen) french fries, has no competition, and certainly Victor's Cafe offers by far the most expensive *palomilla* and Versailles the most popular one; but knowledgeable sources overwhelmingly agree that the *palomilla* served at the small and unsophisticated Islas Canarias has no rival at any price.

The Cubans' biggest fiesta of the year, undoubtedly, is still *Nochebuena*, the Christmas eve party that brings together all relatives. During the weeks prior to this celebration, Cuban supermarkets become stocked with such seasonal delicacies as *sidra* (Spanish cider), chestnuts, walnuts, and *turrones* (rich-tasting nougat, a wide variety of which is always imported from Spain during the month of December). Local supermarkets and restaurants also advertise when it is time to order one's *lechoncito* (piglet) and cooked turkey. More traditional families, however, roast the *lechoncito* themselves. The actual preparation of the menu for the authentic *Nochebuena* begins at least a day before, when the turkey is stuffed and the *lechoncito* is left to marinate over-night in a concoction of garlic, onions, cumin, bay leaves, sour orange, vin-egar, salt, and pepper—the exact proportions of which are based on secret recipes handed down from one generation to the next.

Early on the actual day of this fiesta, the younger men dig a deep hole in the ground and layer it with wood charcoal and several twigs of *guayaba* (guava) for its sweet aroma; on top of this rustic barbecue pit, the *lechoncito* is set in the early afternoon and topped with long plantain leaves and a heavy tin cover to seal in the low heat. One of the more experienced men in the family usually supervises the ritual of roasting the pig, checking often to make sure the slow-burning fire is kept at an even temperature so that the fat has enough time to melt. These activities are still carried out mostly by the men—a clear reminder that the machismo that once prevailed in Cuba has not completely disappeared. After several hours the *lechoncito* is turned, cov-ered once again, and left to roast until the evening. The secret to roasting a pig is patience, but the long wait is justified.

All the while, inside the home, the women are busy preparing *congrí* and *yuca* and decorating the table with trays of *turrones* and other traditional desserts. The *Nochebuena* supper itself is generally served late in the evening. When the family is seated around the table, one of the elders often rises to offer the exiles' traditional *brindis*, a toast which could range from long-winded nostalgic speeches to simple comments about the family. In any case, the *brindis* usually includes an obligatory reaffirmation of the hope that next year's celebration will be held in Cuba. Then the feast starts, and huge amounts of food are gobbled down without regard to its high-cholesterol content; clearly, this is not the day to watch one's diet. After supper, many families exchange the Christmas gifts laid around the tree and the traditional *nacimiento* (nativity scene). Some then rush to attend the midnight *misa de gallo* (the mass held to commemorate the birth of Christ). The traditional celebration concludes with a silent prayer for the departed.

The life Cubans enjoy in South Florida appears to have no end. Every year new activities, often inspired by the cultural legacy brought from their homeland, are organized for their ever-expanding population. Any journey through South Florida, however, would not be complete without including a short trip to nearby Key West, a community dotted with such historic mementos of Cuba's past and present history as the San Carlos, a landmark where Martí came to collect funds for Cuba's war of independence last century, and La Casa del Balsero, a memorial to the rafters who never made it across the Straits of Florida. At the southernmost tip of Key West stands a sign that reminds one and all that only ninety miles across the water lies Cuba, the island still yearned for by the exiles.

NOTES

1. Gustavo Pérez Firmat, *Life-on-the-Hyphen: The Cuban-American Way* (Austin: University of Texas Press, 1994), 8.

2. For a critical survey of the academic literature on Cuban emigrés, see Silvia Pedraza-Bailey, "Cubans in Exile, 1959–1989: The State of the Research," in *Cuban Studies Since the Revolution*, ed. Damián J. Fernández (Gainesville: University Press of Florida, 1992).

3. The assumption that the acculturation of immigrants follows a somewhat linear path has been challenged from several perspectives. See José I. Lasaga, "La juventud del exilio y la tradición nacional cubana," *Exilio: Revista de Humanidades* (Otoño-Invierno 1967); Alejandro Portes and R. L. Bach, *Latin Journey: Cuban and Mexican Immigrants in the United States* (Berkeley: University of California Press, 1985).

4. E. F. Kunz, "The Refugee in Flight: Kinetic Models and Forms of Displacement," *International Migration Review* (Summer 1973): 125–46.

5. Silvia Pedraza, "Cuba's Refugees: Manifold Migrations," in *Origins and Destinies: Immigrations, Race, and Ethnicity in America*, ed. Silvia Pedraza and Rubén G. Rumbaut. Belmont: Wadsworth, 1996), 263.

6. Carlos M. Alvarez, "Lo contextual y lo afectivo-simbólico en la identidad cubana del sur de la Florida," in *Cuba: Cultura e identidad nacional* (Havana: Universidad de la Habana, 1995), 113.

7. Preliminary findings from an ongoing research study about the identity of young Cubans suggest that a major correlation exists between their retention of Spanish-language proficiency and the presence of grandparents in their households. Carlos M. Alvarez, C. Curbelo, and Rafael Martinez: "La identidad cubana entre jóvenes adultos del sur de la Florida" (forthcoming).

8. See Portes and Bach, *Latin Journey*; Alejandro Portes and Leif Jensen, "What's an Ethnic Enclave?: The Case for Conceptual Clarity," *American Sociological Review* 52 (December 1987); and Victor Nee and Jimmy Sanders, "On Testing the Enclave-Economy Hypothesis," *American Sociological Review* 52 (December 1987).

9. For an insightful discussion of the role "improvisation" played among Cuban exiles, see Alejandro Portes and Alex Stepick, "Change without a Blue Print," in *City on the Edge: The Transformation of Miami*, ed. Alejandro Portes and Alex Stepick (Berkeley: University of California Press, 1993).

10. Although this process is conventionally referred to as "acculturation," in the case of the Miami Cubans, it would be appropriate to consider "cultural negotiations" the give-and-take dynamics of the exiles vis-à-vis the dominant culture.

11. To call it a myth is not to question the relevance of a popular belief that, "without reflecting an objective reality, defines an intra-psychical and cultural reality." Fernando González-Reigosa, "Mitos y símbolos de las naciones cubanas: ¿Por qué los cubanos no pueden ser posmodernos?" Paper presented at the Fifth Congreso Internacional sobre Culturas Hispanas en los Estados Unidos, Alcalá de Henares, Madrid, July 1992.

12. The term "frozen generation" in fact was coined by psychologist Fernando González-Reigosa in the 1970s to refer to exiles caught within the time warp of the enclave. Fernando González-Reigosa, "Las culturas del exilio cubano," *Reunión: Boletín del Intituto de Estudios Cubanos* 89–90 (September-October 1978), 1 ff.

13. See Portes and Stepick, *City on the Edge*.

14. Gonzalez-Pando, Miguel, "La Busqueda de una conciencia generacional," *El Nuevo Herald*, October 25, 1993.

15. Gonzalez-Reigoza, "Las culturas del exilio cubano."

16. Rubén G. Rumbaut, "The Agony of Exile: A Study of Migration and Adaptation of Indochinese Refugee Adults and Children," in *Refugee Children: Theory, Research and Service*, ed. Frederick L. Alhearn, Jr., and Jean L. Athey (Baltimore: Johns Hopkins University Press, 1991), 61.

17. Ibid., p. 61.

18. Pérez Firmat, 13–14.

19. For a more complete discussion of Cuban exile literature, see María Cristina García, *Havana USA: Cuban Exiles and Cuban Americans in South Florida, 1959–1994* (Berkeley: University of California Press, 1996), 169–207; Carolina Hospital, ed., *Cuban American Writers: Los Atrevidos* (Princeton, N.J.: Ediciones Ellas/Linden Lane Press, 1988).

5

The Emigrés' Economic Miracle

To understand the keys to Cuban-American success, one must
look to . . . distinctive national traits, such as intuitive talent to
size up problems and find creative solutions; flexibility to adapt
without mental blocks or ethnic complexes; audacity in taking
risks to achieve objectives; and a warm, engaging personality
that generates enthusiasm and wins support.

—*Nestor Carbonell-Cortina*[1]

*For some years now, the quick prosperity of Cuban emigrés in South Florida has
attracted the attention of academics and journalists. Calling it the Cuban success
story or the Cuban economic miracle, most investigators begin to study the development of the exile community at its 1959 outset. That perspective, however,
may be too narrow. For a better understanding of this phenomenon, various
historical, geographical, sociocultural, and contextual factors that combined to
promote their economic performance must also be taken into account.*

HISTORICAL ROOTS

The accumulated human capital of which Cubans were long beneficiaries
before coming to the United States played a crucial, if often neglected, role
in the early economic achievement of the exiles. Their enterprising spirit and
adaptable nature, critical traits in their national character for centuries, figured prominently in the economic success experienced by the first two waves
of emigrants.

Origins of the Cuban Enterprising Spirit

The exiles' present story, arguably, has its roots in Cuba's past. Hence, to understand their exploits in the United States, it becomes necessary to consider their historical background—long before they were forced into exile. Allowing for requisite differences in time and place, the Cuban Americans responsible for today's economic feat are not too dissimilar from their parents, who laid the original business foundations of South Florida's Cuban enclave in the 1960s and 1970s; their grandparents, who led prerevolutionary Cuba to the forefront of Latin America's economic development in the first half of this century; or even their earlier ancestors, who initiated the island's commercial surge hundreds of years ago. They all share the same enterprising spirit.

Cubans, indeed, are not newcomers to the fields of business and foreign trade. As far back as the eighteenth century, their entrepreneurial skills were already turning the small Spanish colony into a hub of international commerce in this hemisphere. Not surprisingly, Cubans were the first in the Hispanic world to embrace the industrial revolution and, despite Spain's efforts to restrict the island's trade relations with other nations, they developed clandestine contacts with traders from England, France, Holland, and the North American British colonies. It was obvious that Cuba's insular geography always conspired against the official intentions of the Spanish empire to isolate the island's entrepreneurial class from the rest of the New World and Spain's European adversaries. Cuba, granted, was never endowed with gold, silver, or precious stones, but this lack of natural resources simply spurred the creative talent of its people.[2]

After the former British North American colonies gained their independence in 1776, Cubans were allowed for the first time legal and direct commercial access to the United States' market. As the eighteenth century came to a close, a Cuban-born bourgeoisie, whose economic interests were growing less dependent on Spain, was already emerging, just as sugar for the American market was beginning to replace tobacco as the island's main export commodity. Those commercial prospects quickly transformed the colony into a veritable plantation economy that, although still under the political domination of the decadent Spanish empire, had gained a significant measure of economic autonomy. From the dawn of the new century, those profiting from the nascent sugar industry belonged to the new criollo class, the Cuban-born descendants of the Spaniards' autocracy that ruled the colony.[3]

That criollo elite lost much of its fortune while leading Cuba's long war of independence, which began in 1868 and stretched until 1898, when the

United States entered the conflict and ended Spanish rule on the island. The brief period of American domination concluded in 1902, and Cuba finally became a sovereign nation. Although the island Spain left behind was economically ruined, Cuban entrepreneurs were able to restore the country's economic health in a few decades. Hence, Cuba quickly leapt to the top of the Latin American continent. Throughout the first half of this century, the enterprising spirit of Cubans was responsible for their country's remarkable business development. Although politically troubled, the country Fidel Castro found in 1959 was economically rich and technologically advanced. Indeed, Cubans were relying upon their enterprising spirit long before they arrived in the United States after the revolutionary takeover.

Once in exile, early labor market conditions in South Florida persuaded many experienced, as well as new, Cuban entrepreneurs to favor the fledgling business opportunities their own presence had made possible rather than accept underemployment in the bottom rungs of the more competitive Anglo economy. That tendency was reinforced by the social and occupational mobility that characterize the U.S. economy and its available capital markets. A mere decade after the Cubans settled in South Florida, their enterprising spirit already thrived within its free market economy, as evidenced by the thousands of small businesses established in the Cuban enclave throughout the Adjustment Stage (1965–1973). At the time, a similar wave of Cuban businesses were also emerging in other exile colonies throughout the United States.

The Cubans' Adaptable Nature and the Challenge of Exile

On the surface, Cuban emigrés may have appeared unprepared to meet the challenge of a new land where language and customs seemed so different from their own. That notion, however, is not entirely correct. The emigrés may have brought no money, but they carried an ample supply of human capital. In addition, in the case of the initial exodus, many were familiar with the United States and had contacts in America; this was not terra incognita to that vintage of entrepreneurs and professionals who left Cuba right after the revolutionary takeover.

As islanders constantly exposed to outside influences, Cubans had developed a characteristic openness to other cultures long before they arrived in the United States. Contrary to the homeland experiences of most ethnic migrations to America, Cubans were used to interacting with different nationalities, particularly to engage in trade. As a result, by the time the 1959 revolution took place, Cubans had developed a culture that was highly adaptable to change, for reasons based mainly on history and geography.

As the first point of entry into the Spanish colonial possessions in the New World, the island always had a way of drawing people from the Iberian peninsula and beyond. Some called this an attraction, but Cubans preferred to describe it as a seduction. In any case, Cuba had grown into a cosmopolitan microcosm long before Fidel Castro appeared on the national scene. Despite its luscious landscape, pearly beaches, and cane fields, all the abundance of its shops and all the vibrancy of its economy, the island's flavor and soul definitely came from its multiethnic population whose features and tones were brought from all over the world—Spain, Central Europe, the Mediterranean basin, the Orient, Africa, and, of course, the United States.

The Cuban descendants of people of such diverse origins and histories seemed to cast the infinite variety of physiognomies and complexions of their society. Indeed, away from their original homes and free to make their own rules in the young country, wave upon wave of newcomers intermingled, resulting in the combination of different bloodlines that is evident in the present-day Cuban population. The blending of nationalities also show the extent to which contradictory customs, beliefs, and traditions became integrated into a national culture, as evidenced, for example, by the practices of santería, a syncretized religion in which the names and images of African *orichas* were interchanged with those corresponding to Catholic saints.[4]

We brought from Cuba a culture that was rooted in traditional Hispanic values, but much more eclectic because it was highly influenced by the blacks. That Cuban culture was already an adaptation of Hispanic culture to the requirements of modern times, and that facilitated the exiles' adjustment to America. (Translation of author's interview with anthropologist Mercedes Sandoval)

Cubans had always manifested an uncanny ability to reconcile what appeared to be conflicting, to change according to new circumstances; therein lies their adaptable, opportunistic nature, a trait that facilitated the early exiles' rather successful adjustment to a somewhat foreign milieu. It was all part of the cultural baggage they brought. For though largely penniless upon their arrival, historical experiences had prepared their national character to meet the challenges of exile. And, not surprisingly, that is just what they did once they arrived here. In just one generation, these enterprising and adaptable emigrés created what has been labeled the Cuban economic miracle.

MIAMI'S CUBAN ECONOMIC ENCLAVE

Two of every three Cuban exiles currently live in Florida. Precisely because of this concentration, research on the exiles' economic dynamics in the United States has focused primarily on that area. The emigrés' decision to settle in South Florida following the 1959 revolution was influenced by long-standing geopolitical factors. To begin with, the respective histories of Cuba and Miami appear to have developed along somewhat parallel courses: Each was once ruled by the Spanish empire, each has been a haven for refugees and visitors from the other, and each has attracted different people from all over the world. After the Cubans arrived in the United States, contextual forces promoted, at first, the establishment of a sociocultural and economic enclave in Miami and, then, the city's emergence as the gateway to Latin America. Both developments contributed to the so-called Cuban economic miracle.

Miami's Economy before the Arrival of the Cubans

At the beginning of the sixteenth century there were only native Tequestas in South Florida. The conquistadores, the first white men to come, spoke Spanish; later, they brought blacks from Africa. When other white men who spoke English came, most of the local Tequestas and Spaniards left to seek refuge in nearby Cuba. Ever since, these two land areas separated by the Straits of Florida have kept in close contact.

At the outset of this century, nearby Havana was already a thriving commercial metropolis while Miami was still a wasteland in which white, brown, and black workers toiled together in mosquito-infested marshes. Miami's pioneers knew they were clearing those low lands for the impending arrival of civilization, but what they could not imagine was that a Cubanized cosmopolitan city would one day rise from those barren tracts. But that was Miami's manifest destiny. Blessed as well as victimized by its geographical location, Miami was meant to be a place in which the inhabitants of the Old and the New World, North and South America, Europe and Africa, would all come together. Some were attracted by the area's tropical winters; others, by the allure of easy money schemes and highly speculative land deals; and still others by the everything goes permissive atmosphere of Miami, the Magic City. Most of today's residents, however, were thrust upon these balmy shores by the political and economic misery of their lives elsewhere, but that was to come somewhat later.

In Miami's early days, Bahamians and southern blacks provided the labor with which a white elite built dreams that often proved as ephemeral as sand castles by the seashore. Toward the end of the 1930s, regular ferry and airplane service to Cuba was inaugurated. By the 1950s, Miami had long shed its frontier town image to become a service-oriented resort catering mostly to winter visitors and retirees from the cold industrial centers of the Northeast as well as wealthy Cubans and Latin Americans from south of the border. Then came the Cuban emigrés.

Miami's Economy after the Cubans Arrived

In the wake of the arrival of the initial Cuban exodus, Miami began to undergo another dramatic metamorphosis. Its seasonal tourist economy developed into a thriving center for international business activity in just two decades. The changing economic dynamics of the emerging city did not stop there; the fury of the forces unleashed by the newly arrived Cubans continued to affect not only the Magic City's economic profile, but its very identity.

In a sense, Miami today remains an American city because it is located within U.S. territory and abides by its laws and political system. In other significant sociocultural and economic dimensions, however, it has become a Latin American metropolis. The majority of its residents are now foreign born and speak Spanish, and the city's business foundations link present-day Miamians to Latin America probably more than to any other region of the United States. Cuban exiles have certainly taken care of that.

It is difficult to imagine that so profound a transformation could have been completed in less than two generations, but that was actually all it took for Miami to heed the call of its geopolitical destiny. Soon after the arrival of the first Cuban emigration wave (1959–1962), the city's economy took off in a southern direction at a dizzying pace. And it has never looked back. Right at the beginning, the exiles found their first jobs in the only economy then in existence: the established Anglo business sector.

> Very quickly we found out that banks would not hire me despite my 16 years of banking experience. So, as soon as we found out that banking was not in the cards at that point, it was a matter of finding whatever job there was. I found my first job as an inventory clerk in a shoe factory, Alewa Shoe Corporation. I was with the shoe factory for a year and a half. Soon, I became bookkeeper, then office manager, then controller, and then vice president. . . . During that year and a half, I continuously went to banks for interviews. (Author's interview with banker Carlos Arboleya)

Soon thereafter, even as they centered their efforts in the business development of the Cuban enclave and in import-export activities with Latin

America, most Cubans continued to find employment outside the exile economy. Given the interconnectedness of the South Florida market, the overall effect of that initial exodus was dramatically felt throughout the entire area; the transactions the exiles had with the mainstream economy far outweighed what Anglo residents spent within the fledgling Cuban enclave.[5]

Miami also benefited from the millions of dollars the federal government poured into the local economy in that period—some of it covertly to finance the enormous anti-Castro operations of the Central Intelligence Agency (CIA) and more still to help Dade County Schools cope with the impact of tens of thousands of incoming Cuban students.[6] The magnitude of this external injection of funds became a significant variable that produced secondary economic repercussions throughout South Florida as a result of the multiplier effect. The contribution that this exogenous variable represented in terms of additional income and supply stimulated a corresponding increase in the demand for goods and services and precipitated a veritable frenzy of small business openings and new construction throughout the Adjustment Stage (1965–1973). Both developments, in turn, reinforced the consolidation of the Cuban enclave, which grew from a quaint ethnic neighborhood to a complex, though not quite autonomous community.

Still, the considerable degree of economic self-sufficiency attained by this largely segregated enclave occurred as a result of two critical characteristics of the initial exodus: First, it represented a vertical sampling of Cuba's pre-Castro society, and, as such, it was capable of supplying almost all the basic goods and services demanded by the exiles; second, the economic system encountered by those exiles on their arrival in South Florida was not much different from the one prevailing on the island before the revolution. From a socioeconomic perspective, therefore, the quasi-independence of the consumer-oriented business and service network established by the early exiles in Miami replicated rather faithfully Havana's organizational and technological structure. Being a cross section of Havana's professional, technical, and entrepreneurial class, the emigrés, once transplanted to Miami's similar market, generated an economically thriving enclave.

> All of a sudden we came with our teachers, our doctors, our nurses, our friends, even our nannies—everyone. It was like taking a segment of one society and putting it in another place, but just for a little while—until we could all go back to Cuba. Some of those who came had once been prosperous in Cuba even if they arrived here without any money. But they brought their intelligence, their knowledge, and they worked to become prosperous again. . . . And all of a sudden they constructed a community that became economically successful. (Author's interview with radio personality Margarita Ruiz)

Indeed, the incipient community developing on this side of the Straits of Florida during the Transition Stage (1962–1965) was, on a smaller scale, a mirror image of the Havana of old—socioculturally familiar and economically viable to the exiles.

> After the failure of the 1961 Bay of Pigs invasion and the missile crisis, Cubans realized that their stay in the United States—and especially Miami—was going to be for a long time. And then, they had to start trying to create a new life for themselves and for their families. In the first years, they just tried to survive. After that, without losing my interest in Cuba, I started looking for a job and went to New York. (Author's interview with retired banker Luis Botifoll)

The arrival of approximately 300,000 new exiles in the freedom flights during the Adjustment Stage (1965–1973), about half of whom settled in Miami, provided the critical mass for the consolidation of the enclave, and that, in turn, acted as further reinforcement to its business development. By the early 1970s, once the exiles managed to link with American financing mechanisms and institutions, the small businesses they had earlier established within the enclave were poised to experience a rapid expansion. By the 1980s, they diversified and expanded well beyond Little Havana's original confines. The unending influx, first of additional Cubans, and then of other Latin Americans, kept wages from rising in response to the expanding outcome and income.

In retrospect, even the 1973–1974 national recession may have worked to the advantage of the Cuban enterprises within the enclave. That economic contraction forced many local Anglo firms out of the South Florida market, whereas the Cuban business sector, composed of smaller nonunion companies with lower overhead costs, proved better capable of weathering the temporary crisis. During the following recovery period, the vacuum of sorts left was quickly filled by Cuban firms. This was the case, for instance, in the local construction industry, which witnessed the emergence of stronger Cuban-owned companies by the mid-1970s. From then on, the construction industry, most notably its residential component, became a leading sector in the expanding economic growth of the Cuban community.

Similarly, by that time the international sector was also experiencing a boom, and the small import-export companies started by the Cubans in the previous decade flourished in the 1970s, attracting to South Florida a host of ancillary and complementary services. As the Economic Miracle Stage (1973–1980) went on, freight-forwarding, transportation, and insurance companies exclusively serving the foreign market quickly proliferated. To cap it all, various financial institutions and multinational corporations involved in international transactions moved to South Florida.[7] At the end of the decade, South Florida could count with the entire structure required to support its thriving import-export field. It was no coincidence that by then Miami International Airport was on its way to becoming ninth worldwide in volume of passengers and sixth in air cargo.

Just around then, the celebrated Cuban success story came to life. The accomplishments of those initial two waves of emigrés were impressive enough, but the fact that they had started with almost nothing made their success appear almost miraculous. Less than two decades after their arrival, the exiles had effectively recast Miami and seized control of the bilingual and bicultural metropolis that replaced the old winter resort. During that brief period, South Florida's economic and sociocultural foundations had shifted; Cubans were both the main protagonists and principal beneficiaries of the transformation, although they were no longer the only players.

> I don't think that we, as Cuban exiles, made a conscious decision to gain economic power in our new host society. I think we just did that by way of surviving. As a matter of fact, I think this was a process that took place almost unconsciously by the sheer need of establishing ourselves in this new society. (Author's interview with economist Antonio Jorge)

The statistics show that such a judgment is no mere exaggeration. In the 1980s, the median Cuban American household attained income and earning levels almost comparable to the national norm, and small Cuban-owned businesses led the private sector development in the Greater Miami area. When contrasted with other ethnic minorities, the economic progress of these newcomers appeared even more remarkable. Over 20 percent of all Cuban American households reported incomes in excess of $50,000, more than double the Hispanic average in the United States, and there was one Cuban-owned enterprise for every sixteen Cuban Americans, compared with one for every fifty-eight Mexican Americans, seventy-nine Puerto Ricans, and eighty-four African Americans. Most impressively, this feat was accomplished without a blueprint, as urban sociologist Alejandro Portes has pointedly observed.[8]

These statistics, however, provide only a measure of an amazing success story. A more telling picture is gained by experiencing the actual business life of present-day Miami. From top to bottom, Cuban Americans are directly involved in every economic facet of the community. They head banks and chambers of commerce; lead import-export activities; dominate the small-business sector, the residential construction industry, and various professions;

and supply a highly productive labor force for an ever-expanding economy. This, of course, does not mean that the exiles have managed to build a self-contained economy capable of absorbing the majority of their workforce. What it clearly indicates is that the exogenous forces the exiles embodied have played a more determining role in the transformation of South Florida's economy than the domestic independent variables.

It must be granted, of course, that although the Cuban business sector has grown faster than its non-Cuban counterpart, the largest firms in South Florida are still owned by the Anglo business establishment, even if Cuban Americans are often involved at their highest corporate levels.

> Definitely, the commercial and business activity of the Cuban exile community has been greatly exaggerated. . . . We have a lot of businesses, but they are mostly "mom and pop" operations with very few employees, with limited capital, and with net earnings in small figures. Almost all would certainly qualify in the category of small businesses. (Author's interview with business-man Ramón Cernuda)

The exiles' gains, although substantial by most measures, have come mostly from small and medium-sized businesses that, given the cultural differentiation of the goods and services they offer, find no significant competition from the established Anglo sector. It has been mostly in those culturally differentiated economic activities, which are typically closer to the consumer end of the production chain,[9] as well as in the import-export field, that the exiles have definitely gained a comparative advantage. This point does not diminish in any way the remarkable accomplishments of the Cubans, but it properly qualifies their relative success.

Comparative Economic Impact of Successive Cuban Emigration Waves

What Cubans as a whole have achieved in South Florida and other states in less than four decades may appear extraordinary. But to understand fully this economic feat, it is helpful to look more closely at the particular contributions of each successive wave of emigration over time. That comparative analysis yields an inescapable conclusion: Cubans arriving after 1980 have been unable to replicate the outstanding performance of their predecessors. Indeed, the rapid economic development experienced by the exile community before that milestone year has tended to taper off ever since.

What accounts for those differences? For one thing, the more recent newcomers come from a revolutionary order that dismantled the existing civil society and sharply broke with the pre-Castro past. As a result of that rupture, the *Marielitos* and the more recent *balseros* (rafters) may have been somewhat disinherited from the enterprising legacy of which their precursors in exile, as well as their early ancestors on the island, had been recipients. Those mostly young refugees who left Cuba after its society had been radically transformed, in other words, had been formed by the revolutionary experience and thus may have suffered varying degrees of deprivation in terms of business traits deemed crucial to succeeding in a free enterprise system.

In addition, the sociocultural and idiosyncratic characteristics of those raised under the communist regime set them apart from earlier Cuban exiles. This was the case, in particular, with the group of 125,000 refugees who arrived during the 1980 Mariel boatlift. In terms of demographics and value orientations, the *Marielitos* were more likely to approximate the typical profile of other economic refugees; much like those, the *Marielitos* were often younger and less educated; they were also victims of stigmatization upon arrival. The unjust rejection they suffered from the established Cuban community added to the problems they faced. As could have been predicted given their socioeconomic background, the *Marielitos* were also unfamiliar with life in America. All these factors made their economic integration much more difficult; they tended to remain bound to low-paying jobs in the enclave economy and continued to patronize its business and professional network long after the more successful Cuban Americans had deserted the culturally differentiated cocoon. As professionals, business owners, or managers, the upwardly mobile members of initial exodus may have continued to derive substantial income from the Cuban sector of the economy, but they preferred to make their own expenditures in the more sophisticated high end of the mainstream sector.

The comparison between the early exiles and the more recent refugees strongly suggests that their respective historical background and social class origins played crucial roles in their economic behavior in America. Such drastic differences in economic performance cannot be accounted for in terms of the timing of their arrival and contextual factors alone. This comparison also indicates that as soon as the initial exodus attained a measure of success, its members moved away from the ethnic ghetto to enjoy all the privileges of an affluent lifestyle—living in wealthy suburbs, dining at haute cuisine restaurants, shopping at exclusive stores, traveling abroad, and so on. In the end, the socioeconomic gap that separated the groups in pre-Castro Cuba was not substantially bridged in the United States, although the *Marielitos*, once they overcame the dubious reputation that haunted them for years,

ultimately demonstrated individual initiative and hustle of their own somewhat reminiscent of the previous Cuban emigration waves.

The above is not meant to be a judgment of the *Marielitos*, the more
recent *balseros*, or those refugees who will likely continue to come from Cuba.
But this comparative analysis does provide a persuasive clue to the relative
weight of the various factors involved in the much-celebrated Cuban success
story. If it is true that at the beginning much of the exiles' business success
within the enclave was triggered by the solidarity of their shared exile identity,
it is equally valid to assert that the impressive economic gains of the Cuban
Americans cannot be exclusively accounted for by the forces existing within
their enclave.

FACTORS EXPLAINING THE CUBAN EXILES' SUCCESS

Trying to assess the relative weight of the different variables affecting the
economic performance of Cuban emigrés during their first two decades in
South Florida has become a prolific academic industry. Several hypotheses
that hinge on the preeminence of one factor or another have been advanced.
Most investigators, regardless of their respective disciplines, tend to identify
more or less the same variables, although each explanation differs in how the
importance of these variables is ultimately prioritized.[10]

Establishing a hierarchy among all factors involved in the development of
the capital of the Cuban Exile Country, of course, is like comparing apples
and oranges. How does one balance the effects of quantifiable factors, like
the advantage of a concentrated exile market in the Miami enclave, with
subjective factors, like the bond created by their political identity? And what
about the roles their enterprising legacy and their adaptable character have
played in their progress in America?

Though not necessarily in the order presented below, the following factors
may help to explain the success of the Cuban emigrés in the initial two
decades of exile. It must be emphasized that this particular time frame—
1959 to 1980—was not chosen arbitrarily; after the Economic Miracle Stage
(1973–1980), the enclave was already a much-celebrated economic reality.
Thereafter, the prosperity of the Cuban business sector may have tapered off
somewhat.

The Exile Political Identity

If the initial foundations of Miami's bilingual and bicultural recasting can
be traced to the establishment of the Cuban enclave, the bond holding it

together was unquestionably the exiles' collective sense of identity. The passion with which they held on to their political idiosyncrasies as exiles shaped their early orientation and determined their most momentous decision of the Survival Stage (1959–1962): to remain in Miami. That initial exodus stayed in Miami because, from here, they awaited Castro's defeat.

Later, in the Transition Stage (1962–1965), when they were forced to accept the unlikelihood of going back to a free Cuba any time soon, the exiles did not let that realization undermine their commitment to an improbable cause. Rather, drawing strength from their political beliefs, they set out to reach their practical ambitions in the United States with all the fervor of a holy war. During the Adjustment Stage (1965–1973), the adaptable exiles shifted direction without giving up the old ideological cause that had brought them into exile; in essence, they tried to rebuild their lives in America without dismantling their essential core values.

Although motivational analysis is highly complex in nature, a strong correlation between the exiles' political identity and their economic aggressiveness seems to be suggested by the available empirical evidence and experiential consensus.[11]

> Our sense of identity was related to our economic success. If we had not kept together; if we had disseminated throughout the United States; if we had blended with the surrounding community; if we had not built an enclave of our own; if we had not created a market for ourselves, then we would not have been economically successful. (Author's interview with Antonio Jorge)

As reluctant immigrants, the humiliation of their political defeat, in effect, may actually have hastened their efforts to carve a territory of their own in Miami. And it was from that enclave that they set out to prevail in the economic arena, a goal they certainly strived for with characteristic political conviction. Assuming a surrogate role as self-appointed representatives of capitalist democracy, they celebrated every Cuban cafeteria, bakery, and supermarket that opened in Little Havana and other exile colonies as victories of the free enterprise system over communism. That crusading spirit led to the creation of a booming Cuban enclave that, by the beginning of the Economic Miracle Stage (1973–1980), may have surpassed the volume of goods and services produced on the entire communist island.

The 1980 Mariel exodus, in a sense, burst the proverbial bubble. The *Marielitos* were different from the exiles who had migrated to the United States in the first two emigration waves. Arguably, the demographics of the latecomers did not conform to the upwardly mobile orientation of the earlier exiles. But neither were they moved by the same crusading political spirit: They were political refugees, not political exiles. It would be misleading, however, to attribute the *Marielitos'* unremarkable economic performance solely to a somewhat different sense of identity, for other more determining sociocultural factors may have accounted for their group's lack of early economic success.

Social Class Origins of the Emigrés

The initial wave of exiles who arrived during the Survival Stage (1959–1962) and, to some extent, the second emigration wave which arrived during the Adjustment Stage (1965–1973) had come mainly from the upper and middle strata of Cuba's prerevolutionary society. As such, they brought significant human capital in terms of education, professional experiences, and value orientations that were consistent with the free enterprise system awaiting them in the United States.

> The initial Cuban exodus to the U.S. was disproportionally concentrated in the area of people with high education—entrepreneurs who later found it relatively easy to take up roots in this country, find gainful employment and start new businesses. . . . This was a tremendous loss for the Republic of Cuba, but a tremendous gain for Miami. Because of this importation of human capital, Miami over the years has become known as the place where the Cuban economic miracle took place. This success was remarkable and relatively unique in its magnitude and in the rapidity with which it happened. (Author's interview with Florida International University president Modesto Maidique)

But these were not the only benefits the early Cuban exiles would derive in America from their privileged origins. After losing their worldly possessions and social standing, those upper and middle class emigrés yearned to reclaim the socioeconomic position they once enjoyed in Cuba. That psychological itch was a critical factor that urged early exiles to apply their business and professional experiences to succeed in their new lives.

> Definitely, there are cultural and psychological elements that were very rooted in us, and they have been responsible in a major way for our success in the United States. (Author's interview with Antonio Jorge)

Although largely destitute upon arrival, the Cuban exiles held on to the value orientations and self-confidence that tend to characterize upwardly mobile professionals and businesspeople everywhere. They also upheld rich traditions that for centuries had nurtured the national character of their socioeconomic class in Cuba. Beginning in the traumatic Transition Stage (1962–1965), they tapped those inner resources to uplift their declining sense of self-worth and overcome their humiliating fate. And since many of them had come from the classes more up to the task of laying the business foundations of the Miami enclave, that was precisely what they did. Education, professional background, value orientations, and psychological motivations, all held together by their exile identity, spurred their determination during the early years of exile. Only by succeeding could they bolster their wounded individual pride and avoid becoming a forgotten bunch of losers.

> That was a tremendous standing in mental health. The Cubans did not accept the role that comes with the label of being *gusanos* [worms]. Instead, they turned it around and made *gusanos* a good word. And I think it has to do with a sense of pride, and a sense of, "I am not what the Communist system is expecting me to be." (Author's interview with Mercedes Sandoval)

Their social class origins also set them apart from most refugees coming to America. Unlike other Latin Americans who, lacking in relevant educational backgrounds and business experience, are largely forced to rely on sacrifice and hard effort, those first Cuban exiles resorted to their ample professional and entrepreneurial skills to control their own economic fortunes in America almost from the start. The exiles' adamant refusal to accept assimilation into the bottom layers of society, as is usually the case for most immigrants and refugees, drove them to set up small businesses and become masters of their own future in America. Furthermore, they instilled in their children a high regard for education. In 1980 Cubans under thirty-five years of age showed the highest rates of school enrollment of all Hispanic groups, higher even than the general U.S. population.[12]

The critical role their social class origins played in the initial development of the Cuban Exile Country can be further assessed by comparing the experiences of consecutive waves of Cuban emigrés. Cuban refugees who have arrived since the 1980 Mariel boatlift never matched the phenomenal economic performance of the upper and middle class exiles who preceded them. Neither the *Marielitos* nor the rafters possessed the same socioeconomic advantages because they came from a communist society where ideological correctness counted most. By just stepping off the boat that brought them to America, most *Marielitos* and rafters experienced a sudden improvement in their living standards, whereas the majority of the initial exodus left behind a socioeconomic position higher than the one awaiting them.

Concentration in South Florida

Despite the Cuban Refugee Program's resettlement effort, which started in 1961 and reached its peak in the late 1960s, most early exiles decided to settle in Miami with hopes for a quick return to Cuba. When those hopes were shattered during the Transition Stage (1962–1965), their increasing numbers in Little Havana provided the human ingredient for building an ethnic enclave catering almost entirely to themselves. It can be argued ad infinitum whether the Cuban enclave was the result or the cause of the rapid business development during the Adjustment Stage (1965–1973). One and the other, however, seemed inseparable, for the developing enclave and its continuing attraction to increasing number of exiles acted as mutually rein-forcing factors in the early success achieved by Cubans.

Since the outset, the cultural resiliency of the enclave—hence, its very economic viability—was nurtured by the concentration of a culturally ho-mogeneous population of exiles and the measure of success they achieved almost from the start. The convergence of larger numbers of emigrés on a rather small, geographically fragmented area retarded the acculturation pro-cess of those within the enclave. Because that initial exodus represented the critical cultural link to the past, their early progress also strengthened the likelihood of perpetuating self-defining cultural attributes such as language, traditions, value orientation, political idiosyncrasies, and, of course, sense of identity.

Upon this cultural cocoon were laid the business foundations of the en-clave. These developments attracted additional emigrés who arrived in the freedom flights (1965–1973); the "fresh" newcomers, in turn, reinforced Cuban cultural patterns associated with *cubanía* and provided a growing supply of labor and a captive consumer market to sustain the consolidation of the enclave.

> There is a continuous renewal of what it means to be a Cuban. Every wave, every boat that comes directly from the island, and every Cuban that comes through a third country to Miami, in some way renews the Cuban culture. (Author's interview with Modesto Maidique)

> The Cuban exiles are the only minority that I know of that have been able to create or re-create the atmosphere of the land they left. . . . Miami is a place where Cubans come and can read newspapers in Spanish . . . drink *café cubano* and *guarapo* (sugar cane juice), and as more Cubans come, they keep bringing sort of a refreshing view of what's happening in Cuba. (Author's interview with Georgetown University professor emeritus Luis Aguilar León)

Even after the freedom flights ended in 1973, the number of Cubans kept increasing as a result of the influx of exiles who returned from other American cities where they had been relocated. Demographers found this acceleration of the trend toward concentration in South Florida during the 1970s especially significant, because it ran contrary to the tendency toward geographic dispersion exhibited by Puerto Ricans and Mexican Americans during the same period.[13] By that time, clearly, the enclave had attained the critical mass necessary to support the expansion of its small business and service network.

> In U.S. history, you have an immigration. . . . When that immigration settles down, have children and their children have children, a new generation grows up; they start speaking English and reading English and the old language is forgotten. Well, what happened in South Florida is completely different. The Cuban immigration hasn't stopped yet. We had an influx in the early 60s, one in the 70s, a big one in the 80s, and we are having one now that will probably increase with time. (Author's interview with *The Miami Herald*'s former president Roberto Suárez)

At the conclusion of the Economic Miracle Stage (1973–1980), the boundaries of the enclave extended well beyond Little Havana, and by then, Miami's foreign-born population also included thousands of Latin Americans. Only at that point did the "American" firms become belatedly aware of the economic potential of the Cuban market—certainly too late to catch up with exile firms that had gained a comparative advantage in the enclave.[14]

In retrospect, the causal mechanisms providing for the economic growth South Florida experienced in the aftermath of the initial Cuban exodus appeared to run contrary to the prevailing models in modern consumer-oriented societies. In the case of the exiles, the growth process in the volume of production and income was triggered by the inflow of a largely destitute population and workforce, an effect that would not have worked but for the huge concentration of a Cuban population in Miami. In fact, the hypothesis that the Cuban economic miracle stands as a clear case of the operation of Say's Law, according to which an increase in supply may generate a corresponding increase in demand that in turn absorbs the additional output, has been advanced by Antonio Jorge and Raúl Moncarz.[15]

> If we had gone to New York, most probably we wouldn't have been able to do what we did. New York is a big capital with too many people in all kinds of businesses, but Miami was a little place, dedicated to tourists. There was nothing here. A significant factor in our development was that we were too many people and created our own market; we didn't depend, to start a busi-

ness, on the American community. We depended on ourselves—and that helped. (Author's interview with Luis Botifoll)

The absorptive labor capacity of their ever-expanding enclave economy was such that wages were kept at stable low levels while productivity increased. Indeed, after a brief hiatus in 1970, when Dade County accounted for "only" 40 percent of all Cubans living in the United States, the Cuban population in this area had steadily increased to 52 percent by 1980 and to 57 percent by 1990. By then, Miami had emerged as the third largest and most prosperous Hispanic community in the country.

Reliance on Informal Networks and the Private Sector

From the outset, the exiles developed an informal business, professional, and service network that went hand in hand with the early establishment and subsequent expansion of the Little Havana enclave and other exile colonies. The strength of such a network may have been based on its economic viability, but sociocultural and ideological factors also played crucial roles in its consolidation. The exiles favored this informal economy because it saved them money, extended credit, and delivered services in Spanish by people familiar to them.

In addition, to patronize the struggling fellow exiles was generally seen as a way of helping each other. On a practical level, of course, this solidarity translated into jobs and triggered a strong multiplier effect.

Beyond that of the family, a purely economic network was created in Miami and other exile colonies. If I needed a roofer, well, I went to a buddy of mine who's from my hometown, and he's sure to give me a discount to have me as a client; of course, he'll charge me much less than an "American" would, but will still make some money. After a while, "Americans" involved in many of the trades and services started to leave because they simply couldn't compete. This personal network helped to "stretch" family income among the exiles, since many could have performed services "on the side" for small fees or barter their services. (Translation of author's interview with Mercedes Sandoval)

In those early days, the exiles rarely consulted the "yellow pages" when they needed a service; instead, they relied on personal contacts for referrals. A wide range of technical and professional workers, from doctors and accountants to electricians and beauticians, offered services underground because they were not yet licensed to practice legally in this country. Since transactions more than likely were in cash and not reported to the Internal

Revenue Service, the informal network depended on mutual trust between service providers and their satisfied clients—a trust the solidarity of their shared exile identity immediately created. This highly personal style of doing business proved invaluable in furthering the economic progress of the enclave. Many of these clandestine efforts in time developed into small firms.

Cultural and historical attitudes brought from Cuba also played a significant role in the establishment of this informal network. Its early development, for instance, may have been aided by the Cubans' essential distrust of government. Government antagonized them in Cuba and confused them here. Furthermore, Cubans felt no right to claim their fair share of public jobs, particularly since they considered themselves exiles just waiting to return home. Under such conditions it may have been somewhat natural to keep a safe distance from the public sector, despite the fact that a number of Cubans received assistance from the federally funded Cuban Refugee Program. That attitude partly persisted even after they gained a significant measure of political clout in South Florida; the exiles remained the Hispanics least likely to be employed in the public sector and the most likely to be self-employed.[16]

> Unlike most other minorities, the Cubans did not flow towards the public sector. Rather, they developed their own businesses and established an economic enclave of their own, primarily concentrated in commercial activities. Small businesses catering to Cubans in a homemade market so to speak made for that Cuban enclave, which has been the secret of the Cuban success. . . . I don't think that we as Cuban exiles made a conscious decision to gain economic power in our new host society. We just did that by way of surviving. As a matter of fact, I think this was a process that took place almost unconsciously by the sheer need of establishing ourselves in this new society. (Author's interview with Antonio Jorge)

What many exiles did was to join the fledgling service network or start small businesses. This decision proved a blessing in disguise, for it allowed them to develop and consolidate the economic foundations for their own enclave. In retrospect, this reliance on the private sector, albeit on its informal fringes, was a central factor in promoting their economic success in South Florida. Only much later, after the exiles acquired political power, did they become deft at obtaining Small Business Administration loans and government minority contracts.

Role of the Traditional Family

The family was unequivocally the preeminent social institution in Cuba. Perhaps because their country was constantly subject to political calamities,

Cubans' patriotism was a rather abstract ideal. They revered their nation, but their practical devotion certainly remained with the family. This dual loyalty made sense. In light of the excesses and vices that plagued successive governments, Cubans often felt encouraged to "circle the wagons" around family.

Before Castro's revolution, the family stood at the center of daily existence. Theirs was not the nuclear family so dominant in American society, though. The prevalent pattern then was that of the extended family, in which parents and children shared their home life with several relatives, each of whom contributed to their welfare. The result was a strong family structure that proved uniquely efficient. The family, more than the school, was the institution that cared for the upbringing and socialization of the young, for passing cherished values from one generation to the next, and for upholding traditions. In times of hardship, the family was always there to help. It protected its members from the arbitrary political system and supported them when they faced a personal crisis, such as job loss or illness. The family, not the state, took care of the elderly, the disabled, and the infirm.

When a young man and woman married, the couple frequently lived under the solidaristic roof of the extended family, at least until they had children or became economically independent. In addition to the benefits the family rendered in the affective domain, the material advantages derived from such a social organization were plentiful, as responsibilities were shared among all its members. For those struggling to make ends meet, of course, the extended family was often the best way for getting ahead in Cuba. But even among the well-to-do, three-generation families, if for traditional rather than economic reasons, continued to be the norm until 1959. Truth be told, a few years before the revolutionary takeover, American sociocultural influences on the island had begun to erode the traditional prevalence of this family structure, most notably among young professionals and the prosperous middle class.

Under Castro's revolution, the extended family institution suffered a serious crisis. Uprooting and separation weakened family ties. As the state took control over society, the role of the family in most people's lives dramatically decreased. In exile, on the other hand, the need for survival revitalized the extended family. In addition to helping the newly arrived exiles survive, that family structure softened its members' sense of loss and lessened their feelings of sociocultural isolation in the new and often alien land. Anyone who could get a job in those days did, including former upper and middle class women unaccustomed to outside employment in Cuba. Interestingly, the high participation of women in the labor force has been identified as a primary factor in the remarkable economic performance displayed by the two earlier Cuban emigration waves. As sociologist Lisandro Pérez first suggested, the real Cuban success story "may rest more on a generalized family work ethic than on the individual cases of meteoric social mobility."[17]

> The Cuban female started participating in the labor force with greater significance than practically any minority group in the United States, and practically like the dominant white female, which meant that there were two incomes coming into the family instead of one. (Author's interview with Mercedes Sandoval)

Quantitative studies based on the 1980 U.S. Census strongly support this assertion. The proportion of women holding jobs was higher for Cubans than for any other minority group in the United States and almost equal to that of Anglo women; not surprisingly, Cubans led all other groups in the percentage of family units with two or more workers, a pattern that has been maintained over the years.[18] Census figures for 1980 rather than more recent statistics are used here because, by that benchmark year, the first two emigration waves had established themselves, and the economic enclave was already a reality.

According to the 1980 U.S. Census, the proportion of relatives older than sixty-five years within exile families was an incredibly high 30.7 percent (the national norm was 8.9 percent). These statistics demonstrate the prevalence of three-generation family units among early Cuban exiles. The socioeconomic advantages of this pattern seem obvious: The larger-sized households contributed more income, for the elderly often qualified for Social Security benefits and the Cuban Refugee Program's assistance. Grandparents who did not hold outside employment took over many child-rearing chores, freeing parents to work unencumbered by such responsibilities. In the extended family, grandparents also became the central agents for the perpetuation of cultural values and traditions. Not surprisingly, preliminary research indicates that the presence of grandparents within the household bears a direct correlation to the retention of Spanish-language proficiency among American-born Cuban children.

Miami's Location Relative to Latin America

By settling in Miami, the initial exodus was able to take full advantage of this area's geographical proximity to the largely untapped Spanish-speaking markets south of the border. From the start, the exiles guessed that their language, cultural similarities, and previous business contacts with Latin

Americans would provide unique economic opportunities for them. They were right, and then some.

> The location of Miami, relative to the rest of the Latin-American countries, gives a special advantage to being bi-lingual . . . the education and entrepreneurial inclination of the Cubans created in Miami, I think, a unique situation that has given Cubans, political and economic power faster than any other immigrant group in the history of the U.S. (Author's interview with Modesto Maidique)

In reality, the establishment of the first international trade activities in the mid-1960s resulted from the Cuban entrepreneurs' early recognition of the potential of that foreign market, as well as their knowledge of the types of American goods and services that would appeal to Latin Americans. The exiles were familiar with the needs of Latin societies because, just a few years earlier, they had been part of a similar society. Hence, it was not difficult for Cubans to become the factor that catalyzed Latin America's potential demand into effective demand. Once those international links were established, foreign trade activities rapidly increased and diversified along a wide-ranging field that included consumer, business, and professional goods and services.

In a matter of a few years, the enterprising Cubans succeeded in adding a thriving import-export component to the economic foundations of the entire South Florida region. Certainly, given the interdependence between the enclave and the mainstream economy, the prosperity of the former spilled over into the latter. In fact, though the forces that triggered the import-export boom originated with the exiles, the resulting intermarket transactions with the overall economy by far surpassed those taking place within the enclave itself. This contention is supported by the higher growth and investment rates and the lower unemployment rate experienced throughout South Florida in the 1960s and 1970s in comparison to the national economy.

During that period, greater Miami gained a comparative advantage in the import-export field, replacing New Orleans as the main commercial port to points south, and ultimately emerged as the gateway to Latin America. By their second decade in exile, Cuban entrepreneurs had established hundreds of thriving import-export businesses that catered to that region. The synergy created by the international field attracted financial institutions and multinational corporations involved in foreign trade to South Florida. Miami's bilingual and bicultural reputation, in turn, acted as a magnet for thousands of Latin Americans who came as tourists, investors, immigrants, and refugees, and who made Spanish not only the home language of the majority of the local population, but a veritable lingua franca for conducting business as well.

NOTES

1. Néstor T. Carbonell-Cortina, "The Cuban-Americans: Past Achievements and Future Hopes," paper presented at the National Association of Cuban-American Educators, Miami, 17 August 1991.

2. How Cuba overcame its paucity in natural resources is somewhat reminiscent of the "challenge-and-response" dynamics with which Arnold Toynbee, in "A Study of History," explained the development of advanced societies.

3. For an excellent discussion of the historical roots of the Cuban exiles' economic success, see Leví Marrero, *Raíces del milagro cubano* (San Juan: Ediciones Capiro, 1984).

4. Santería, also referred to as Afrocuban religion, sprouted among the island's large black slave population during colonial times. *Orichas* are the gods they brought from Africa.

5. This point must be underscored, for it has been mistakenly assumed that the development of Miami's Cuban enclave took place at the expense of the overall local economy; the opposite was actually the case.

6. Estimates of the amounts the CIA spent in South Florida are not available. But taking into account that its Miami operation in those days was second only to the CIA's Langley headquarters in Virginia, they must have been substantial. The Cuban Refugee Program poured over a billion dollars into the local economy.

7. By 1980 greater Miami could boast more international banks than any other American city but New York.

8. Alejandro Portes and Alex Stepick, *City on the Edge: The Transformation of Miami* (Berkeley: University of California Press, 1993).

9. Forward linkages in the production chain are those said to be closer to the consumers and generally less complex and capital intensive than backward linkages, which connect intermediate goods to raw materials and, ultimately, to capital goods and manufacturing.

10. Portes and Bach have given preeminence to structural factors arising from the human capital the exiles brought from Cuba and to their high concentration in Miami; Pedraza stresses the assistance offered to the exiles through the Cuban Refugee Program; Pérez notes the economic viability of the exiles' extended-family structure.

11. The solidarity of the shared exile identity has produced quasi-monopolistic conditions in the Cuban market for certain culturally differentiated goods and services with low elasticity of substitution relative to competing markets.

12. Lisandro Pérez, "The Cuban Population of the United States: The Results of the 1980 U.S. Census of Population," *Cuban Studies* 15, no. 2 (Summer 1985): 1–18.

13. Ibid.

14. The strongest case for such an advantage was provided by culturally differentiated brand products and businesses that were popular in Cuba and reappeared in exile, for example: Bacardi, Café Pilón, Materva, Conchita, Restaurante Centro Vasco, and La Gran Vía.

15. Antonio Jorge and Raúl Moncarz, "International Factor Movement and Complementarity: Growth and Entrepreneurialship under Conditions of Cultural Variation," in *Research Group for European Migration Problems, R.E.M.P. Bulletin,* ed. G. Beyer (The Hague, September 1981).

16. Pérez, "The Cuban Population of the United States."

17. Ibid., 16.

18. The relatively low fertility rates among exile families may be explained by the high participation of Cuban women in the labor force.

6

Politics of the Emigrés

The political culture of the exile community in south Florida evolved in response to events in both Cuba and the United States. Cuban emigrés engaged in both exile politics and ethnic politics; as exiles, they tried to shape the political developments in the homeland, and as immigrant citizens they tried to shape their local environment.

—María Cristina García[1]

POLITICAL PROFILE

Authoritarian Political Culture and Caudillismo

Since the beginning, the political culture of the Cuban Exile Country has nurtured a hybrid variety. The grafting onto American stock of a Cuban strain susceptible to authoritarianism produced an offshoot of incredible political hardiness but marked with a recessive flaw: That first crop in exile retained a sour aftertaste reminiscent of its Cuban lineage, which it passed on to succeeding political harvests.

In Cuba, the authoritarian penchant for political intolerance was often deemed a necessary evil to ward off revolutionary excesses. The first emigrés brought that mind-set to the United States, where it was allowed to thrive under the guise of their anti-Castro spirit.

Because communism took over our homeland, as long as a communist regime exists in Cuba we are technically at war. For that reason, I think we have a right to be extremists, but that's strictly because we're at war. (Author's interview with radio personality Margarita Ruiz)

We are constantly being criticized for being too aggressive—they call us right wing reactionaries. And I guess to a large degree, maybe it's true. I mean, I am reactionary and I'm reactionary anti-Castro because of our life experiences. (Author's interview with Florida State Senator Mario Díaz Balart)

Beneath this single-minded attitude, the emigrés have always held contrasting political ideas, which they usually kept to themselves. Since all that actually bonded their politics in exile was their anticommunism, Cubans considered political pluralism a luxury they could ill afford. The appearance of political unanimity, though forced—or enforced, some would rather say—fostered an exile political culture that revived old authoritarian excesses through which Cuba's ship of state had sailed perilously until its ultimate shipwreck in 1959.

The predominant idea in Cuban exile politics is that you need absolute unanimity in order to confront the totalitarian government in Cuba, and that only this unanimity gives us the strength to face the Castro government. As a result, there is very little space for tolerance, for the respect of the plurality of ideas, for a free flow of political ideas in the exile community. (Author's interview with publisher Ramón Cernuda)

In their diaspora, the exiles seemed damned to remain adrift in troubled political waters, as if their national destiny could never set them free from the dark undercurrents of authoritarianism. They rationalized that there are historical moments or exceptional circumstances when a people must rally together to face a common enemy, and the imposition of measures restricting freedom may be deemed necessary; the consensus among Cubans was that exile qualified as one of those extraordinary cases. Political dissent was thus suppressed by an anti-Castro establishment strong enough to dictate its official line to the rest. Given the political turbulence that *el exilio* has always faced, expressing different views, even on how to fight their bearded nemesis, invited controversy. Those who dared to dissent publicly from the exiles' hard line were often pressured to conform—or else risk being labeled communist sympathizers.

Being a liberal in the Cuban community would generally give you a lot of grief. I've known people here that have suffered very severe consequences because of it. I think that it has given me less grief . . . because I was a Bay of

Pigs veteran and presided over their association on two occasions; I think that I have suffered less than most other people. But it's not been easy; there have been times when people have said that I am a communist, which basically everybody knows that's not true. (Author's interview with political activist Alfredo Durán)

The most controversial by-product of the holy war against Castro is perhaps the glorification of violence as an acceptable political tactic. Terrorist incidents have periodically erupted within the Cuban Exile Country although such extreme tactics have been directed primarily against pro-Castro targets.

The terrorist era of the seventies was a direct by-product of the change of U.S. policy in the sixties and how it affected the Cuban exile community. I was involved in anti-Castro operations in the seventies and in the eighties, and I was involved in intelligence operations and in counter-intelligence operations. And I was involved in some violent activities that I don't particularly consider terrorist; I consider them legitimate acts of war. (Author's interview with militant activist Enrique Encinosa)

Some liberal and pro-díalogo emigrés have also been victims of the terrorist attacks conducted by their more extremist countrymen, particularly during the wave of indiscriminate political violence that shook the exile community in the 1970s. Since then, however, hard-line exiles have claimed that the responsibility for such extreme acts falls on communist infiltrators bent on discrediting the anti-Castro movement. Given the "long arm" of the Cuban revolution, it is probable the culprits have come from both camps.

Because I'm independent, outspoken, courageous . . . five years ago the corner of my garage was bombed. And that bomb was placed to intimidate me. I think the culprits should be brought to justice; I demand that. But that bomb was a blessing in disguise, and whoever did it, did me a favor. 'Cause already I was a public figure, the bomb converted me into an obligated reference for newspaper people, for writers, for politicians, for clergymen, for dissidents, for students, for researchers, you name it. (Author's interview with Miami Dade Community College professor María Cristina Herrera)

It is not that Cuban emigrés do not believe in democracy; most exiles would say they passionately believe in it. In their excessive zeal, however, those who perceive themselves in the political majority often feel compelled to deny the rights of minorities. This right-or-wrong political counterpoint has nurtured an intransigent streak that tends to allow the imposition of one view, albeit the most popular, over all others. Fidel Castro himself illustrates that authoritarian obsession for political unanimity. The bearded messiah-turned-dictator, who it has been said embodies the best as well as the worst qualities of Cuba's body politic, shamelessly summarized this ominous stance—"Within the revolution everything; outside the revolution nothing." Heirs to a political tradition plagued with such authoritarian intransigence, the exiles were early victims of the same tendencies that had wreaked havoc on their nation during the republican period. Not surprisingly, they generated in exile political specters somewhat akin to those that had cursed their own fate on the island.

Although their political thought had been rooted in liberal ideological traditions since the eighteenth century, Cubans' actual political attitudes belie those origins.[2] Given the Cuban republic's murky political history, it is perhaps understandable that, once in exile, Cubans would again try to stymie debate and repress dissent. Often the exiles appeared not to know any better. In their fight against an enemy that did not quibble about resorting to totalitarian methods, they felt utterly justified in wielding like tactics. It would lead them to replicate here what they thought they were escaping from: an authoritarian political culture that relied on contrived unanimity as a first line of defense against their common enemy.

> Cuban exiles are a lot more tolerant than we have been given credit for. As we understand it, free expression is a two-way street; so, when pro-Castro elements come to Miami to provoke us, we have responded by staging our own protests against them or by boycotting their activities. But that's not being intransigent; what we have done is exercise our constitutional rights to dissent from the views of Castro sympathizers. (Author's interview with retired banker Luis Botifoll)

Sadly, they seem to have missed the larger point: Having lost their homeland to totalitarianism, it now behooves them to underscore their differences vis-à-vis Castro's regime, and to base their cause in the most absolute respect for freedom.

> The most subversive notion that could be advanced within the exile community in the eyes of Cuba today would be the fact that this is a heterogeneous exile, that people think in a variety of ways. Mind you, supposedly, when we came here it was precisely to be able to do that. We came here because we didn't agree with the party line. (Author's interview with Miami Film Festival director Natalio Chediak)

The narrow attitude with which the emigrés approached political debate, ironically, never carried over to the economic sphere, where the exiles pay homage to free market ideology and revere open competition as a sacred tenet. This sharp contrast between economic and political idiosyncrasies may partly explain why their free enterprise convictions led them to so much business success everywhere they settled, while their authoritarian politics undermined the promotion of their cause among advocates of democracy.

Although the Cuban emigration always harbored different ideological hues and beliefs, this diversity remained concealed beneath the monolithic surface of *el exilio*. Even those who arrived in the initial exodus held contrasting political points of view. That very first vintage that settled in the United States right after Castro's 1959 takeover, the partisans of the deposed ancien régime, were a mixed ideological batch themselves; all they shared was having collaborated with General Fulgencio Batista, the caudillo who ruled during much of the republic's previous twenty-five years.[3] For a while, the *batistianos* outnumbered the mostly nonpolitical upper class vintage that soon followed them to the United States. Thereafter, the radicalization of the revolution also forced into exile a more heterogeneous representation of the Cuban middle class as well as disenchanted members of Castro's own 26th of July Movement, and friction arose between the *batistianos* and *fidelistas*. In both camps, nevertheless, a wide variety of ideological constituencies found political quarters: Among them were social and Christian democrats, conservatives, liberals, and repentant revolutionaries; anti-American nationalists who opposed American imperialism, and *plattistas*[4] who defended U.S. hegemony over the island. Free expression of such divergence, however, was sacrificed for what the exiles perceived represented the common good of their cause.

During the formative period of *el exilio*, the traditionally authoritarian tendencies brought from Cuba may have been reinforced by the exiles' early dealings with the Central Intelligence Agency (CIA), an institution not particularly known for its pluralistic practices. From the beginning, American officials barred *batistianos* from key positions in the Consejo Revolucionario Cubano, the coalition of exile organizations being hammered together by U.S. operatives in 1960. Although the rationale for excluding those identified with Batista's disgraced regime was based on their lack of appeal to Cubans on the island, the CIA's heavy-handed demeanor was clearly resented by some exile leaders. Under the charged political climate that prevailed, the CIA proceeded with its plan for the invasion, while the exiles' reservations were quelled by the urge to fall in line. For the sake of expediency, therefore, the exiles became wholly dependent on the CIA, and out of misconstrued loyalty to their American ally they accepted a subservient position. Since then, the anti-Castro movement—and the Cuban Exile Country itself—has been imprinted with a lasting authoritarian character. The exiles would never be able to overcome such extreme political tendencies.

> I have been an opponent of the Cuban government for 34 years. I am a Cuban national and the Cuban government does not allow me into my own country; I have been refused entry into my country four times. I am definitely opposed to the totalitarian, one-party system prevailing in Cuba—the Cuban government knows it and the extreme right wing in exile also knows it. But one extreme needs the other to justify their intransigent positions. And when someone like myself, not aligned with either extreme, speaks up, it bothers them, [because] it simply confuses the black-and-white images that each side wants to impose. (Author's interview with Ramón Cernuda)

An authoritarian political culture often begets totalitarian regimes which, in turn, beget revolutions that ultimately tend to beget caudillos. That vicious cycle can repeat itself over and over again ad nauseam. Cuba has had its share of totalitarian regimes, revolutions, and, of course, caudillos—charismatic strongmen who appear to incarnate the messianic hopes of Cubans. Indeed, caudillismo was part of the political legacy of four centuries of Spanish colonial rule; not surprisingly, that tradition was carried forth by the brave Cuban patriots who freed their country from the Spaniards in the late 1800s but could never free themselves from the yoke of authoritarianism. Since its birth, the Cuban republic has been held captive to a mentality that glorifies the exploits of its larger-than-life heroes rather than the civic virtues of its ordinary citizens.

Since Cuba became an independent nation in 1902, caudillos have mostly dominated Cuba's history: General Gerardo Machado, from 1928 to 1933; General Batista from 1933 to 1944 and from 1952 to 1959; and Castro since 1959. Authoritarian rule was periodically interrupted during brief spells, but not long enough for a truly democratic culture to take hold in the young nation. The caudillos' personal magnetism and their dictatorial methods, in effect, frustrated the development of a civic spirit grounded on the preeminence of the rule of law. Cubans could be for or against the dictator on duty, but their personal allegiance or opposition has been explained primarily in terms of blind faith to men rather than ideological convictions.

> Cubans . . . often build their hopes around men, mostly certain strong leaders. (Translation of author's interview with Communist Arnaldo Escalona)

The essential political characteristics of Cubans can be judged by the people who have governed them. . . . When it was time to vote, Cubans would let their political passions get the best of them. (Translation of author's interview with political leader Carlos Márquez Sterling)

The tendency to coalesce around individuals instead of ideals was part of the political baggage brought to the United States by the first exiles. Once here, exile political leaders emphasized their personal anticommunism rather than their commitment to democratic practices, and anti-Castro slogans were mistakenly equated with democratic beliefs. As a result, cynics may point out, the exiles can sing the democratic gospel by heart, but it is not so evident that they know how to dance to it—not without an authoritarian band leader, anyway. The emigrés, in fact, often state that what the Cuban Exile Country has lacked is a leader capable of matching Castro's own prowess, an unabashed confession that confirms how well the ancestral specter of caudillismo has survived in exile. Paradoxically, Cubans on both sides of the Straits of Florida have been subjected to similar authoritarian pressures: In exile, American democratic institutions ameliorated their impact; on the island, devoid from such external constraints, those pressures fully developed into tyranny.

The Emigrés' Early Political Dilemma

Since the intention of the initial wave of exiles was to return to Cuba shortly after toppling Castro, their politics for some time centered exclusively on that effort. As temporary boarders in this country, they kept themselves detached from American politics except for a consuming interest in U.S. policies vis-à-vis the Castro regime. Being foreigners, they could not have participated in this country's political life even had they wished to, and they did not wish to in those early days.

Even after their hopes of returning to their homeland were shattered by the outcome of the 1961 Bay of Pigs invasion and the 1962 missile crisis, they still remained largely isolated from America's politics. They followed local elections, and certainly President Kennedy's betrayal of the cause of Cuban freedom predisposed the exiles against the Democratic party, but since few of them were American citizens all they could do was express their political predilections among themselves.

Cubans and Cuban Americans associate the Bay of Pigs fiasco with the Democratic administration. It was an administration that didn't come through for us. No matter what happened, we were so young as a community, and those scars were so raw, that somehow—it's subliminal—we thought: Democrats, they're all communists or socialists. (Author's interview with businesswoman María Elena Toraño)

During the Adjustment Stage (1965–1973), after the passage of the 1966 Cuban Adjustment Act facilitated adopting permanent resident status—a prerequisite for applying for American citizenship and, in turn, acquiring voting rights—a handful of exiles became more involved in their adopted community. This was evident by the late 1960s, when the creation of the Greater Miami Coalition, a broad effort that sought representation from all segments of the South Florida community, offered the exiles an opportunity to participate in local affairs.

The establishment was represented in the Greater Miami Coalition, and they had two blacks and two Cubans—Bernardo Benes and I. We started by addressing the necessity to have Spanish-speaking personnel in places like hospitals, the Police Department, the Fire Department. . . . We had a big fight trying to get Spanish-speaking people in those places. (Author's interview with Luis Botifoll)

I think that I was selected by the Greater Miami Coalition as a token Cuban, but they made a mistake: I was no token. . . . I was probably the first Cuban American who strongly opposed discrimination. . . . I was at the forefront of the social activists while Leslie Pantín Sr. and Luis Botifoll started the business contact with Anglos. I think that the Greater Miami Coalition was dissolved by the then executive vice-president of the United Way because the Cuban American committee was taking too much power. (Author's interview with banker Bernardo Benes)

The Greater Miami Coalition, nevertheless, helped the exiles focus on the issue of discrimination for the first time. Shortly thereafter, similar concerns would lead to their initial political involvement in South Florida. Despite their reservations about President Kennedy's handling of the Cuban issue, a group of young emigrés recognized that, because of the Democratic party's overwhelming dominance in Florida politics, it represented their best option.

A group of Cuban Americans formed the first Democratic Club, which was recognized by the Democratic party of the state of Florida. And the reason that club was formed was to influence the political leadership of this state to listen to the needs of the Cuban community. Among those needs at that time was getting licenses for doctors, trying to get better social services for the

Cuban community and all that, and we thought a good vehicle to do that was through the political process. (Author's interview with Alfredo Durán)

The Cuban anti-Castro establishment at the time, however, considered the decision to take U.S. citizenship to mean electing to give up the fight to free Cuba—by then, admittedly, a fight that was mostly rhetorical. In a closely knit community like Miami's Cuban enclave, where peer pressures tended to keep most exiles in line, pledging allegiance to the American flag was deemed a treason to Cuba. Indeed, the choice between remaining politically disenfranchised exiles or adopting American citizenship represented a dilemma of moral proportions. The decision to switch citizenship, particularly among old militants and die-hard freedom fighters, emerged as a sort of litmus test of an exile's true patriotism.

During the Economic Miracle Stage (1973–1980), the advent of a new Cuban American consciousness among the younger generation began to erode the exiles' staunch stand against participation in American politics. This new Cuban American offshoot, however, still had to contend with old exile idiosyncracies deeply rooted in an obstinate anti-Castro spirit. Whether younger Cuban Americans fully shared that all-consuming obsession or not, they recognized that to mobilize the exiles to participate in American political life they would have to appeal to their concern for Cuba. The trauma of changing patriotic allegiances less than two decades after their arrival in the United States was thus justified by an expedient argument: Acquiring U.S. citizenship and registering to vote would afford the exiles the opportunity to work within the political system to influence U.S. policy toward Cuba.

Cubans first started becoming heavily involved in local politics in the late seventies. And since the liberation of Cuba was and really continues to be our number one concern, we naturally aligned ourselves with the Republican party because this party had such a strong anticommunist message. (Author's interview with U.S. Congresswoman Ileana Ros Lehtinen)

Although it was a far-fetched possibility at the time, the prospects of influencing U.S. policies toward Cuba resonated with the crusading spirit of *el exilio*. Once so persuaded, the exiles thrust themselves into local campaigns with the same determination with which they had previously refused to do so. This drastic shift from mere observers to enthusiastic participants owed much to the fact that Manolo Reboso and Alfredo Durán, arguably the first Cuban Americans to become active in Miami's politics, had participated in the Bay of Pigs Invasion and were prominent members of the Association of

Bay of Pigs Veterans. Given the strong anti-Castro credentials of these two
political pioneers, their endorsement of Anglo candidates carried enough
weight among the few registered Cuban voters to make a difference at the
polls.

From then on, Cubans in South Florida clearly became split between exile
politics and ethnic politics—although both camps, at least at a rhetorical
level, remained focused on the issue of Cuba's freedom. As a whole, however,
the emigrés have never really given up their loyalty to their homeland. They
appear to have acquired a dual political identity, which is evidenced by the
ease with which they have integrated elements of both political cultures into
their anti-Castro discourse. In retrospect, they were unconsciously redefining
how to remain Cubans outside of Cuba's own territory.

ETHNIC POLITICS IN THE MIAMI ENCLAVE

Political Empowerment

Their patriotic dilemma over the citizenship question finally resolved, the
exiles, particularly the younger ones, became active in local elections—at first
not as candidates themselves but as voters and power brokers. Much like
other disenfranchised immigrant minorities in America, they were early prey
to the electoral pandering of Anglo politicians and their Cuban American
strategists who, realizing the blurred line that separated exile politics and
ethnic politics, kept hammering at the Cuban issue. For a while, it was
unmistakenly American ethnic politics at its traditional worst.

During the Adjustment Stage (1965–1973), when Cubans still lacked the
votes to elect their own candidates, their high turnouts and bloc voting patterns could nevertheless become a factor in closely contested races. In those
early days, established politicians, including Democratic Congressmen
Claude Pepper and Dante Fascell, who regardless of their party affiliation
and liberal records catered to the emigrés' hard line on Cuba, could always
count on the exiles' support. Reboso, Durán, and other Cuban Americans
would bring Anglo candidates to the Cuban enclave, where enthusiastic
crowds welcomed the candidates and provided the ideal setting for photo
opportunities to the contagious beat of Cuban music.

Appealing for Cuban votes often became a surreal spectacle, as candidates
for local and state office delved into issues of U.S. foreign policy over which
they had absolutely no jurisdiction even if elected. Typically, American politicians condescended to the exiles' penchant for anti-Castro rhetoric instead
of addressing problems related to the actual posts for which they were run-

ning. This pattern of putting foreign issues above local concerns, once instituted, continued to dominate electoral priorities among the exiles. Perhaps
only in South Florida's Cuban community could candidates for city council,
circuit judge, and state legislator win or lose an election solely on the basis
of their foreign policy platforms.

This is not to say that those initial campaigns did not serve a useful purpose; if nothing else, they offered Cubans a first opportunity to learn how
American campaigns were organized and to develop incipient political machines in Miami, Hialeah, Westchester, and other pockets of Cuban voters.
At the same time, Cuban American power brokers gained influence in the
eyes of the Democratic powers-to-be who, in turn, reciprocated through the
common practice of political patronage. Reboso and Durán, the first Cuban
American officeholders, owed their respective appointments to midterm va-
cancies in the Miami City Commission and the Dade County School Board
to grateful Democratic politicians.

> We were first appointed by the establishment, but the establishment was re-
> acting to political and economic pressures that we were able to assert. Some-
> times our power appeared to be much more than it really was; it was like
> playing with mirrors. That's the way it basically happened. (Author's interview
> with Alfredo Durán)

By the end of the Adjustment Stage, the Cuban vote within small municipalities like Miami and Hialeah, where city races were nonpartisan, had
already succeeded in electing a few Cuban Americans.

Political Obstacles

What Cuban American candidates could not manage at the time was to
attract support from non-Cuban voters within districts dominated by Democratic incumbents. That became obvious when Democrat Alfredo Durán,
who had earlier been appointed to the school board, ran to retain his seat in
1974. Even with the overwhelming support of Dade's Democratic political
establishment, Durán was not able to win his party's nomination for a second
term in South Florida's first ethnically divisive campaign involving Cubans.

> We had passed bilingual education for the first time, which was ultimately
> what did me in . . . and what was debated [during the campaign] was the
> bilingual education program; some of the things said were that I wanted to
> make everybody dance the *cucaracha* [a Spanish song] in the school system,
> and that I wanted to make everybody sleep a siesta after school. In other words,

bilingual education became the central issue and I, the Democratic incumbent, lost the Democratic party's nomination. (Author's interview with Alfredo Durán)

This campaign crushed the electoral hopes of many Cuban American Democrats. By 1976 Cubans in both parties accounted for just under 10 percent of Dade County's registered voters, too insignificant a percentage to elect their own candidates in Democratic-controlled countywide primaries. On the other hand, Cuban Americans realized that they could be nominated in the Republican primaries, even if the prospects of winning a general election as Republican candidates were then nil in Dade's entrenched Democratic districts. The rejection of Dade's Democratic voters would soon prove costly to that party: By default, Cubans started drifting toward the then-fledgling local Republican party, where their presence was warmly welcomed and their conservative beliefs better appreciated—and in so doing, Cubans began to erode the complete domination Democrats had enjoyed in South Florida since reconstruction days.

Just remember that when Jimmy Carter became President . . . the majority of the Cuban American electors were Democrats. Then, the Cuban American community switched. . . . And that did affect the political face of South Florida to the extent that the two members of Congress who come from districts that are majority Cuban Americans are now Republicans; and all the State House members and State Senators from fundamentally Cuban American districts are also Republicans. (Author's interview with U.S. Congressman Lincoln Díaz Balart)

The case of Lincoln Díaz Balart, then an aspiring Cuban American lawyer who in the 1970s had presided over the state's Young Democrats, illustrates why most Cubans opted to swell the Republican ranks. Despite his political talent and active involvement in Florida's Democratic politics, Díaz Balart could not win even his party's nomination to the Florida Legislature. After several unsuccessful attempts as a Democrat, he decided to switch parties; as a Republican, he gained a house seat in the mid-1980s.

I always wanted to serve in public office. Yes, we started in the Democratic party. But with time we realized that in the Democratic party we were not welcome, so we switched. The shift occurred, and then the overwhelming majority of Cuban Americans were no longer Democrats; they became Republicans. (Author's interview with Lincoln Díaz Balart)

Díaz Balart and his fellow Cuban American Republicans still faced another formidable obstacle to their political aspirations: having to run in multiple-member and at-large electoral districts that diluted the Cuban voting potential. As drawn at the time, Dade's legislative and congressional districts had been gerrymandered to protect the mostly white male Democratic incumbents. As a result, the growing Cuban population continued without fair political representation of their own in South Florida's electoral process, particularly in the state legislature and in the U.S. Congress.

Indeed, by the end of the Economic Miracle Stage (1973–1980), there was only one Cuban-born state representative, and none had reached the state senate or the U.S. Congress. This underrepresentation also affected African Americans who, much like Cubans, were concentrated within their own sections of Dade County but had to run in larger districts where they had been traditionally defeated. Sharing the same predicament, Cuban Americans and African Americans struck an unusual alliance and set out to challenge a gerrymandered system that undermined the constitutional doctrine of "one person–one vote."

Reapportionment and Redistricting

In order to account for demographic changes, the U.S. Constitution provides that legislative districts be redrawn every ten years. Their reapportionment into districts of substantially equal populations with new boundaries that would take into consideration their racial and ethnic composition was thus required following the 1980 Census. These actions were supposed to end the underrepresentation of Cubans and African Americans in South Florida's electoral process.[5]

Changes having such profound effects, however, have never come easy to minorities. Since boundary lines do tend to slant electoral outcomes, the political powers-to-be closely controlled that process in order to perpetuate the power of incumbency; historically, Florida legislators prepared redistricting plans and the governor signed them without much regard for the voting rights of minorities. That "old boys" network began to crumble after passage of the 1965 Voting Rights Act, which required new reapportionment plans to reflect racial and ethnic minority requirements. Under the act, particularly as later amended, the Florida Supreme Court, the U.S. Department of Justice, and the federal courts could step in to ensure the legal fairness of the redistricting process.

The 1982 congressional amendment to the Voting Rights Act gave added impetus to the empowerment of minorities in Dade County. Whereas before minorities had to show "intent to discriminate," the new rules clarified that a violation could be established if the "totality of the circumstances" leading to nomination or election had denied equal and open participation to racial, color, or language minorities. Under such federal mandate, two of the major barriers to the empowerment of minorities came down: the at-large districts, which had forced Cubans and blacks to run countywide for the Dade County Commission and the school board, and the multiple-member districts from which candidates for the state legislature and U.S. Congress were elected.[6] Once the old system was torn down and new single-member electoral districts were redrawn, Cuban Americans led Republicans to the state capital and to the U.S. Congress.

> All of a sudden, we jumped to Tallahassee where we got six or seven or eight Cuban American state legislators elected, and then to the Senate. And then you had a Cuban legislative caucus. Then, first with Ileana [Ros-Lehtinen], and later with Lincoln [Díaz Balart], we had representation at the federal level. (Author's interview with María Elena Toraño)

> I was first elected to the State Legislature in 1982, then re-elected in '84. In '86 I ran and was successful in that campaign for the Florida Senate and then, when Claude Pepper passed away in 1989, I had the opportunity of becoming the first Hispanic woman in Congress. (Author's interview with Ileana Ros Lehtinen)

The struggle for political empowerment, however, was just getting started. Since South Florida's Hispanic population continued to increase during the 1980s, reapportionment and redistricting were again necessary after the 1990 Census, which found that approximately half of the county's population was Hispanic—the other half was divided between blacks (30 percent) and non-Latin whites (20 percent). The redistricting contest in 1992 centered on the boundary lines of Hispanic minority districts, which Democratic legislators tried to limit in order to retain control of the state house of representatives and the state senate, but by then they were fighting a losing battle against the tide of history as embodied by the ever-increasing Cuban American population.

Cuban Americans, of course, can be expected to continue voting almost exclusively for their own candidates.[7] As a result, in the 1990s, Cubans—and Conservative Republicans, at that—emerged as a dominant political force in South Florida's political landscape, breaking the virtual monopoly once enjoyed by Anglo Democratic incumbents. At present, Cuban Americans control the mayoral posts and city council seats in Miami and Hialeah,

Dade's largest municipalities, as well as in Coral Gables, Sweetwater, West Miami, and Hialeah Gardens. In addition, the city managers of Metropolitan Dade County and the cities of Miami and Miami Beach, as well as the superintendent of Dade County Schools, are also Cuban born; half of Dade's legislative delegation is composed of Cubans; and two Cuban Americans, Ileana Ros Lehtinen and Lincoln Díaz Balart, have been elected to the U.S. Congress.[8]

This dramatic shift in the local political balance of power has favored Cubans at the expense of Dade County's other constituencies. African Americans have fared better than Anglos, since the leveling of the political playing field has also helped their empowerment. The major losers have clearly been the Anglos, a development that has precipitated backlash reactions, white flight, and further polarization of the community along ethnic and language lines.

> What was very painful for me . . . was every time I saw those bumper stickers that said: "Will the last American Leaving Miami, bring the American Flag." Here I was, a Cuban American born in Ft. Lauderdale, Florida, as American as apple pie. . . . I still have a bumper sticker here that says: "Will the last bigot leaving Miami, please see me for gas money." (Author's interview with Mario Díaz Balart)

The Politics of Bilingualism

Since the 1970s, bilingualism has surfaced as the great divider of South Florida's sociopolitical fabric. Long before the English Only Movement became a hot political issue elsewhere in the nation, language was already a "code" word used by those who resented the sweeping advance of Cubans in South Florida. Although the debate over the relationship between Americans' common tongue and their national interest seemed largely a rhetorical one at the time, its implications were far from innocuous; the politics of bilingualism had direct relevance on free public education for all, the respect for and the limits of cultural pluralism, and ultimately on the empowerment of language minorities. These underlying issues represented a more significant challenge to the core values of America's society—thus, the language debate's potential for political conflict.

Obscured by such polemics was the fact that Cubans in South Florida were learning English faster than other immigrants had ever done before— the catch being that the exiles were also maintaining Spanish and using it not just to observe traditions at home but to their economic advantage in the market place.[9] This pattern of language usage has been evident since the Cuban Exile Country was still in its infancy, long before the exclusion of Cubans from public jobs and services began to be challenged. In the early 1970s, such advocacy groups as the Spanish American League Against Discrimination (SALAD) and the Cuban National Planning Council (later renamed Cuban American National Council) began to play a significant role in uncovering and denouncing discriminatory practices against Dade's Spanish-speaking minorities.

> At the local level, we had the creation of organizations such as the Spanish American League Against Discrimination (SALAD), which attempted to redress some of the discrimination Cubans were being subjected to; and at the national level, we started the Cuban National Planning Council, to work both in Miami as well as in other Cuban American communities across the nation. We began conducting research on policy analysis and on the needs of Cuban Americans. (Author's interview with Cuban American National Council president Guarioné Díaz)

Significantly, these organizations helped to catalyze a new sociopolitical awareness among Cuban Americans—certainly their first serious departure from the traditional exile politics of Cubans at the time. As early as 1974, an emerging crop of Cuban American activists accused the Dade County manager of ignoring federal mandates for Spanish-language services and demanded a larger share of county jobs. SALAD's founder Javier Bray, however, was not merely interested in extracting piecemeal concessions from the public sector; he was actually charging that America had never been the mythical melting pot. In contrast to the traditional nation-building myth based on assimilation, Bray submitted the concept of Americanism as a process of orchestrating the immigrants' diversity into something unique, "without asking anyone to give up what they were."[10]

> Whereas before many people did believe in the idea of the melting pot as the nation-building approach to one language and one dominant role model of which we could not really be a part of because we're very different, we said, "Wait a minute! We have important contributions to make, and one of these contributions is our language. We must be included in an efficient way in our schools and society." (Author's interview with Javier Bray, founder of the Spanish American League Against Discrimination)

Although the philosophical foundations of the new Cuban American militancy was consistent with the civil rights' movement of the 1960s, it marked such a departure from the exiles' anti-Castro obsessions that it attracted only an elite of well-educated, younger, more liberal exiles; the rest regarded this activism with suspicion, since it did not squarely address the issue of Cuba. In more subtle ways, ironically, the new Cuban American militancy was compatible with the exiles' early contention that their interest was to remain Cubans without forsaking their language, their culture, and their national identity. Truth be told, given the political idiosyncracies of the exiles, their outlook and dynamics from the onset had sharply contrasted with the traditional experiences of other language minorities. Not lacking in self-confidence, the exiles often considered themselves better than not only other immigrants but mainstream Americans as well.

THE AMERICANIZATION OF EXILE POLITICS

The momentous events that ushered in the Diversification Stage (1980–1990) sparked a deep transformation of the political culture of the Cuban Exile Country. In the wake of the 1978 *Diálogo*, latent ideological rifts that had remained hidden beneath the surface of the exile community were radically exposed; the 1980 Mariel boatlift brought over a generation of Cubans raised under Marxism; and in 1981 the creation of the Cuban American National Foundation (CANF) took the anti-Castro crusade to a new level of sophistication. The combined effects of these three events began to erode old patterns that had so far dominated the politics of Cuban exiles and further erased the already-blurred line separating exile politics from ethnic politics. From then on, mainstream political practices were put to work on behalf of the exile cause.

> In the eighties, the exiles begin a new stage that some would call more mature. Their political activities shift to Washington with the objective of using U.S. power to isolate Cuba and apply more pressures against the regime by means of an intensified economic embargo. During the period, the exiles also prevailed upon the U.S. Congress to fund Radio Martí. (Translation of author's interview with Ramón Mestre, director of *El Nuevo Herald*'s Op-ed pages)

During the 1980s, *el exilio* appeared to show some evidence of political maturity, while its strategies to shape developments on the island split into two broad and irreconcilable camps: the *dialogueros*, who advocated negotiations to bring a peaceful transition to democracy in Cuba, and the *intransigentes*, who wanted to crush Cuba's revolutionary regime out of existence. Although these two strategies could well have complemented each other within a broader effort to free Cuba, such a pluralistic approach was incongruous with the authoritarian political culture of the Cuban Exile Country. By all objective accounts, the hard-liners represented the majority view— and they clearly intended to silence the pro-dialogue minority.

A parallel development of great significance was the creation of the Cuban American National Foundation, a well-financed operation that took exile politics out of the ghetto and into the halls of the U.S. Congress, where it launched a sophisticated public relations campaign to influence U.S. policies toward the Castro regime.

> We were very conscious that at that point we had to win a political battle against Castro in the country in which we are living. We realized pretty soon that to influence the U.S. political system, we must copy . . . the Jewish model, and we became very close-allied with the Jewish lobby and the Jewish movement in Washington.
>
> We changed the whole strategy of Cubans in exile. We provided a new route and new sense of direction. . . . I have to be honest, I never dreamed when we founded the Cuban American National Foundation that two years after we were going to have the President of the United States here in Miami having dinner with us and attending a Cuban rally . . . and that we were going to establish an excellent relationship with the leaders of Congress. (Author's interview with Cuban American National Foundation chairman Jorge Mas Canosa)

The gravitational pull of the Cuban American National Foundation, or *la Fundación*, attracted hundreds of successful exile entrepreneurs who contributed large amounts to finance its lobbying efforts in the nation's capital. The organization thus emerged as a formidable political and economic force as well as a stronghold of conservatism and free market economy—displaying along the way what its critics characterized as heavy-handed tactics.

> The achievements of a political group must be weighted against its defects. . . . The most severe—and accurate—critics of the Foundation point out that, first, it perpetuates *plattista* traditions by rendering to the U.S. fundamental decisions about Cuba's future and destiny; and, second, that its actions denote a lack of democratic, pluralistic convictions. It is a very effective, very well organized group whose projection is fundamentally authoritarian. (Translation of author's interview with Ramón Mestre)

Undaunted by charges that its millionaire leader, Jorge Mas Canosa, embodied the traditional Cuban caudillo, the foundation nevertheless pressed on with its political agenda, prevailing upon the U.S. Congress to establish Radio Martí, a Radio Free Europe type of broadcast to incite the Cuban people to free themselves from communism. Later, the foundation also lobbied successfully for the passage of the 1992 Cuban Democracy Act and the 1996 Cuban Liberty and Democratic Solidarity Act, both of which further tightened the three-decade-old U.S. embargo on Cuba. The ensuing clash over the appropriateness of the embargo turned it into the definitive issue separating *dialogueros* and *intransigentes.*

> The most important contribution that we have made is not Radio Martí, is not the financial resources that we brought in; it's actually a new strategy, a new way of thinking and a very strong sense of pride in what Cuban exiles have been able to accomplish. (Author's interview with Jorge Mas Canosa)

While the self-described "moderate" *dialogueros* have tried to challenge the foundation by opposing its hard line against Castro, they have not been able to match the preeminence *la Fundación* enjoys among the exiles. Its deep pockets, the professionalism of its lobbying operation, and the support it enjoys within the Cuban American business and political establishment have consolidated the Cuban American National Foundation to a point where the debate for and against the foundation often distracts from other exile issues. In all fairness, *la Fundación* has been blamed for the common political practice of rewarding friends and punishing enemies, but because within the Cuban Exile Country only the Cuban American National Foundation wields enough power to get away with such tactics, it is often resented.

> Sometimes the American press misinterprets our passion and our enthusiasm and our character for some kind of intolerant behavior. I am a passionate individual because I am Cuban. I have a lot of enthusiasm and strong opinions because I have gone through very strong experiences. When you have to leave your country, when you have to leave behind your family, when you see your relatives and your best friends executed or thrown in jail . . . you're going to have strong opinions. To achieve what we have, we had to step on a lot of toes. (Author's interview with Jorge Mas Canosa)

For all its power, however, the foundation may have stepped on the wrong toes when it clashed with *The Miami Herald.* Their somewhat cozy initial relationship had deteriorated into bitter recriminations by the early 1990s, dragging their respective principals, Jorge Mas Canosa and David Lawrence, Jr., into a feud that probably helped neither adversary. Their confrontation started when *la Fundación* strongly objected to the newspaper's coverage of

Cuba and Cuban Americans; that led *the Herald* to question Mas Canosa's views on freedom of the press. *La Fundación* then blanketed South Florida with bumper stickers reading, "I don't believe *The Herald.*" The newspaper responded with strong editorials questioning Mas Canosa's commitment to free expression.

Although the tactics employed by the Cuban American Foundation have frequently invited acrimonious controversy, there is no denying its effectiveness. It has virtually dictated the U.S. agenda vis-à-vis the communist island, and the fact that it has managed to do so under Republican as well as Democratic administrations makes their record all the more impressive. In historical perspective, the foundation revived the political hopes of the exiles by fulfilling a dream that barely two decades earlier had seemed just a convenient rationalization to bring the exiles into the political life of their adopted country: influencing U.S. policy toward Cuba.

It has certainly been a long journey since the days when Reboso and Durán escorted Anglo candidates through Little Havana's disenfranchised neighborhoods. What remains to be seen is whether at the end of their mercurial political journey in America the exiles will succeed in overcoming the authoritarian tendencies that doomed their predecessors on the island. Should they manage that elusive feat, the exile experience would have delivered Cubans from their ancestral specters.

NOTES

1. See María Cristina García, *Havana USA: Cuban Exiles and Cuban Americans in South Florida, 1959–1994* (Berkeley: University of California Press, 1996), 120.

2. See, for example, the anthology of Cuba's liberal thought: Beatriz Bernal, ed., *Cuba: Fundamentos de la Democracia* (Madrid: Fundación Liberal José Martí, 1994).

3. General Batista, who emerged from the 1933 revolution that deposed General Machado, was in turn deposed by the 1959 revolution led by Castro.

4. *Plattista* is a derogatory label used to denote someone who shows allegiance to America's imperialist designs toward Cuba. The term derives from the despised Platt Amendment of 1902.

5. For a concise, yet comprehensive, discussion of the legal issues and political implications of redistricting in Florida, see The Cuban American Policy Center, *Laws and Politics in Florida's Redistricting* (Miami: The Cuban American National Council, 1992).

6. Although multimember and at-large districts are not inherently unconstitutional, the "totality of the circumstances" has often shown that they deny minorities the opportunity to elect candidates of their own choice.

7. There have been few exceptions to Cuban Americans' bloc voting: Steve Clark

defeated Cuban Miriam Alonso in the race for mayor of Hispanic-dominated Miami in 1992; in the same year, Bruce Kaplan defeated Cuban Conchy Bretos in a predominantly Hispanic county district. For a well-documented analysis of bloc voting patterns among Cubans, see The Cuban American Policy Center, *Ethnic Bloc Voting and Polarization in Miami* (Miami: The Cuban American National Council, 1991).

8. Several Cuban American officeholders have not resisted old political vices inherited from Cuba's tainted republican past, and charges of corruption have forced several of them out of office. The most notorious case may be that of Hialeah's powerful mayor Raúl Martínez, who was accused, in federal court, of accepting bribes. Ironically, Martínez was later reelected before he was cleared of the charges.

9. Despite the fact that over 50 percent of Cubans spoke English "very well" or "well" by the 1980s, an overwhelming majority of them still preferred to speak Spanish at home.

10. A provocative discussion of the politics of bilingualism in Dade County can be found in James Crawford, *Hold Your Tongue* (Wesley, 1992), 93–100, 118–20.

Epilogue

The Cuban Exile Country in the Post-Castro Era

Anticipating developments in the Cuban Exile Country after Castro's demise seems a safer exercise than projecting when that long-awaited event will actually occur. Certainly, the once-prevalent expectation that a collapse of the communist regime could trigger a massive return of exiles to the island no longer seems plausible. All projections indicate that the result of such an event will instead be another wave of refugees from Cuba—despite America's determination not to let that happen. Indeed, the history of the Cuban exiles is now so profoundly linked to South Florida that their presence here seems permanent and irreversible.

> I suspect that a lot of the second generation, the "last generation," is not going to really go back. I've been hearing that we're going back to Cuba for over 30 years. I have a wait-and-see attitude. People here think that they're going to go back to the old Cuba, but you can't go home, and definitely there is no more home for us in Cuba. (Author's interview with businesswoman Cruz Hernández Otazo)

The die-hard, older exiles, however, still nurture dreams of returning; and the recent resurgence of the patriotism of yesteryear gives comfort to their race against time.

> Definitely, I would like to be a part of the reconstruction of Cuba. I have lived that dream throughout my more than three decades in this country. . . . We have to have a sense of our own identity. . . . To be or not to be? Are we Cuban exiles or not? After the fall of Castro, if we don't go back, is there any

rationale, is there any justification, for calling ourselves exiles? I don't think so myself. (Author's interview with Antonio Jorge)

In all likelihood, Miami appears bound to become even more Cubanized and Havana more Americanized when Castro disappears from the political landscape. The most probable outcome suggests that both cities would draw so close that they will be viewed as one region sharing a unique transborder, bilingual culture. Despite the natural reservation of many non-Cubans, Cuban Americans certainly love that scenario, for they anticipate becoming the bond connecting both sides of the Straits of Florida in a post-Castro era.

> *El exilio* will play a very important role in a future Cuba. From an economic perspective, if there is peace and calm in the post-Castro era, Cuban Americans will be constantly traveling and creating a second residence in the island. Gradually, they will develop economic links between the U.S. and Cuba, and Miami will emerge as somewhat of a Cuban city—second only to Havana. From a political perspective, Cuban Americans will also become extraordinarily significant given their capacity to influence U.S. legislation toward Cuba. (Translation of author's interview with *Plataforma* founder Carlos Alberto Montaner)

If that comes to pass, Cuban Americans could no longer consider themselves exiles—although, given Cuba's traditional penchant for political instability, South Florida could once again become a haven for a new vintage of political exiles. What seems certain is that, as always, developments on the island will continue to determine the future of Cuban Americans living in the United States. Even two generations after the 1959 revolution, their destiny still appears inexorably linked to Cuba's.

Appendix I: Statistical Summary

Table 1
Number of Cubans in the United States in 1990 (by year of immigration)

Years of Immi-gration	No. of Cubans	% of Cubans	% of Immi-grated Cubans
1987–90	33,837	3.3	4.9
1985–86	16,963	1.6	2.4
1982–84	23,163	2.2	3.4
1980–81	125,313	12.0	18.2
1975–79	33,256	3.2	4.8
1970–74	109,731	10.5	15.9
1965–69	173,287	16.6	25.1
1960–64	174,275	16.7	25.3
1950–59	50,956	4.9	—
Before 1950	16,406	1.6	—
Born in U.S.	285,244	27.4	—
Total	1,042,433	100.0	100.0

Source: U.S. Bureau of the Census, *U.S. 1990 Census*, Public Use Microdate Sample, 5 percent, weighted. See Pedraza, 1996, 267.

Table 2
Percentage of Cuban American Residents in Four Key States and in the Remaining United States in 1980 and 1990

State	1980	1990
Florida	58.5	64.6
New Jersey	10.1	8.1
New York	9.6	7.1
California	7.6	6.9
Remaining United States	14.2	13.3

Source: U.S. Bureau of the Census, *1980 and 1990 Census of Population*, General Population Characteristics, Table 63, 1983, and Summary Tape File 1A, 1992.

Table 3
Cities Where More Than Three-Fourths of Cuban Americans Are Concentrated

City	Percent
Miami	56
New York	15
Los Angeles	6

Source: The Cuban American Policy Center, 1994b, 1, 11.

Table 4
Cuban Americans Living in Dade County, Florida, in 1960, 1970, 1980, and 1990

Year	Percent
1960	23.6
1970	38.8
1980	50.5
1990	54.0

Source: U.S. Bureau of the Census, Summary Tape File 1A, Metropolitan Dade County Planning Department, Hispanic Profile: Dade County Florida, Research Division 1986. See The Cuban American Policy Center, 1994a, 12.

Table 5
Percentage of Cuban Americans with English Proficiency in 1980 and 1990

Proficiency Level	1980	1990
Very Well	40.3	50.1

Proficiency Level	1980	1990
Well	21.0	18.1
Not Well	21.4	18.7
None	17.3	13.1

Sources: U.S. Bureau of the Census, *1980 Census of Population*, Public Use Microdata Sample A, One-in-a-Thousand Sample for the United States, 1980; U.S. Bureau of the Census, *1990 Census of Population*, Public Use Microdata Sample, 1990.

Table 6
Language Preference at Home among Cuban Americans in 1980 and 1990 (in percent)

Home Language Preference	1980	1990
English	7.2	10.4
Spanish	92.8	89.6

Sources: U.S. Bureau of the Census, *1980 Census of Population*, Public Use Microdata Sample A, One-in-a-Thousand Sample for the United States, 1980; U.S. Bureau of the Census, *1990 Census of Population*, Public Use Microdata Sample, 1990. See also The Cuban American Policy Center, 1994b, 25.

Appendix II: Summary of the Stages of Development of the Cuban Exile Country

SURVIVAL STAGE (1959–1962)

This stage begins with Fidel Castro's takeover.

The exiles develop a political identity and concentrate on deposing Castro.

They accept any jobs in order to survive.

U.S.-Cuba conflict escalates into military confrontation.

TRANSITION STAGE (1962–1965)

This stage begins in the wake of the Bay of Pigs Invasion and the Cuban missile crisis.

Hopelessness sets in as the exiles realize they will not be returning to Cuba.

The CIA cuts off support to exile freedom fighters.

The first Cuban businesses open in South Florida.

Thousands of exiles resettle in other cities in the United States.

ADJUSTMENT STAGE (1965–1973)

This stage begins when Castro opens the port of Camarioca to the exiles.

The United States initiates open-arms immigration policy toward Cubans.

The freedom flights bring 300,000 new exiles to the United States.

The foundations of the Cuban enclave in Miami are consolidated.

Smaller Cuban colonies form in New York, New Jersey, and California.

ECONOMIC MIRACLE STAGE (1973–1980)

This stage begins when Castro puts an end to the freedom flights.

Miami's Cuban enclave experiences an economic boom.

The exiles adopt American citizenship and become involved in politics.

Cuban American consciousness emerges among younger exiles.

Cuban Americans serve as the engine for Miami's Latinization.

Anglo white flight starts when bilingualism polarizes South Florida.

DIVERSIFICATION STAGE (1980–1990)

This stage begins in the wake of the 1978 Dialogue between Castro and the exiles.

The Mariel boatlift brings 125,000 new refugees to the United States.

The Cuban Exile Country is divided over exile trips to the island.

Cuban Americans become a political force in South Florida.

Cuban American National Foundation (CANF) lobbies U.S. Congress to create Radio Martí.

Cuban American businesses expand beyond Miami's initial enclave.

POST-SOVIET STAGE (1990–PRESENT)

This stage begins with the cessation of Soviet economic assistance to Cuba.

Hopes for Castro's demise revived while exile groups become linked with the internal opposition.

Cubans take to the sea in rafts; 32,000 are detained in Guantanamo.

The Clinton administration ends the open-arms immigration policy toward Cubans.

The CANF lobbies U.S. Congress to tighten the embargo.

Appendix III: Notable Cuban Exiles

Liz Balmaseda. Cuban-born and Miami-educated journalist for *The Miami Herald, Newsweek*, and NBC. Her sharp, insightful columns on the complex life of the Cuban American community have won several national awards, most notably a 1993 Pulitzer Prize. In 1996 she was honored by the American Cancer Society as one of Miami's Most Dynamic Women.

José Basulto. Left Cuba as a teenager after the revolutionary takeover, but infiltrated back into the island to prepare internal resistance for the Bay of Pigs Invasion. Since then, Basulto's unwavering commitment to Cuba's freedom has guided his life in exile. In the early 1990s, he founded Brothers to the Rescue, a humanitarian effort to rescue Cubans leaving their country in small rafts.

Luis Botifoll. Considered the dean of the Cuban American community. Botifoll's accomplishments span more than fifty years. In Cuba, he distinguished himself as an attorney and media executive; in South Florida, he rose to prominence as a banker and civic leader. The chairman emeritus of Republic National Bank (Miami's largest) has devoted himself to civic service since his retirement two years ago. He currently serves as chairperson of the "Amigos" of the Cuban Living History Project.

Frank Calzon. Born in Cuba and educated at the universities of Rutgers and Georgetown. The director of the Freedom House's Free Cuba Center, Calzon has been a tireless advocate for human rights and a peaceful transition to democracy in his native country. Since 1975 he has also been the executive director of *Of Human Rights*.

Willy Chirino. Born in Pinar del Rio, Cuba. He came to the United States as one of the 14,000 unaccompanied minors who were part of Operation Pedro Pan. He started playing his own music in Miami as a youngster, and today, after composing over 100 songs, he is considered the "salsa king" by thousands of his fans. He also heads the Chirino Foundation, a nonprofit group devoted to helping children throughout the world.

Nestor Carbonell Cortina. True to family tradition, has always shown a passion for learning and for public service. After studying at Harvard and the Universidad de Villanueva, he came to the United States and participated in the Bay of Pigs Invasion. Since then, Carbonell has remained active in the struggle for a free Cuba and has authored several books. He currently lives in Connecticut, where he is an executive for Pepsico, Inc.

Manuel Jorge Cutillas. Educated at Rensselaer Polytechnic Institute. He began a lifelong career with Bacardi in 1955. After Castro's takeover, Cutillas settled in the Bahamas, where he supervised the company's plant. In 1992 he became president, CEO, and chairman of the board of the Bacardi and Martini Rossi group of companies, the world's largest liquor manufacturer. He is a member of the "Amigos" of the Cuban Living History Project.

Mario Díaz-Balart. The youngest of four brothers, including Congressman Lincoln Díaz-Balart, banker Rafael Díaz-Balart, and national TV reporter José Díaz-Balart. Republican Senator Mario Díaz-Balart has risen to prominence in Florida politics. He is also president of Gordon Sloan Díaz-Balart, a leading South Florida marketing and public affairs firm.

Remedios Díaz Oliver. Came with her family from Cuba in 1961. She began her Miami career as an accounting clerk and, after a few years, rose to the presidency of her company. In 1991 she and her husband, Fausto, founded All American Containers. She serves on several boards of directors and remains active in the civic life of the community.

Elena Díaz-Verson Amos. Born in Havana in the 1920s. She came to the United States as an exchange student in the 1940s. After her marriage to John B. Amos, a fellow student at the University of Miami, the couple moved to Columbus, Georgia, and founded a company that eventually became American Family Life Assurance Corporation (AFLAC). Her involvement in philanthropic and humanitarian causes has earned her many national and international awards.

Emilio and Gloria Estefan. Arguably the first couple of the Cuban Exile Country. The Estefans' successful musical career has catapulted them to wealth and international fame. To many Cuban Americans, however, Emilio and Gloria remain role models of the local kids who made it big. The Estefans live in Miami with their family.

Enrique C. Falla. Released from a Cuban prison where he served two years for his participation in the Bay of Pigs Invasion. He earned bachelor's and master's degrees from the University of Miami. Upon graduation, he began a career with the Dow Chemical Company, and he is now executive vice president of the company and a member of its board of directors.

Andy García. Born in Havana. He came to the United States at the age of five and attended Florida International University and spent several years performing in regional theater productions before moving to Los Angeles in the late 1970s. Once Hollywood discovered him, García became an instant movie star featured in dozens of productions such as *The Godfather: Part III*, for which he won an Oscar nomination.

Aida Levitan. Holds a Ph.D. in Spanish literature. Levitan has distinguished herself in public service and business. As executive vice president of Sanchez & Levitan, she has been nationally recognized for her work in the area of Hispanic marketing, advertising, and public relations. Levitan, who lives in Miami, is a founding member of the "Amigos" of the Cuban Living History Project.

Modesto A. (Mitch) Maidique. Born in Cuba and educated at the Massachusetts Institute of Technology and Harvard University, where he later taught. Maidique is a renowned authority on the management of high-technology enterprises. In 1986 he became president of Florida International University, the fastest growing public university in the United States.

Jorge Mas Canosa. Born in Santiago de Cuba. He was forced into exile at an early age for his opposition to the dictatorships of Batista and Castro. His business accomplishments and political activities on behalf of Cuba's freedom have made him the most influential member of the Cuban Exile Country. Mas Canosa is chairman of the Cuban American National Foundation and of MasTech, Inc., a public engineering contracting firm.

Bob Menendez. Born in New York, of Cuban exile parents. He began his political career as mayor of Union City, New Jersey. He served as a state senator from New Jersey between 1986 and 1992, when he was elected to the U.S. Congress. Menendez has lately acted as a spokesman for the Clinton administration's Cuba policy and, in 1997, became assistant "whip" of the House.

Carlos Alberto Montaner. Left Cuba after escaping from Castro's jails. He studied at the University of Miami and taught literature at the University of Puerto Rico before moving to Spain, where he has continued his prolific writing career. Arguably the most influential and intellectual Cuban exile, Montaner has dedicated his life to the cause of Cuban freedom.

Ileana Ros Lehtinen. Born in Havana. She came to the United States fleeing communism when she was seven years old. She studied at Miami Dade Community College and Florida International University. In 1982 Congresswoman Ros-Lehtinen began her political career when she was elected to the Florida House of Representatives. She was elected to the U.S. Congress in 1989, becoming the first Hispanic woman to serve in that body.

Carlos Saladrigas. Came from Cuba at age twelve through Operation Pedro Pan, the largest international transfer of unaccompanied minors on record. He studied at Belen Jesuit School and later earned an MBA from Harvard. In 1984 he founded the VINCAM Group, a pioneer in the employee leasing industry. His company went public in 1996 and today is one of the largest Hispanic businesses in the nation. Saladrigas and his wife, Olga, have been active in United Way, the board of Belen, and the "Amigos" of the Cuban Living History Project.

Selected Bibliography

Alvarez, Carlos M. "Lo contextual y lo afectivo-simbólico en la identidad cubana del sur de la Florida." In *Cuba: Cultura e identidad nacional*, 113–22. Havana: Universidad de la Habana, 1995.

———. "La identidad cubana entre jóvenes adultos del sur de la Florida." Forthcoming.

Amaro, Nelson, and Alejandro Portes. "Una sociologia del Exilio: Situación de los grupos cubanos en los Estados Unidos." *Aportes* 23 (January 1972): 6–24.

Aragón, Uva de. *La mujer cubana: Historia e infrahistoria (el Exilio)*. Coral Gables, Fla.: North-South Center, University of Miami Press, 1996.

Arboleya, Carlos. "The Cuban Community in 1980: Coming of Age, as History Repeats Itself." Miami: 1980.

Behar, Ruth. "Juban América." *Poetics Today* 16, no. 1 (Spring 1995): 151–70.

Bernal, Beatriz, ed. *Cuba: Fundamentos de la Democracia*. Madrid: Fundación Liberal José Martí, 1994.

Botifoll, Luis J. "How Miami's New Image Was Created." Paper presented at the Conference to the Cuban National Planning Council, Institute of Interamerican Studies, University of Miami, Coral Gables, Fla.: 27 January 1984.

———. *Introduction to the Future of Miami*. Miami: Laurenty, 1988.

Carbonell-Cortina, Néstor T. *And the Russians Stayed: The Sovietization of Cuba*. New York: William Morrow, 1989.

———. "The Cuban-Americans: Past Achievements and Future Hopes." Paper presented at the National Association of Cuban-American Educators, Miami, 17 August 1991.

Clark, Juan M. "The Exodus from Revolutionary Cuba (1959–1974): A Sociological Analysis." Ph.D. diss., University of Florida, 1975.

Clark, Juan, José I. Lasaga, and Rose S. Reque. *The 1980 Mariel Exodus: An Assessment and Prospect*. Washington D.C.: Council for Inter-American Security, 1981.

Cortina, Rodolfo J. "Lenguaje e identidad." In *Hispanos en los Estados Unidos*, edited by Rodolfo J. Cortina and Alberto Moncada, 105–12. Madrid: Ediciones de Cultura Hispánica, 1988.

Crawford, James. *Hold Your Tongue*. Reading, Mass.: Addison-Wesley, 1992.

Cuban American Policy Center. *The Cubanization and Hispanization of Metropolitan Miami*. Miami: The Cuban American National Council, 1994a.

———. *A Demographic Profile of Cuban Americans*. Miami: The Cuban American National Council, 1994b.

———. *Ethnic Bloc Voting and Polarization in Miami*. Miami: The Cuban American National Council, 1991.

———. *Hispanic National Groups in Metropolitan Miami*. Miami: The Cuban American National Council, 1995.

———. *Laws and Politics in Florida's Redistricting*. Miami: The Cuban American National Council, 1992.

Encinosa, Enrique. *Cuba en guerra*. Miami: The Endowment for Cuban American Studies of the Cuban American National Foundation, 1994.

Franqui, Carlos. *Retrato de familia con Fidel*. Barcelona: Editorial Seix Barral, 1981.

García, María Cristina. *Havana USA: Cuban Exiles and Cuban Americans in South Florida, 1959–1994*. Berkeley: University of California Press, 1996.

Gonzalez-Pando, Miguel. "Doing Business." In *Greater Miami: Spirit of Cuban Enterprise*, edited by Miguel Gonzalez-Pando, 40–69. Fort Lauderdale, Fla.: Cooperfield, 1996.

———. "La basquedo de una conciendin generacional." *El Nuevo Herald*, 25 October 1993.

González-Reigosa, Fernando. "Cuban-American Cultures and Psychotherapy: A Clinical Psychological Study." In *Appreciating Difference: Reading in the Psychology of Cultural Diversity*, edited by J. Toomer, 157–61. Lexington, Ky.: Ginn, 1986.

———. "Las culturas del exilio cubano." *Reunión: Boletín del Instituto de Estudios Cubanos* 89–90 (September–October 1976): 1–11.

———. "Mitos y símbolos de las naciones cubanas. ¿Por qué los cubanos no pueden ser posmodernos?" Paper presented at the Fifth Congreso Internacional sobre Culturas Hispanas en los Estados Unidos, Alcalá de Henares, Madrid, July 1992.

Gupta, Akhil, and James Ferguson. "Beyond Culture: Space, Identity, and the Politics of Difference." *Cultural Anthropology* 7, no. 1 (February 1992): 6–23.

Hamada, Tarek. "Reflections on a Revolution." Interview with Silvia Pedraza. *Dissent* (Fall 1983): 13–16.

Hospital, Carolina, ed. *Cuban American Writers: Los Atrevidos*. Princeton, N.J.: Ediciones Ellas/Linden Lane Press, 1988.

Jorge, Antonio, and Raúl Moncarz. "International Factor Movement and Complementarity: Growth and Entrepreneurialship under Conditions of Cultural Variation." *Research Group for European Migration Problems, R.E.M.P. Bulletin*, edited by G. Boyer. The Hague, September 1981.

———. "The 1990s: Hispanics in South Florida." Paper presented at the North American Economics and Finance Association, American Association Meetings and National Association of Hispanic Professors of Business and Economics, Atlanta, 28–30 December 1989.

Jorge, Antonio, Jaime Suchlicki, and Adolfo Leyva de Varona. *Cuban Exiles in Florida: Their Presence and Contribution.* Miami: University of Miami, North-South Center, 1991.

Jorge, Antonio, Jorge Salazar-Carrillo, Raúl Moncarz, and Irma Tirado de Alonso. "The Cuban Entrepreneur and the Hispanic Market: Myths and Realities." Paper presented at the Allied Social Science Associations Annual Meeting, New Orleans, 28–30 December 1986.

Kotkin, Joel. *Tribes: How Race, Religion and Identity Determine Success in the New Global Economy.* New York: Random House, 1992.

Kunz, E. F. "The Refugee in Flight: Kinetic Models and Forms of Displacement." *International Migration Review* 7 (Summer 1973): 125–46.

Lasaga, José I. "La tradición del exilio y la tradición nacional cubana." *Exilio: Revista de Humanidades* (Otoño-Invierno 1967).

Lee, Everett S. "A Theory of Migration." *Demography* 3, no. 1 (1966): 47–57.

Marrero, Leví. *Raíces del milagro cubano.* San Juan: Ediciones Capiro, 1984.

Moore, Martha T. "New Breed CEO Markets Locally—Worldwide." *USA Today*, 8 February 1996.

Nee, Victor, and Jimmy Sanders. "On Testing the Enclave-Economy Hypothesis." *American Sociological Review* 52 (December 1987).

Pedraza, Silvia. "Cuba's Exiles: Portrait of a Refugee Migration." *International Migration Review* 19 (1985): 4–34.

———. "Women and Migration: The Social Consequences of Gender." *Annual Review of Sociology 17* (1991): 303–25.

Pedraza, Silvia, and Rubén G. Rumbaut, eds. *Origins and Destinies: Immigration, Race, and Ethnicity in America.* Belmont: Wadsworth, 1996.

Pedraza-Bailey, Silvia. "Cubans in Exile, 1959–1989: The State of the Research." *Cuban Studies since the Revolution*, edited by Damián J. Fernandez, 235–57. Gainesville: University Press of Florida, 1992.

Pérez, Lisandro. "The Cuban Population of the United States: The Results of the 1980 U.S. Census of Population." *Cuban Studies* 15, no. 2 (Summer 1985): 1–18.

Pérez Firmat, Gustavo. *Life-on-the-Hyphen: The Cuban-American Way.* Austin: University of Texas Press, 1994.

Portell Vilá, Herminio. *Historia de Cuba en sus relaciones con Estados Unidos y España.* Havana, 1938.

Portes, Alejandro. "Social Origins of the Cuban Enclave Economy." *Sociological Perspectives* 30 (1987): 476–85.

Portes, Alejandro, and R. L. Bach. *Latin Journey: Cuban and Mexican Immigrants in the United States.* Berkeley: University of California Press, 1985.

Portes, Alejandro, and Leif Jensen. "What's an Ethnic Enclave?: A Case for Conceptual Clarity (Comments on Sanders and Nee)" *American Sociological Review"* 52 (December 1987).

Portes, Alejandro, and Alex Stepick. *City on the Edge: The Transformation of Miami.* Berkeley: University of California Press, 1993.

Puente, Maria. "Spanish Leads Way in Foreign Language Study Boom." *USA Today*, 20 March 1996.

Rieff, David. *The Exile: Cuba in the Heart of Miami.* New York: Simon & Schuster, 1993.

Rumbaut, Rubén G. "The Agony of Exile: A Study of Migration and Adaptation of Indochinese Refugee Adults and Children." In *Refugee Children: Theory, Research and Service*, edited by Frederick L. Alhearn, Jr., and Jean L. Athey, 61. Baltimore: Johns Hopkins University Press, 1991.

Santiago, Fabiola. "Crucial para Miami el Español, dice estudio." *El Nuevo Herald*, 19 March 1996.

Wheat, Jack. "Demand for Bilingualism Translates into Surge in Spanish on Campus." *The Miami Herald*, 5 February 1996.

Index

About the Author

MIGUEL GONZALEZ-PANDO is the founder of the Cuban Living History Project at Florida International University. He came to this country in 1960 and joined the Bay of Pigs invasion, as a result of which he was caught and held prisoner. Upon his release from a Cuban jail two years later, he returned to South Florida. He is the editor of *Bilingualism in a Multicultural Society* (1975), *Greater Miami: Spirit of Cuban Enterprise* (1995), and *Miami: Gateway to the Americas* (1996).